MEMORANDA

Presented to the

LYTTON COMMISSION

BY

V. K. WELLINGTON KOO, *Assessor*

VOLUME II

Published by The Chinese Cultural Society,
743 Fifth Avenue, New York City

PRINTED IN THE UNITED STATES OF AMERICA
BY J. H. FURST COMPANY, BALTIMORE, MARYLAND

CONTENTS TO VOLUME II.

MEMORANDUM

ON

THE SO-CALLED ANTI-FOREIGN TEACHING IN CHINESE SCHOOL BOOKS

Document No. 16   Peiping, June 1932

MEMORANDUM ON THE SO-CALLED ANTI-FOREIGN TEACHING IN CHINESE SCHOOL BOOKS

1. Criticism of Chinese school books.
2. Many books cited in the Japanese pamphlets not officially approved text-books.
3. Citations not found anywhere.
4. Distorted translations.
5. Passages in no wise anti-foreign.
6. Undefined passages.
7. Criticism of imperialism and of its excesses in China.
8. The Opium War.
9. Other so-caleld anti-foreign teachings.
10. Unique position of China. Privileges of foreigners. Concessions. Leased territories.
11. Chinese reactions to the inequality of relations.
12. Development of the national spirit in China.
13. Examples of foreign countries.
14. Japanese school books.
15. Revision planned.

APPENDIX:

Anti-foreign materials appearing in primary and middle school text-books compiled or approved by the Japanese Board of Education.

MEMORANDUM ON THE SO-CALLED ANTI-FOREIGN TEACHING IN CHINESE SCHOOL BOOKS

1. **Criticism of Chinese school books.** A number of passages from Chinese text-books have been translated and cited by the Japanese in an effort to show that elementary education in China is anti-foreign in nature.

The Japanese have issued two pamphlets on the subject. The one printed by the *Herald Press* of Tokyo, is under the title of *Anti-Foreign Education in China.* The other, which is more elaborate, is entitled *Anti-Foreign Teachings in New Text-books of China,* and was published by the *Sokokusha Press* of Tokyo. These pamphlets have been presented by Japan to the Commission of Inquiry. The present Memorandum will answer the points raised in these publications, and especially the second one.

2. **Many books cited in the Japanese pamphlets not officially approved text-books.** The educational institutions established by the Chinese Government only use those text-books which are approved by the Ministry of Education. But a large number of the quotations cited in the Japanese pamphlet are taken from publications which do not appear on the list of the approved text-books as, for instance, *The National Humiliation Reader,* cited on pages 5, 10, 15, 21, 23, 25, 26, 30, 32, 33, 41, 58, 67, 71, 82, 91, 98, and 109 of the second Japanese publication. In fact out of the 67 different cases which are cited, only 27 were taken from text-books approved by the Chinese Ministry of Education, the remaining 40

being taken either from text-books which were not approved or from books published by individuals whose existence even is not known to us.

3. **Citations not found anywhere.** A certain "History of Two Fishermen of the Liaotung Peninsula" reproduced on pages 38-39 as an example of anti-foreign teaching was supposed to have been taken from the *Higher Grade National Language New Doctrine Text-Book*, 3, XXII. We have tried to find the text complained of, but in vain.

4. **Distorted translations.** Frequently, the translations submitted by the Japanese are not accurate. The text is distorted instead of being a faithful translation. For instance, (1) on page 2, there is a passage "In 1884 France plundered Annam . . .", when the Chinese text should be translated "In 1884 France took Annam . . ." (2) On page 36, "Having seen our country placed under such oppression Chinese citizens must take steps to *rebel* against Japan . . ." The exact translation should be "When China is so oppresesd by Japan, her citizens should find some means of resistance." (3) On page 37 ". . . and other anti-Japanese incidents," does not exist in the Chinese text! (4) On page 54, there is the quotation "first, the alliance of leading nations for a *world-revolution*," for which the correct translation should be "first, the alliance of leading nations of the world which are *pioneers of revolution.*"

5. **Passages in no wise anti-foreign.** Many of the texts cited by the Japanese publications are not in fact anti-foreign in nature. For instance, the descriptions (pages 15-21 of the second publication) relative to the Opium War and the signing of the Treaty of Nanking are meant to show the defects of the former Imperial Government, the frequent disharmony among the high officials, the

lack of patriotic sentiment in many of them, and their cowardice before the British forces.

The description of the landing of the Germans at Kiaochow (pages 28-30) is a bitter criticism of the self-sufficiency, ignorance and the lack of courage of the Chinese generals of the Imperial days.

On page 25, a Burmese complains that his country was invaded and conquered by British forces because "the Chinese Government did not send a single soldier for its rescue." On page 45, the loss of Annam is attributed to the incompetence of Chinese diplomacy. Page 32 relates how the French entered Annam at the request of a pretender to the throne of that country. These texts are not subject to valid criticism.

6. **Undefined passages.** The description on pages 96-101 of a wealthy Chinese in America who deprecates his own national origin after the Americans have shown him friendliness and eventually receives spiteful treatment served to his compatriots from these same Americans is meant to show that the blame is equally distributed.

In the dialogue between the two fishermen of the Liaotung Peninsula (pages 38-39), the older one complains that since its occupation by the Russians (1898) and by the Japanese (1905), life has become more difficult. But it may be observed that there is hardly any little fishing village in Western Europe where one does not hear similar regrets of the passing of the "good old days."

7. **Criticism of imperialism and of its excesses in China.** Pages 43-55 are devoted to a description of the imperialism of the great colonial Powers. The policy called "Imperialism" is perhaps denounced in terms a little too harsh, but surely the language is not so excessive as that used by the socialist press in various parts

of the world. We can understand how some foreigners might feel hurt by the manner in which the conduct of their mother country is judged by others. But they should understand that colonial expansion cannot be viewed in the same light by the countries which sponsor it and reap benefit from it, and by the nations which are its victims.

As examples of these "imperialist excesses," the Shanghai incident of May 30th, 1925 is cited on pages 8 and 53, and the Japanese occupation of Tsinan in 1928 is referred to on page 41.

In this connection it should be noted that even among foreigners there are many who agree that the police of the International Settlement on May 30th, 1925, was not sufficiently cool and showed little forbearance.

As regards the Tsinan incidents, we believe that they arose from the provocative attitude of Japan and the ill-considered measures adopted by her troops.

We do not see anything to criticise in the manner in which these facts are related in the text-books criticised by the Japanese.

8. **The Opium War.** The War of 1842 and the Treaty of Nanking are also mentioned in several of these books. But among Englishmen there are those who do not consider the "Opium War" as particularly just, nor do they entirely approve the action of the British Government of that period in resorting to force in order to impose upon another people the traffic in a drug which saps its vitality.

9. **Other so-called anti-foreign teachings.** If we eliminate from the critical memorandum which the Japanese Government has distributed to the members of the Commission all the passages which we have just mentioned, little remains of the so-called anti-foreign teaching complained about.

May we request the Commission, however, also to take into consideration the following observations?

10. Unique position of China. Privileges of foreigners. Concessions. Leased territories. In the first place, there is no question that China occupies, even at the present moment, a unique and abnormal position in the family of nations. It is the only country where the privileges of extraterritoriality, of consular jurisdiction, and of exemptions from various fiscal obligations, are still enjoyed by the nationals of a few great Powers. It is the only country where foreigners possess municipal concessions in which they exercise quasi-sovereign rights of administration. It is also the only country where many Powers have leased territories which bear great resemblance to colonies.

These concessions and leased territories are portions of sovereign Chinese soil which have been taken away from us by armed force or by such diplomatic pressure as frequently amounted to the threat of armed force. The great majority of the inhabitants of these regions are Chinese, and it is largely due to the labour, industry and the means of the Chinese that the concessions and leased territories owe their present prosperity.

11. Chinese reactions to the inequality of relations. This state of affairs creates between the Chinese and the foreigners, on our own soil, unequal relations which seriously prejudice the dignity of our national existence. Such conditions only exist in China and have no analogy elsewhere. This being the case, it is not surprising that some Chinese have developed a special attitude towards the non-equal treatment of their nation by other nations. This is only natural for a country having any self-respect.

12. Development of the national spirit in China. It has been necessary to awaken the masses, to make them understand the dangers of their past apathetic attitude, to develop a patriotic spirit in them, and to indicate to them what the national aims should be and how to attain them by peaceful and legitimate means.

13. Examples of foreign countries. For that reason, we have had recourse to a methodology which has been universally employed abroad, that is to say, the exaltation of the patriotic sentiment. The history of Europe tells us that the best way to heighten this sentiment is to lay stress on the national characteristics of a people.

Is it surprising then that we should have followed Europe's example and attempted to transform "the heap of sand", to which Dr. Sun Yat-sen has compared the inarticulate mass of the Chinese nation, into a solid body, by subjecting it to a process of nationalization which is sometimes excessive perhaps but certainly necessary in order to give birth to a new and vigorous nationhood? One must remember that the history of China offers, unfortunately, only too many cases of privileges wrested from her through the employment of force.

14. Japanese school books. It is fair to ask whether Japan, who reproaches us to-day did not use identical methods during the period in which she suffered from similar abuses of which we are complaining. Did she not cultivate during the first twenty years of the Meiji era a certain amount of what she now calls antiforeignism? Did she not resent as keenly as we do the impairments of her national sovereignty? And even to-day, liberated as they have been from the hindrances of the former unequal treaties, does Japan show in her teaching of history and in her press that equanimity which she believes to be lacking in us?

In this connection we have asked our Ministry of
Education to make a survey of the text-books used to-day
in the governmental educational institutions in Japan.
The work has been done in haste and we have been able
to examine only a limited number of these books. We
have, however, noticed a great number of passages in
which episodes in the history of Japan's foreign relations
and the policies of certain Powers are related in a way
which is not very complimentary to the nations concerned.

We give, in the appendix, a translation rendered as
literally as possible of some of these selections and we
believe that the Commission will be impressed by their
astonishingly bad taste, frequently approaching effron-
tery, in many of these instances.

15. **Revision planned.** In order to impress sound
ideas on juvenile and unenlightened minds, one has to
give them an impassionate turn, and is thus liable sometimes to exceed the limits of moderation. Some of the
authors of other text-books may have erred in this
respect. There would be, therefore, no objection on
China's part to re-examine the school-books already
approved by the Ministry of Education and to introduce
such revisions as are really necessary. As regards
passages concerning our neighbour state, however, these
revisions will not probably be very thorough-going unless
and until the deliberately provocative attitude of the
leaders of Japanese public opinion towards us changes
for the better. Nor is it reasonable to expect us to
accomplish very much through the revisions of our text-
books if measures are not adopted by the Japanese
themselves to eliminate anti-Chinese teachings in their
school-books.

Peiping, June 25th 1932.

APPENDIX.

ANTI-FOREIGN MATERIALS APPEARING IN PRIMARY AND MIDDLE SCHOOL TEXT-BOOKS COMPILED OR APPROVED BY THE JAPANESE BOARD OF EDUCATION.

I. Concerning more than one foreign country.

1. *Japanese History Text-book for Primary Schools,* Volume II. Compiled by the Japanese Board of Education.

Lesson 2:

"Political views suddenly changed and the Emperor himself led his troops against the *barbarous foreigners.*"
"We swear to carry out *anti-foreignism.*"
". . . a sword which signifies resistance against *foreign barbarians.*"
"Foreign ships often *invaded* our shore or entered our ports resorting to *barbarous activities.* We must resist them . . . *anti-foreignism* flourished . . . when Emperor Jinko came to the throne, an order to *attack all foreign ships* was issued."
"*Anti-foreignism* intensified."
"The fire of *anti-foreignism* sparkled."
"After the Russian *invasion,* British *outrages* continued."

2. *History of Japan for Middle Schools.* Approved by the Japanese Board of Education and published by *Sanshodo Kaboshiki Co.,* Japan.

Chapter 30:

"The British *invasion* . . . Great Britain, Russia and France, relying on the vastness of their countries, resorted to *encroachment with barbarous tactics.*"

3. *National History for Primary Schools.* Compiled by the Japanese Board of Education.

Lesson 47:

"*Anti-Foreignism* . . . by this time the western countries suddenly enlarged their sphere of activities in the Far East . . . repeatedly *hampered* us from all sides, because we refused to have commercial intercourse with her, Russia *invaded* Karafuto Island, Chishima Island, etc.; and British ships also *created trouble* in

Nagasaki; the people, feeling enraged, *advocated anti-foreignism*, the Shogunate, therefore, gave the order to *attack the pirate ships* of the foreign countries."

4. *National History for Primary Schools,* Last Volume. Compiled by the Japanese Board of Education.

Lesson 47:

" In the process of treaty revision . . . these treaties were concluded by Togugawa *under force* which *impaired* our dignity and *violated* our interests . . . thus much regret was caused among the people."

5. *National History for Primary Schools.* Compiled by the Japanese Board of Education.

Lesson 49:

" The fire of *anti-foreignism* was intensified. Iyeshige was compelled to *attack* the foreigners on May 10th.

6. *Japanese Middle School History Text-book.* Approved by the Japanese Board of Education and published by *Sanshodo Kaboshiki Co.,* Japan.

Chapter 49:

" *Anti-foreignism* began."

7. *European History for Middle Schools.* Approved by the Japanese Board of Education and published by *Sanshodo Kaboshiki Co.,* Japan.

Chapter 64:

" Great Britain, France and Russia are our *chief invaders.* Germany, too, is giving her *encroaching tactics* a trial."

8. *Foreign History.* Approved by the Japanese Board of Education and published by *Sanshodo Kaboshiki Co.,* Japan.

Chapter 75:

" In the latter part of the 19th century, western *invasion* of the east gradually increased, thus *imperialism flourished* and *oppression intensified.* Great Britain, France and Russia were our *chief invaders.*"

9. *Japanese History for Middle Schools.* Approved by the Japanese Board of Education and published by *Sanshodo Kaboshiki Co.,* Japan.

Chapter 31:

"By this time our people were highly enraged because of the *interference* of the three countries, namely, Great Britain, Russia, and Germany, but due to the lack of force to resist these three *invaders*, our Emperor issued a proclamation commanding the people to have patience for the struggle of a common cause, and that a day will arrive when they will have their *revenge*."

10. *Japanese History for Girls*, Last Volume. Approved by the Japanese Board of Education and published by *Sanshodo Kaboshiki Co.*, Japan.

Chapter 34:

"*Anti-foreignism* was popularized."
"To us the Ansei Treaty was the most *disadvantageous of the unequal treaties*."

11. Same as above.

Chapter 36:

"Order to *fight* all foreigners."

12. *History of the Western World*. Approved by the Japanese Board of Education and published by *Sanshodo Kaboshiki Co.*, Japan.

Chapter 37: (Conclusion).

"Four hundred years have elapsed since the discovery of the new route and the new world . . . the western peoples emulated with one another trying to *grab* new land and *oppress* the coloured peoples, claiming that they were the superior race. They were very powerful as well as *perverse* and *abusive*."

13. Same as above.

Chapter 42:

"Besides extending their influence beyond the boundary of Europe, the western peoples, in the 19th century, advocated that the white race was the superior race throughout the whole world, thus often resorting to *malicious action* towards the other races."

II. Concerning Great Britain.

1. *Japanese History Text-book for Primary Schools*, Volume II. Compiled by the Japanese Board of Education.

Lesson 2:

"The outrageous activities of the British."
"British ships suddenly *invaded* the port of Nagasaki."

2. *Japanese Middle School History Text-book.* Approved by the Japanese Board of Education and published by *Sanshodo Kaboshiki Co.,* Japan.

Chapter 32:

" The *barbarous British* came after the Russian *invasion.*"
" British ships were often seen sailing near the Japanese coast . . . one ship suddenly *invaded* Nagasaki, *violated* our national law with the utmost *savagery.* Our people were much enraged by these *violent* actions of the British and the Russians and advocated *anti-foreignism.*

3. *History of Japan for Girls.* Approved by the Japanese Board of Education and published by *Sanshodo Kaboshiki Co.,* Japan.

Chapter 18:

"*Invasion* of the Western Countries."
" The British *Invasion* . . . Great Britain and France took advantage when Bengal weakened. Great Britain was stronger and the result was the *invasion of India* and the *conquests of Bengal and Burma,* thus Great Britain became the most powerful western nation in the Orient."

4. *History of Japan for Middle Schools.* Approved by the Japanese Board of Education and published by *Sanshodo Kaboshiki Co.,* Japan.

Lesson 38:

" The *overthrowing* of Bengal."
" The *cruelty* of the British . . . nothing can surpass the cruelty of the British during their *invasion* of India. In Hasting's time, a policy of *stark cruelty and defiance of law* was enforced: his own words were law. There is no equal anywhere in the world to Hasting's cruelty to slaves."

5. Same as above.

Chapter 18:

" Warnings from the North."
" Following the footsteps of the Russian *invasion* . . . the British ships often appeared near our sea-coast. In the 5th year of Bunka, one British ship suddenly entered Nagasaki and created all sorts of *disorders* and *violated* our law . . . afterwards British ships often anchored near our shore and *robbed* our people . . . therefore, they were highly enraged, and from advocating naval defence they advocated *anti-foreignism.*"

III. Concerning Russia.

1. *Japanese History Text-book for Primary Schools,* Volume II, Compiled by the Japanese Board of Education.

Lesson 2.

"*The Russian Invasion.*"
"The Russian *invasion* of Karafuto and *forceful occupation* of Yetorotu Island are *outrageous activities.*"

2. *Japanese Middle School History Text-book.* Approved by the Japanese Board of Education and published by *Sanshodo Kaboshiki Co.,* Japan.

Chapter 32:

"Russia *invaded* Ainu and Karafuto."
"Russia often *invaded* us."

3. *History of Japan for Girls.* Approved by the Japanese Board of Education and published by *Sanshodo Kaboshiki Co.,* Japan.

Chapter 18:

"*Invasion* of the Western Countries."
"The Russians *invaded* us by land."
"The Russian *invasion* . . . Russia's *invasion* into Central Asia began in the Ch'ing dynasty; in the 9th year of Meiji a large portion of Central Asia was occupied. Afghanistan was also *invaded.*"

4. *History of Japan for Girls.* Approved by the Japanese Board of Education and published by *Sanshodo Kaboshiki Co.,* Japan.

Chapter 22:

"Russo-Japanese Dispute."
"A mob of unruly Russians often *attacked* and *murdered* the troops of the Japanese defence garrison and Japanese residents in Nikolaievsk."

5. *History of Japan for Middle Schools.* Approved by the Japanese Board of Education and published by *Sanshodo Kaboshiki Co.,* Japan.

Chapter 18:

"Warnings from the North."
"The Russians gradually *invaded* the Chishima Archipelago."

" The Russians established schools in Irkutsk and taught Japanese to the vagabonds with the intention of *invading* Japan."

" The Russians often *invaded* Karafuto, Yetorotu Island and Toshijiri Island, etc."

" Received the warning of Russian *invasion.*"

IV. Concerning America.

1. *Japanese Middle School History Text-book.* Approved by the Japanese Board of Education and published by *Sanshodo Kaboshiki Co., Japan.*

Chapter 34:

" America, backed by *military force, compelled* us to sign *unequal treaties.*"

2. *Japanese History for Girls,* Last Volume. Approved by the Japanese Board of Education and published by *Sanshodo Kaboshiki Co.,* Japan.

Chapter 34:

" Determination of Perry and the apprehension of the Japanese."

" The *pirate ships* of the United States entered our country . . . though the people were greatly dumbfounded, yet they sharpened their swords and shined their armours . . . "

V. Concerning France.

1. *History of Japan for Girls.* Approved by the Japanese Board of Education and published by *Sanshodo Kaboshiki Co.,* Japan.

Chapter 18:

" *Invasions* of the Western Countries."

" The French *Invasion* . . . Expeditionary forces were despatched by France for the *conquest* of Annam, Indo-China and Cambodia. Annam offered resistance and declared war on France."

VI. Concerning China.

1. *History of Japan.* Approved by the Japanese Board of Education and published by *Sanshodo Kaboshiki* Co., Japan.

Chapter 21:

" The Chinese Political Disturbance."

" The Japanese nationals were humiliated when Nanking was occupied by Chiang Kai-shih, the commander-in-chief of the Southern Government and his *barbarous troops.*"

2. Same as above.

Chapter 22:

"The Negotiations between China and Japan."

"Every one of the twenty-one demands is a natural provision" (the Japanese meant to say that the twenty-one demands not only could preserve the territorial integrity of China, but would even maintain peace in the Far East as well. Why is it that the Chinese, they asked, do not recognize our good intentions? Moreover, they continued, the simple-minded students and professional instigators, etc. claim May 7th, the date of the signing of the treaty, as their National Humiliation Day, and create all sorts of nonsense every year! How ridiculous!)

3. *Foreign History Text-book.* Approved by the Japanese Board of Education and published by *Sanshodo Kaboshiki Co., Japan.*

Chapter 11:

"The Chinese Revolution."

"There is no comparison whatsoever between the political organizations of Japan and China. From time immemorial, revolutions may succeed and fail, dynasties may have different names, but there was no fixed geographical name for China. Their people may call themselves Chinese or *Chung-hua*, but this is simply due to their bombastic imagination. As a matter of fact, China, has no fixed name."

4. *National Reader,* Modern Edition, Book X. Approved by the Japanese Board of Education and published by *Sanshodo Kaboshiki Co., Japan.*

"Historical Facts of the Success and Failure of a country."

"From time immemorial, although the Chinese King (sic) called China *Chunghua* and called others barbarians . . . how are we to know that in the future, China of to-day will not be conquered by barbarians? Who could guarantee that?"

5. *Japanese History for High Schools.* Approved by the Japanese Board of Education and published by *Sanshodo Kaboshiki Co., Japan.*

Chapter XLVI:

"The Government of China."

"Our Japanese Government is *far superior to that of China.*"

6. *A Geography Reference Book for Higher Primary Schools,* First Year. Compiled by the Japanese Government.

17

"Manchuria: *Its value as a Colony.*"

" The expansion of Manchuria is limitless and the soil is very rich. There are immense plains and forests, and mineral deposits are to be found everywhere. Manchuria is an excellent place for industrial development. As means of communication are now fast developing, this repository of natural resources can certainly be opened up. It goes without saying that this is undoubtedly the ideal place *for Japanese colonization.*"

VII. Concerning World Peace and the League of Nations.

1. *National Reader,* New Edition, Volume I. Compiled by the Japanese Board of Education.

Lesson 28:

" The Hope of the People."

" The Japanese must not fail to realize what Japan has bestowed upon the world. We must fulfil our duty as the representative of the world powers to find out and inform others of any nation that tries to dictate to others and to suppress or quell it. Thus it will enable us to *control the whole world* after the proud and high-flown countries have been *subdued by* us."

2. *Moral Training Reader for Girls,* Volume 57. Compiled by the Japanese Board of Education.

"National Defence":

" After the Great War, all the countries desired peace and tried every means to avoid international conflicts, resulting in the organization of the League of Nations. Could we avoid war after this? After the death of Napoleon, whose whole life was almost spent in fighting, all the European countries hoped for peace. However, war can not be prevented even after the solemn organization of the League. Therefore, unless the cause of war is eradicated, no organization could restrain us."

3. *Modern Japanese Geography.* Approved by the Japanese Board of Education and published by *Sanshodo Kaboshiki Co.,* Japan.

Map 3. (The map of the Japanese Empire).

" The Neighbours of Japan."

" The map consists of five circles, each with a diameter of 1,000 miles. If the Japanese occupation of the third circle is successful, a large portion of China Proper, the whole of Manchuria, a portion of Mongolia, and more than half of Siberia and a portion of the Philippine Islands will be under the Japanese control. If the Japanese occupation of the fourth circle is successful, the whole of China, half of French Indo-China, all of the Philippine Islands, the whole of the Aleutian Island, all of the Hawaiian Islands and a portion of Borneo will come under the Japanese control. If the occupation of the fifth circle is successful, Japan will have the complete control of Asia and the Pacific Ocean and probably entrench herself in Alaska, Canada and the Pacific coast of America."

VIII. Concerning Disarmament.

1. *Moral Training Reader.* Approved by the Japanese Board of Education, published by *Sanshodo Kaboshiki Co.,* Japan.

Chapter 37: (Conclusion).

"National defence is very important when the cause of war is not yet removed, and the whole world is still on this road (of war). It is not easy to remove this cause, and that is why we are striving to strengthen our armaments. Not only the present Disarmament Conference in Geneva, attended by Japan, Great Britain and United States, will fail to reach the expected result, but, on the contrary, it will give the world the pretext for strengthening their armaments. Permanent world peace is hopeless, we must . . ."

2. *History of the Western World.* Approved by the Japanese Board of Education and published by *Sanshodo Kaboshiki Co.,* Japan.

Chapter 41: (seventh paragraph).

"As a matter of fact, all countries have not neglected their armaments . . . they are doing their utmost to strengthen their power within the limit of their financial power. For instance, Great Britain has recently spent an enormous sum of money for the construction of a naval base in Singapore and the United States, although advocating disarmament on the one hand, was on the other hand, considerably enlarging her air force. Under such circumstances, we must not take things lightly."

MEMORANDUM

ON

CHINA'S EFFORTS IN THE DE-VELOPMENT OF THE THREE EASTERN PROVINCES

Document No. 17   Peiping, June 1932

MEMORANDUM ON CHINA'S EFFORTS IN THE DEVELOPMENT OF THE THREE EASTERN PROVINCES.

CHAPTER ONE.—INTRODUCTION.

1. Propaganda on Japanese efforts.
2. The South Manchuria Railway plays a minor part in development.
3. Factors in establishing peace not related to Japanese efforts.
4. Japan's attempts to hinder development. China's efforts of modernization.
5. Judicial and other reforms.

CHAPTER TWO.—IMMIGRATION AND COLONIZATION.

6. Early history of colonization.
7. Impetus the result of famine in 18th century. Regulations giving encouragement.
8. Phenomenal growth after 1887.
9. Organized emigration since 1907. Regulations of Hsingan Settlement Area.
10. Private organizations sponsoring immigration.
11. The distribution of the settlers.
12. The Hsingan Settlement Area.

CHAPTER THREE.—AGRICULTURE, FORESTRY AND FISHERY.

13. Aspects of agricultural growth of the Three Eastern Provinces.

14. Spread of scientific farming and its effect on the crops.
15. Tussah silkworms and growth of sericulture.
16. Cotton and fruit rearing.
17. Animal husbandry.
18. Timber wealth.
19. Historical view of the lumber industry.
30. The fishing industry.
21. Chinese Government organs helping in the development.

CHAPTER FOUR.—INDUSTRY AND MINING.

22. Industrial encouragement given by the Chinese Government.

1. The chemical industry.

23. Bean oil milling.
24. The ceramic industry.
25. The match industry.
26. Other chemical industries.

2. Flour milling.

27. The old and modern flour mill.
28. The breweries.
29. The sauce and sugar industries.

3. The textile industry.

30. Silk and cotton manufacture.
31. Woollen manufacture.

4. The iron works.

32. The Mukden arsenal and other iron works.

5. The electric works.

33. Sixty power plants.

34. Printing and tannery.
35. Encouragement from Chinese Government.

6. The mining industries.

36. History of mining.
37. The coal mining companies.
38. The various iron works.
39. Gold mines richest in China.
40. Copper mines.
41. Lead and silver mines.
42. The talc.
43. The magnesite.
44. The clay beds.
45. Other minerals.

CHAPTER FIVE.—COMMUNICATIONS.

1. Railways.

46. General view of the railways.
47. The Mukden-Hailung line.
48. The Hulan-Hailun line.
49. The Kirin-Hailun line.
50. The Tsitsihar-Koshan line.
51. The Taonan-Solun line.
52. The Tahushan-Tungliao line.
53. The mileage and amount of business on the lines.
54. Compared with the South Manchuria Railway.

2. Water transportation.

a. SEA TRANSPORTATION.

55. The harbours: decline and fall of Yingkow.
56. Antung.
57. Tatungkou.
58. The principal shipping companies.
59. The Hulutao harbour.
60. The contract for its construction.

b. INLAND NAVIGATION.

61. Navigation on the Sungari and the shipping companies.
62. The Nonni river.
63. The Liao river.
64. The Yalu river.
65. Government shipping organs.

3. Postal and telegraph administration.

66. The postal administration.
67. The telegraph administration.

4. Telephones.

68. The growth of the telephone.

5. Wireless.

69. The growth of the wireless.

6. Roads.

70. Road extension.

CHAPTER SIX.—TRADE AND COMMERCE.

71. History of foreign trade.
72. Reasons in development of foreign trade.

1. Principal items of export and import.

73. Agriculture the basic factor of development.
74. The imports.
75. Advantages of Dairen.
76. Japan deriving benefit from the development of the North-east.

2. Introduction of modern business methods.

77. Improvement in business methods.
78. Modern banks.
79. Modern insurance.

CHAPTER SEVEN.—EDUCATION.

80. Efforts of modernization.

1. Elementary education.

81. Progress in elementary education.
82. Chang Hsueh-liang donating Hsinmin primary schools.

2. Secondary education.

83. Progress in secondary education.

3. Higher education.

84. Higher education a later development.
85. Higher educational institutions.
86. The North-eastern University.

4. Social education.

87. Nature or social education.

5. The Han-ching Endowment Fund for secondary and primary education in Liaoning.

88. Chang Hsueh-liang's interest in educational development.

CHAPTER EIGHT.—CONCLUSION.

89. General conclusions.
90. China's wish to open the North-east to all the countries.

Memorandum on China's Efforts in the Development of the Three Eastern Provinces

CHAPTER I. INTRODUCTION.

1. **Propaganda on Japanese efforts.** The Three Eastern Provinces are an integral part of the Republic of China, where 30,000,000 Chinese have their permanent home and make their living. The story of how these people, originally immigrants from the provinces within the Great Wall, have laboured for the economic development and social advancement of the Three Eastern Provinces during the past few decades has something of an epic grandeur and is yet little known abroad, owing largely to the persistent Japanese propaganda that the present prosperity of the Three Eastern Provinces is entirely the result of Japanese efforts. In support of their claim, Japanese propagandists, either official or otherwise, have repeatedly referred to the existence of the leased territory of Kwantung and the South Manchuria Railway as stabilizing factors in the affairs in the Three Eastern Provinces which enable the Chinese people to pursue their vocations in peace. The cumulative impression produced by these statements in Europe and America is that Japan is responsible for the present economic development of the Three Eastern Provinces.

It is time that something be done to correct the misleading statements of the Japanese, if only for the sake or rendering justice where justice is due. In the first place, the claim that the present prosperity of the Provinces is entirely due to Japan's efforts is against all the teachings of the social sciences. The economic development of a country or of a district, we have been told by sociologists, is due to many factors and never to a single factor. In fact, the truth of this theory is so obvious and so universally recognized that it would seem superflous to restate it. But, unfortunately, the wrong impression created abroad by Japanese propagandists still remains with many people.

2. **The South Manchuria Railway plays a minor part in development.** Japan is never weary of saying that the South Manchuria Railway has contributed greatly to to the economic development of the Three Eastern Provinces. The growth of trade, the development of industry and the increase of immigrants are all attributed to the South Manchuria Railway. We do not deny the fact that the railways have played a part in the prosperity of the Provinces, but we maintain that they constitute only one of the many factors which have contributed to the present prosperity. Of the 3,700 miles of railways in the Northeastern Provinces, 1,800 are owned by Chinese, 1,236 under Sino-foreign joint management, and 700 controlled by the Japanese of which 470 miles, constituting the section between Dairen and Changchun, were built by Russia and transferred to Japan as a result of the Russo-Japanese War and by virtue of the Portsmouth Treaty of 1905. In view of this fact, and granted that the railways have been responsible for the development of the Three Eastern Provinces, the contribution of the South Manchuria Railway is not more than 19 per cent. of the net result.

3. **Factors in establishing peace not related to Japa-**

nese efforts. We do not deny that peace and order has a bearing on the economic development of the Three Eastern Provinces, but the contention of the Japanese propagandists that the security of the Three Eastern Provinces is due to the presence of Japanese troops is scarcely tenable. The Japanese troops before September 18th, 1931, at least, were confined within the railway areas, and instead of maintaining peace and order as Japanese publicists have claimed, we have seen elsewhere [1] they have been, on the contrary, factors of disturbance. The stability of the Three Eastern Provinces is due (1) to its peculiar geographical location and (2) to the efforts of the Chinese authorities. There is not less order and peace along the Chinese-owned railways and the Chinese Eastern Railway than that exists along the South Manchuria Railway because of the efforts of the Chinese authorities.

4. **Japan's attempts to hinder development. China's efforts of modernization.** What Japan has done and is doing in the Three Eastern Provinces is motivated purely by her own selfish interests. She has repeatedly obstructed the investment of foreign capitalists and deliberately blocked the development schemes of the Chinese authorities and nationals. But in spite of this, the Chinese authorities have laboured patiently and energetically for the development of the vast natural resources of the Provinces and the economic well-being of the Chinese people. After the Sino-Japanese War of 1894-5, the administrative system was revised with a view to developing the local districts. Shortly after the close of the Russo-Japanese War of 1904-5, the former Imperial Government brought the administration of the Three

[1] *Vide Memorandum on the " Guards " of the South Manchuria Railway, passim.*

Eastern Provinces into line with that of China Proper by appointing a viceroy with power over these provinces, with civil governors and prefects to assist him. Since then, many reforms in the Government have been introduced, and to-day the administration is modernized in many respects. For instance, men for civil service are recruited largely from among the graduates of modern schools.

5. **Judicial and other reforms.** Judicial reform has kept pace with political reforms. There are 47 modern courts and 22 model prisons in the Provinces to-day. This does not include *hsien* courts. In addition to all this, active measures have been taken to encourage the introduction of municipal government and village self-government. The police system has been modernized and Western methods have been introduced as far as possible into the financial administration of the Provinces.

Apart from political reforms, the last 30 years have registered notable progress in the fields of agriculture, forestry, fishery, education, trade, industry, commerce, communication, colonization and mining, as a result of the efforts of the Chinese authorities. Indeed, the present prosperity of the Three Eastern Provinces is due largely to these efforts, while Japan's part is merely incidental and of a local character, as it is mostly confined to the places along the South Manchuria Railway.

CHAPTER II.   IMMIGRATION AND COLONIZATION.

6. **Early history of colonization.** In the early years of the Ching Dynasty, land in the North-eastern Provinces was allotted to the various "Banners" for cultivation, and the settlers were governed by military law. In the 10th year of the reign of Emperor Shun Chih 1644-1661), an imperial edict was issued encouraging the migration of Chinese to Liaoning. Thousands of people left China Proper for the Three Eastern Provinces as settlers and a great impetus was given to the colonization movement. A change of policy came with the accession of Emperor Chien Lung to the throne who issued a mandate closing the Provinces to the Chinese settlers on the ground that they would adversely affect the habits of living of the Manchu and other tribes.

7. **Impetus the result of famine in 18th century. Regulations giving encouragement.** In the middle of the reign of Emperor Chien Lung (1736-1794), a great famine befell the provinces of Shantung and Chihli causing widespread suffering among the people. Thousands of the famine victims left their homesteads and sought refuge elsewhere. Many of them defied the exclusion law and went to the North-east. At first, they did manual work but later they cultivated land on their own account. With the passing of years, more Chinese found their way to the Provinces until the exclusion law became to all intents and purposes a dead letter. When Emperor Tao Kwang (1821-1850) came to the Throne, an edict was promulgated opening the greater part of the Three Eastern Provinces to Chinese colonization. The barriers were further lowered during the eighth year of the reign

of Emperor Hsien Feng (1851-1861). In the sixth year of the reign of Emperor Kwang Hsu (1875-1908), the Imperial Government promulgated the following three rules for the encouragement of immigration to the Northeast:

(1) Arable land shall be sold at the price of four *chuan* per hundred *mou*, but the amount of land which one person is entitled to buy shall not exceed 1,000 *mou*. In the case of those who cannot afford to buy but who want to till land, they shall pay a tax of 600 cash for every 100 *mou* of land cultivated.

(2) Public uncultivated land shall be given to the people for reclamation and cultivation. Cultivators of such land shall be exempted from the payment of land tax for the first five years, after which they shall be liable to a tax of 600 cash for every 100 *mou* of land cultivated. After a number of years to be determined according to the amount of land cultivated, the land shall become the private property of the cultivators.

(3) Those who wish to migrate to regions adjacent to south Ussuri, where the climate is extremely severe and the land is poor, shall not only be exempted from the payment of land tax, but also be entitled to a subsidy of 32 taels each from the authorities.

8. **Phenomenal growth after 1887.** In 1887, that is, the 13th year of the reign of Emperor Kwang Hsu, all the laws and edicts governing the exclusion of Chinese from the Provinces were repealed, and every corner of this vast stretch of territory was thus opened to Chinese immigrants and settlers. From that year to 1900, the number of settlers from Shantung Province alone totalled 100,000 each year. The population of the Three Eastern Provinces in 1900 amounted to 14,000,000 of which the

Chinese constituted 90 per cent. After the Russo-Japanese War of 1904-5, the Chinese Government offered special inducements to emigrants to the Provinces. In the year 1908 alone (the last year of the reign of Kwang Hsu), 6,300,000 *mou* of land were allotted to settlers from China proper. Several serious famines inside the Great Wall, coupled with the ever-increasing birth rate of the Chinese people, caused this migratory movement to continue after the establishment of the Republic in 1912. The peak was reached in 1927, when more than 1,170,000 people went to the Provinces. The following table [2] speaks for itself.

Year	Settlers Arriving	Settlers Returning	Those Remaining
1923	433,689	240,565	193,124
1924	482,470	200,045	282,435
1925	532,770	237,746	295,024
1926	607,352	323,694	183,658
1927	1,178,254	341,959	936,295
1928	938,472	394,247	544,225
1929	1,046,291	621,897	424,394
1930	748,213	512,793	235,420

9. **Organized emigration since 1907. Regulations of Hsingan Settlement Area.** Since 1907, Chinese immigration to the Provinces not only has received the official guidance and protection of the Chinese Government but has assumed the form of an organized movement. The provincial authorities of Shantung and Chihli have done their best to encourage this movement, while Chekiang has even established a special committee for the purpose. Chinese national railways like the Tientsin-Pukow, Peiping-Mukden, Ssupingkai-Taonan, Taonan-Angangchi, Mukden-Hailung, Kirin-Hailung, Hulan-Hailun and Tsitsihar-Koshan lines have run settlers' trains or offered special rates to assist the colonization tide. Upon

[2] Figures published by the South Manchuria Railway Company.

arrival in the Provinces the immigrants would be looked after by men specially appointed by the government for the task, and given every possible assistance in getting a start. The following regulations governing the colonization of the Hsingan Settlement area are illuminating in many ways:

(1) To facilitate the development of the colonization enterprise, the various provincial authorities will be requested to pick able-bodied men and send them to Hsingan to settle and colonize.

(2) An immigration office shall be established at Taoan and sub-offices at such places as are deemed suitable and necessary.

(3) Where an immigrant comes under the auspices of the Hsingan Settlement Bureau, he shall be provided with food and shelter by the Bureau upon arrival at Hsingan. In the case of those whose coming in sponsored by private organizations, such settlers shall be attended to by the organizations concerned. This also applies to transit arrangements.

(4) When immigrants come under the auspices of the said bureau, circular letters will be sent to the various Provinces, requesting them to make this known to the public, and the Bureau will send delegates with *huchao* (passports) to those Provinces which recruit settlers.

(5) Where private organizations want to assist the movement of settlers, they should write to the Bureau for *huchao*. When such applications are accepted and *huchao* issued, the settlers will be admitted into the settlement area.

(6) As soon as the immigrant (or an immigrant family) arrives at Taoan, he should immediately report his

arrival to the Immigration Office, fill in a blank form, obtain a passport and then go to the district designated by the Bureau.

(7) When immigrants come in groups, each group should elect one to three men as leaders to manage the affairs of a common concern.

(8) The bureau or the organization in charge will negotiate with steamship companies or railways for special rates for the immigrants. This also applies to the luggage of the immigrants.

(9) Save those whose coming is arranged by settlers already in the area, the immigration office shall investigate the needs of the immigrants in regard to agricultural implements, livestock, seeds, etc. and report them to the Settlement Bureau. Aid will be granted on the basis of these reports.

(10) The Settlement Bureau shall dig wells for the immigrants.

(11) Houses for the immigrants will be erected at the expense of the Government in advance of their arrival, or the Government will lend them material and let them erect houses on their own accord. The houses or material so lent shall be paid for by the immigrant in three years, but they may apply for an extension when special circumstances warrant it.

10. **Private organizations sponsoring immigration.** Among the private organizations which assisted in the immigration movement may be mentioned the China International Famine Relief Commission with headquarters in Peiping, the Red Swastika Association of different provinces, the Shantung Charitable Association, the Honan Famine Relief Association and numerous other

charitable bodies in Kirin, Heilungkiang, Liaoning and other Provinces. Shantung guilds in the Three Eastern Provinces have been especially helpful in the way of looking after the welfare of the settlers both on the way and after they have arrived in the Provinces. Dr. Yu Tien-hsiu, a well-known Chinese sociologist, also did much for the cause by starting what he termed a frontier movement. Two-thirds of the settlers came from Shantung and Chihli, and this is understandable when it is remembered that for several years these two Provinces experienced a succession of famines and floods. This and the growth of population led many people to turn to the North-eastern Provinces where life was easy and the settlers were received with open arms.

11. **The distribution of the settlers.** About one-half of the immigrants entered the Provinces through the port of Dairen, while the rest entered through Yingkow, Antung or by the Peiping-Mukden Railway. After arrival in the Provinces, most of the settlers advanced northward by the Chinese Eastern Railway, and after reaching Harbin, they distributed themselves in the various districts of Heilungkiang and Kirin. Speaking of the record year of 1927, two-thirds of the 1,700,000 immigrants who entered the Provinces settled in these two provinces while the rest were scattered along the Yalu River. Only two or three per cent of the immigrants were settled along the South Manchuria Railway. Two reasons may be assigned for this distribution. Firstly, the land along the South Manchuria Railway had been taken up for cultivation long before the Russo-Japanese War so that there is very little left for the late arrivals. Secondly, most of the immigrants were farmers who naturally liked to settle in sparsely populated districts. Again, wages are comparatively high in Kirin and Heilungkiang, and this

was no doubt a strong attraction to many settlers. The
following table [3] shows the distribution of Chinese settlers in the Three Eastern Provinces during the three
years of 1927, 1928, 1929.

	1927	1928	1929	Total.
1. South of Mukden.............	....	....	....	20,000
2. North of Mukden.............	....	....	....	25,000
3. Peiping-Liaoning Railway Region	....	....	....	2,000
4. Ssupingkai-Taonan Railway Region	20,000	15,000	30,000	65,000
5. Upper Sungari River Region..	100,000	80,000	100,000	280,000
South Manchuria				392,000
6. South Line of C. E. R........	25,000	15,000	10,000	50,000
7. Eastern Line, C. E. R........	150,000	80,000	50,000	280,000
8. Western Line, C. E. R.......	100,000	70,000	80,000	250,000
9. Low Sungari River Region...	120,000	120,000	80,000	320,000
10. Ussuri River Region.........	20,000	120,000	....	140,000
11. Hulan-Hailun Region.........	10,000	30,000	40,000	80,000
12. Amur River Region..........	2,000	....	....	2,000
North Manchuria.....................................				1,122,000

12. **The Hsingan Settlement Area.** In connection with
the colonization movement in the Three Eastern Provinces, there is an interesting experiment to which reference has already been made, namely, the Hsingan Settlement Area. This experiment was started in the year
1928 when Marshal Chang Hsueh-liang took charge of
the Manchurian Government following the tragic death
of his father Marshal Chang Tso-lin at Huangkutun, and
decided to carry out a disbandment program. For this
purpose, three artillery regiments were organized into
a settlement army. Beginning with 1929, this army
started to colonize Hsingan. In 1920, the area was
opened up to colonization by civilian settlers. Soldier

[3] *Population movement to the North-Eastern Frontier in China*, p. 22.
By Franklin L. Ho. Published by the Institute of Pacific Relations.

colonization was carried on in accordance with the regulations governing the allotment of land to officers' corps and the settlement army. In the six months from January to June 1931, 30,000 *mou* of land were cultivated through soldier labour.

Civilian colonization work in the Settlement Area was governed by the regulations concerning the allotment of uncultivated land, the organization of rural villages and those issued by the Hsingan Settlement Bureau. In 1930, 83,860 *mou* of uncultivated land were distributed for cultivation. From January to June of the same year, 2,032 able-bodied men, 1,339 aged and children and 1,486 women making a total of 4,857 persons settled in the area. Since then more settlers have come and more land taken up for cultivation owing to the number of material improvements having been made. The future is full of hope for the experiment.

CHAPTER III.   AGRICULTURE, FORESTRY AND FISHERY.

13. **Aspects of agricultural growth of the Three Eastern Provinces.** In 31 years, the population of the Three Eastern Provinces has been more than doubled. In 1900, its was estimated at 14,000,000, but last year it was put at 30,000,000 (according to a conservative estimate). The remarkable development, which is due to the increase of immigration and the proverbial fecundity of the Chinese race, has brought about ever-increasing production and consumption. The astonishing growth of the import trade during the last 30 years is a sufficient proof of the increase of consumption. As regards the increase of

production, the most notable achievement is shown in the
field of agriculture. Arable land in the Three Eastern
Provinces is placed at 54,900,000 acres. In 1914, 19,700,-
000 acres of land were under cultivation. To-day there
are 32,000,000 acres under cultivation. In order to see
that all the available land in their territory is put under
cultivation, the provincial authorities of Kirin, Heilungkiang and Liaoning adopted special regulations which
permit a man to cultivate the uncultivated land of another and acquire ownership thereof after a designated
number of years. This is known as *Ch'iang Keng* or colonization by competition. It has already produced satisfactory results. The following table [4] shows the increase
of cultivated land in the Provinces:

Year	Cultivated land	Arable land (In million acres)	Per cent. of the Cultivated land
1914	19.7	64.9	35.9
1915	19.3	54.9	35.1
1916	19.3	54.9	35.1
1917	24.8	54.9	45.1
1918	25.1	54.9	45.7
1922	26.1	54.9	47.5
1923	26.7	54.9	48.6
1924	27.4	54.9	49.8
1925	27.9	54.9	50.9
1927	28.5	54.9	51.9
1926	28.5	54.9	51.9

**14. Spread of scientific farming and its effect on the
crops.** With the introduction of modern agricultural
implements from abroad, farming in the Provinces has
taken on a more scientific character in recent years. The
International Harvester Export Company of Chicago
has opened a branch office in Harbin which sells tractors
to many modern farms in different parts of the Prov-

[4] Hsiao Chu: *Manchuria, a Statistical Survey.* Reprinted in *Problems
of the Pacific, 1929*, p. 384.

inces. In 1915, the annual cereal production of the Three Eastern Provinces amounted to 404,493,000 bushels. In 1929, this figure jumped to 786,799,338 bushels and valued at $200,000,000. This surprising development of agriculture which is the basis of the prosperity of the Provinces is entirely due to the industry of the 30,000,000 Chinese who have laboured year in and year out for the development of this vast stretch of territory of their own country. This point deserves the careful attention of those who wish to understand the basic cause of the present prosperity of the Provinces. The following figures [5] show the increase of production of various crops in the Three Eastern Provinces from 1914 to 1927:

Production of main crops in the Three Eastern Provinces (in million bushels).

	Soya				Sorghum	Wheat	Total
1914..	2.1	29.9	21.5	13.2	2.9	86.0	12.7	185.3
1915..	12.3	32.7	16.5	13.1	3.3	81.0	11.2	170.1
1916..	13.0	36.6	17.4	13.2	3.3	89.6	16.6	189.7
1917..	8.5	33.7	18.5	13.2	1.7	91.4	15.2	182.2
1918..	8.2	32.3	20.2	14.6	2.1	93.7	13.3	184.2
1922..	17.0	88.7	60.5	82.6	8.4	125.3	31.1	413.6
1923..	12.6	118.3	68.4	64.0	9.0	135.3	28.5	436.1
1924..	14.5	114.7	48.0	81.0	8.6	137.4	21.1	425.3
1925..	16.7	143.3	72.6	125.6	19.1	171.7	34.1	581.1
1926..	15.5	111.6	62.9	123.5	16.9	143.7	36.3	510.4
1927..	14.9	158.7	69.5	133.9	19.8	175.6	34.8	605.1

15. **Tussah silkworms and growth of sericulture.** The rearing of tussah silkworms is one of the special industries for which the Provinces are famous, the annual output of pongee making up more than 70 per cent of the total production of the country. This industry was first introduced into the Provinces by settlers from Shantung in the reign of Emperor Chia Ching when they brought with them tussah silkworms. As many of the mountains

[5] *Ibid.*, p. 385.

were uncultivated, tussah trees were planted whose leaves were used to feed the tussah silkworms. Sericulture at once received a great impetus. In recent years, modern methods have been introduced into the industry with the result that the annual production reaches the astonishing figure of 10,000,000,000 cocoons and has a cash value of $30,000,000.

16. **Cotton and fruit rearing.** Next to the tussah silk industry is cotton growing. The annual production of cotton is estimated at 30,000,000 pounds. Thanks to the initiative of the Mukden Spinning Mill, some 150,000 Chinese farmers have grown American cotton with extremely gratifying results. As a consequence of the lead given by returned students of agriculture from America, fruit-growing also is being carried on in an extensive scale. Many modern orchards have been established in different parts of South Manchuria, and these turn out many varieties of fruits. The growing of American apples in the Provinces is attended with great success.

17. **Animal husbandry.** Finally, the Three Eastern Provinces are particularly adapted for grazing; as a matter of fact, many Chinese farmers take this up as a sideline. According to the statistics for 1928, there were in the Provinces 15,000,000 cattle, horses, sheep, donkeys, mules and pigs having a production value of something like 10,000,000 Haikwan taels a year.

18. **Timber wealth.** Of the four timber-producing districts of China, the North-eastern Provinces are the largest. Indeed, they abound in forests, and the best known of these are the Kirin, Hsingan and Sungari forests. The following table [6] will give us some idea of the timber wealth of the Provinces:

[6] *Second Report on Progress in Manchuria, 1930*, pp. 164-165.

Forest District	Area in acres	Present estimate of in cubic feet. timber
The right bank of Yalu and along the Hun River	2,403,889	3,623,326,800
Upper parts of the Sungari Valley	3,521,146	8,740,360,000
Tumen Valley	2,040,295	4,204,008,000
Hurka Valley	1,556,060	4,209,509,000
Lalin Valley	1,553,141	3,004,898,000
Eastern section of C. E. R.	5,967,754	8,982,965,500
Sanhsing district	12,941,704	26,153,018,000
Great Hsingan Range	34,308,680	56,000,000,000
Little Hsingan Range	24,506,200	35,000,000,000
Total	88,798,869	149,918,085,300

19. **Historical view of the lumber industry.** From time immemorial, the forests of the Three Eastern Provinces had been considered as national property, and it was not until the fourth year of the reign of Emperor Kwang Hsu (about 1878) that the public was allowed to fell trees on payment of a tax. In 1902, that is, the 28th year of the reign of the same emperor, a Company was organized with a capital of $200,000 subscribed jointly by the Government and the public for the purpose of developing the timber resources of the Yalu River region. The Company flourished for a time. During the Russo-Japanese War, Japan occupied the Company though a Chinese concern, and confiscated all the lumber in stock. In 1908, an agreement was signed between China and Japan providing for the establishment of a joint Sino-Japanese company to exploit the timber resources of the Yalu River region. As a result of this agreement, the Yalu Timber Company came into existence. Later the Chung Tung Hai Ling Company and the Cha Mien Lumber Company were formed in North Manchuria both of which were Sino-foreign joint enterprises.

Then followed a period of reckless felling of trees with little regard for the conservation of forest resources.

The Chinese authorities became alarmed and decided to put an end to this form of exploitation. In recent years the Government has been paying a great deal of attention to afforestation. On the one hand, model afforestation stations were established in centrally-located districts, and on the other hand, nurseries were opened in order to assure a regular supply of seedlings. At present there are six model stations and 36 nurseries in various parts of the Provinces. The work of afforestation of the district magistrate has since become one of the important items of local administration. Private organizations also have done their best to promote the movement, the success of which may be evidenced by the young forests which are springing up in many parts of the Provinces.

20. **The fishing industry.** The coastal fishing industry of the Provinces is confined to the Yellow Sea and the Pei Hai coasts. Along the Yellow Sea coast there are at least 2,500 families engaged in the fishing trade, making a force of about 7,500 persons with 2,493 fishing crafts. In the Pei Hai coast fishing region there are about 1,400 families and 8,300 persons. The fishing boats are estimated at 1,430. The annual output of fish is put at $3,000,000. Japanese fishermen using Port Arthur and Dairen as their base of operation often enter the territorial waters of China and engaged in fishing in utter disregard of International Law. This is a cause of frequent complaint on the part of the Chinese fishermen whose trade has suffered thereby. In recent years the Government Bureau for the protection of Chinese fishing boats frequently urged the fishermen to invest money in modern fishing crafts, and as a result 79 of these boats have been bought and are now engaged in the fishing trade. A fishermen's guild and also an association for the relief

of the fishing population have been organized in addition to a fishery school. The fishing industry appears to be in for a period of extraordinary development.

Fresh-water fishing is also well developed in the Provinces. The Yalu, the Nonni, the Sungari, the Ussuri, the Mao Tan Kiang, the Hulun Lake, the Heilungkiang and the Ching Po Lake are all rich in fish. The frozen fish produced in North Manchuria during the winter season has a wide market, but owing to the rapid growth of population, the annual production of marine products still falls far short of the demand and a large quantity of such products has to be imported to meet the need.

21. **Chinese Government organs helping in the development.** It is worth noting the various institutions which the Chinese Government has established in the Provinces for the encouragement of agriculture, forestry and fishery. In the first place, there is the Department of Industry which is the highest administrative organ of each Province. There are three departments in the Provinces corresponding to the Three Provinces of Liaoning, Kirin and Heilungkiang. These all have on their staffs experts who draw up plans for the development of the three leading industries. Secondly, there is the Bureau for the Protection of Fishing Crafts which is entrusted with the administration of coastal fishery. It maintains a coastal guard for the protection of Chinese fishermen.

Thirdly, the Irrigation Bureau has as its object the encouragement of irrigation projects and the cultivation of paddy fields. Fourthly, there are many agricultural associations in the Provinces which have been established for the promotion of the common interests of the tillers of the soil. These are divided into provincial, district and village associations.

Fifthly, many agricultural experiment stations have

been established under official auspices. In Liaoning there are five such stations. Kirin has ten, Heilungkaing two and Harbin one. One of the objects of the stations is to improve the seeds of the farmer, and in this connection several experiments have been successfully carried out. In Kirin alone eleven stations have been established to handle the exchange of seeds between the different Provinces and districts. With regard to the problem of agricultural education, there is a College of Agriculture in the North-eastern University of which the staff consists of graduates from American colleges. In addition, there are many training institutes which offer short courses to those interested in the development of scientific agriculture. Vocational schools also offer agricultural courses; in fact, many of the experiment stations are run by graduates of these schools.

CHAPTER IV. INDUSTRY AND MINING.

22. **Industrial encouragement given by the Chinese Government.** The Three Eastern Provinces are blessed with abundant mineral resources, and labour there is cheap. For thirty years the Government has been exerting its best to promote and encourage various industries so that many enterprises have been able to make rapid progress. Machinery has been introduced into most factories, and improved methods have been adopted by various handicrafts. Among those which have already established a firm footing in the Provinces the most successful are the chemical industry, flour milling, textile industry, iron works and the electric enterprises.

1. The Chemical Industry.

23. **Bean oil milling.** The bean oil milling is of old origin. Since the middle of the seventeenth century manual labour was used to make bean oil and bean cakes out of soya bean with very good results. The year after the Sino-Japanese War, in 1896, an Englishman began to introduce mechanical installations for one of the Chinese oil mills at Newchwang, thus inaugurating the manufacture of oil by machinery. Later at the beginning of the twentieth century a Chinese invented "the screw process" which was used widely in the oil mills established at Dairen, Newchwang, Changchun, Harbin, Antung, and other towns along the railway lines. The capital invested aggregated $80,000,000 and the total annual output was 12,000,000 bean cakes, and 353,880,000 kilograms of bean oil. The following table [7] shows the latest figures about bean oil milling in the Three Eastern Provinces:

Bean Mills in Manchuria.

	Number of Mills	Bean-cake (pieces) produced daily	Capacity of Bean Oil. (kilograms)
Dairen	39	218,100	654,300
Newchwang	22	38,634	115,902
Antung	26	53,726	161,298
Harbin	40	83,125	239,348
Along Railways in South Manchuria.	297	130,170	394,713
Along Railways in North Manchuria.	28	46,165	126,325
Total	452	569,920	1,691,886

24. **The ceramic industry.** The ceramic industry has shown marked progress in the past ten years. Factories for the making of cement, glass, pottery, tiles and bricks have sprung up in rapid succession. The quality of these manufactured articles is not inferior to those imported

[7] *The Manchuria Year Book 1931*, pp. 118-119.

from abroad. The Chao-Hsin Ceramic Industrial Company at Mukden, capitalized at $480,000, is the most successful enterprise of its kind. It has two departments, one for tile and brick making and the other for crockery. The number of workmen is over one thousand. The annual output of bricks and tiles is 10,000,000 pieces, and of crockery, 5,000,000 pieces. As their prices are reasonable and their quality is good, they are sold throughout the Provinces. Classes for apprentices are attached to the factories where they are taught the art of making pottery. These factories are organized on a modern scientific basis.

25. **The match industry.** The match manufacturing enterprise was first started in 1907 at Changchun as a Sino-Japanese concern. Later on match factories were started by Chinese at Kirin, Mukden, Yingkow and other places. The best-known is the Huilin Match Factory at Mukden. There are now seventeen match factories in the Provinces. Their annual output totals 773,470 boxes. Owing to severe competition on every hand, these match-making factories have divided up into the following three groups:

Organization	Name	Location	Nationality	Annual Output	
T h e Chinese Match Industrial Unions	Huilin Match Co.	Mukden	Chinese	Boxes	73,470
	Sanming Match Co.	Yingkow	"	"	77,020
	Shensheng Match Co.	"	"	"	66,200
	Kuantung Match Co.	"	"	"	56,170
	Tsengchang Match Co.	Kirin	"	"	43,670
	Chinhua Match Co.	"	"	"	32,350

Organization	Name	Location	Nationality	Annual Output
	Taifeng Match Co.	"	"	" 30,000
	Paoshan Match Co.	Changchun	Japanese	" 45,000
	Changchun Match Co.	"	"	" 45,000
Swedish Owned	Dairen Match Co.	Dairen	Swedish	" 30,000
	Jihching Match Co.	Changchun	"	" 36,350
	Kirin Match Co.	Kirin	"	" 70,570
Independent companies	Yuanhua Match Co.	Antung	Chinese	" 44,000
	Chenhsing Match Co.	Hulan	"	" 32,000
	Mingyuan Match Co.	Ashiho	"	" 43,670
	Luchang Match Co.	Tsitsihar	"	" 30,000
	Jihtsun Match Co.	Dairen	Japanese	" 18,000

Total.................................Boxes 773,470

Owing to the activities of the Swedish Match Company, competition in the match manufacturing field was keenly felt in the Provinces. The Chinese Government came forward to devise ways and means in order to protect the interests of all the match enterprises concerned. As a result a system of monopoly was established and carried out. A bureau known as The Match Monopoly Bureau was established on May 1st, 1931. This Bureau entrusts the Chinese Match Industrial Unions with the purchase and sale of all products of the match companies. But the marketing prices are fixed by the Bureau.

26. **Other chemical industries.** There are other industries manufacturing dyestuff, soap, and medical supplies. They are found in all large cities where they have well-

18

equipped and up-to-date factories. So far no reliable statistics are available. The first paper manufacturing mill was started in December, 1930, with a capital of $1,000,000. It has a very promising future. As for the refined salt industries there are four salt fields at Ying-kow, with a daily output of 18,000 catties.

2. Flour Milling.

27. **The old and modern flour mill.** Flour-milling is one of the most important industries in the Provinces. There are both old-style and modern flour mills. Modern flour mills were first established in 1903 at Harbin. In later years more and more flour mills sprang up to meet the demands at home. As the World War had entirely cut off the importation of foreign flour, more flour mills came into existence. For instance, up to the year 1928, there were about fifty mills in the Provinces of which about forty were found in Harbin and along the Chinese Eastern Railway with an annual production of 16,000,000 sacks of flour.

28. **The breweries.** The brewing industry is a very profitable enterprise in the Provinces. *Kaoliang* is chiefly used in the breweries which have been established in practically all the principal cities and towns. According to investigations made in 1929, there were eight breweries in the city of Mukden with a total capital of $180,000 and the annual production of the *kaoliang* gin amounted to 2,700,000 catties; and of fruit syrup, about 10,000 dozen bottles valued at $400,000. In Changchun, there were six breweries, with an aggregate capital of $280,000 and their annual output was 3,600,000 catties. In recent years, the brewing of beer and soda water has been a very profitable business. There are the Pawangszu Soda Water Co., Yinho Soda Water Co., Peiyang Soda Water

Co. at Mukden, and the Hulan Sugar Mill and Brewery at Harbin. Along the Chinese Eastern Railway, there are four breweries turning out from about 100,000 to 500,000 bottles yearly.

29. **The sauce and sugar industries.** The sauce and sugar industries have a story of more than twenty years. The sauce business enjoys a wide market and consequently is profitable. The best kind of sauce is made in the trade training department of the First Jail at Mukden. The sugar manufacturing industry was first attempted in 1906. At that time the agricultural experiment station first made its appearance so that the sugar manufacturing business was not successful. In the year 1909, the Chinese Government first established the Hulan Sugar Factory at Harbin. But owing to the scarcity of sugar beets, the output was greatly limited. This enterprise has been taken over by the Provincial Bank of the Three Eastern Provinces, and now it is undergoing a process of reorganization.

3. The Textile Industry.

30. **Silk and cotton manufacture.** The spinning and weaving industry comprises three classifications, tussah silk, cotton and wool. Silk filatures have been opened at Kaiping, Hsiuyen, Chuangho, Hsifeng, Antung, Mukden and other districts, the best being in Mukden, but most of the factories are in Antung. The Chunyi Silk Weaving Co. was established in 1920 at Mukden with a capital of $250,000. It has 400 filatures and 150 looms, and its annual output is 8,000 rolls of pongee and 300 piculs of silk. At Antung there are thirty-seven silk factories with capital ranging from $10,000 to $30,000 and workmen numbering from one to six hundred. They have from 100 to 600 looms and their output every year aggre-

gates 10,000 boxes of silk and 600,000 catties of silk waste. The silk annually exported from the Provinces is valued at 10,000,000 Haikwan taels.

The cotton industry is centered in Mukden, Yingkow, Antung, Changchun, Harbin and other large cities, but the largest weaving factory, established in July, 1920, is at Mukden. This factory is capitalized at $4,500,000, and occupies 280 *mou* of land. It is equipped with a 600 horse-power boiler, and an electric motor furnishing an electric power of 1,000 kilowatts. There are 20,000 spindles, 200 looms, 5 sock and stocking machines, and one dyeing machine. Its present output comprises cotton cloth, cotton and dyed fabrics, thread socks and stockings. Every year it turns out 15,000 bales of cotton piece goods, 480 bales of dyed fabrics, 150,000 rolls of cotton cloth, and 9,500 dozens of socks or stockings. There are 1,300 workmen in the whole plant. That it is under competent management is shown by the fact that although most cotton mills in the country are running at a loss, this undertaking is a great financial success.

31. **Woollen manufacture.** The annual wool output in the Three Eastern Provinces is 30,000,000 kilograms. The best-known of the woollen factories is the Yu Ching Teh Woollen Factory at Harbin, established in May of 1922, with a capital of one million dollars. It is equipped with dynamo and the necessary machinery. It employs over 300 workmen. The factory anually turns out 91,400 blankets of various sizes and qualities, 125,000 yards of woollen goods, valued at $1,500,000. Besides receiving from the Government special encouragement this factory is exempted from taxation.

4. The Iron Works.

32. **The Mukden arsenal and other iron works.** The

Mukden Arsenal is recognized as the best iron works in the Provinces. This plant occupies 3,200 *mou* of land. It comprises the bullet factory, rifle factory, shell factory, gun factory, powder factory, foundry and fire-engine factory, seven in all. In the year 1930, this arsenal had a staff of 1062 men and employed 8050 workmen. This plant is the best of its kind in the whole country. Next comes the workshop attached to the North-eastern University. It was started in 1925 with a capital of $1,750,-000. Its present equipment comprises lighter cranes and thirteen movable platforms, nineteen generating engines, seven electric engines, 207 Dynamo-electric machines. Thus equipped it can turn out various passengers and freight cars, working machines, various implements and tools. It can also repair engines, iron-work machines, steam engines and dynamos. Then there is the workshop at Huangkutun connected with the Peining Railway similar to the North-eastern University workshop, only on a smaller scale. According to the investigations made in the year 1929, in Mukden district alone there were 26 iron works, with a total capital of $3,000,000.

5. The Electric Works.

33. **Sixty power plants.** There are about sixty power plants in the Three Eastern Provinces. With the exception of those under foreign or joint Sino-foreign control and management, the purely Chinese-owned enterprises make up more than half of the total number. The Mukden Power Plant is equipped with five dynamos having 9,600 kilowatts and serves 200,000 consumers. It enjoys a very profitable business. Next comes the power plant at Harbin with similar equipment as the Mukden Plant, but it has fewer consumers. This plant also runs the street cars in Harbin making substantial profit. The Muk-

den Tram-Car Company is under municipal management. Though it is a fairly successful enterprise its service needs to be extended to yield greater profit. Besides
these power plants, there are other electric enterprises
under private or Government ownership. Steps are being
taken to start similar establishments in distant or remote
districts.

34. **Printing and tannery.** Among the printing establishments set up to meet the needs of the rapid cultural
advancement in the Three Eastern Provinces, mention
should be made of the printing department connected
with the North-eastern University, the Tungchi Printing
House, and the Hsinhua Press, each with a capital over
$100,000. The tanning business has also been making
rapid headway, like the North-eastern Tannery and
Chunghua Tannery at Mukden, and the Shuanghoshen
Tannery at Harbin. The last named company, established
in 1922, with a capital of one million dollars, has become
widely known for the high quality of its goods.

35. **Encouragement from Chinese Government.** The
Chinese Government has shown great interest in the
new enterprises by extending to them special considerations in the form of reduction of taxes or the abolition of
duties entirely. With such favourable circumstances,
the Chambers of Commerce have been able to promote
many industrial enterprises. The industrial development of the Three Eastern Provinces is therefore being
greatly accelerated.

6. The Mining Industries.

36. **History of mining.** It is a well-known fact that
the vast territory of the North-eastern Provinces is famous for its minerals. Besides its abundance of coal and
iron, there are gold sands, talc, magnesite, lead, copper,

and clay. The mining industry had already reached a high stage of development as far back as the tenth century during the Pohai regime, and later on, during the Manchu dynasty, particular attention was paid to the coal and gold mining. Since the establishment of the Republic the Government has been even more interested in promoting the mining industries. The results so far have been gratifying. We shall give a more detailed account in the following paragraphs.

37. **The coal mining companies.** According to the estimates of mining experts, the coal deposits for the whole of the Three Eastern Provinces are in the neighbourhood of 1,556,243,000 tons: 1,174,006,000 in Liaoning; 138,850,000 in Kirin; and 243,387,000 in Heilungkiang. The coal mines registered are 387 in Liaoning; 270 in Kirin; and 26 in Heilungkiang. According to the 1930 statistics, the total output of all the active coal mines in this region was 10,040,652 tons. With the exception of the Fushun and Yentai mines managed entirely by the Japanese and the collieries at Penshi, Muling, Chalannar, and Laotaokou, run by both Chinese and foreigners on a co-operative basis, all the other coal mines are entirely operated by the Chinese.

(1) The North-eastern Mining Administration is the largest of its kind in the North-east. In 1919, it took over the operation of the Pataohao coal-fields; in 1928, it took over the Fuchowan coal mines; and in 1931, the Hsi-an mines. These three mines were merged and reorganized into a limited mining company. The following table shows the capital, land area and the daily output of each of these mines.

The Location of Mines	Capital	Area (in mou)	Daily output (in ton)
Pataohao Coal Mines.........	$3,600,000	5,400	250
Fuchow " "	2,000,000	21,929	800
Hsi-an " "	1,400,000	9,600	800
Total...................	$7,000,000	36,929	1,850

(2) The Chinkou Mine:—The Chinkou Mine covers an area of 1,405 *mou*. It was first started by a merchant named Chow Wen-kwei, but owing to lack of capital it became a joint enterprise with the Shen-hai Railway, both parties furnishing capital aggregating $1,350,000. It was reorganized as a company, and its output rose to 95,430 tons in 1927.

(3) The Weimingshan Coal Mine, covering an area of 1,332 *mou*, was started by a merchant called Li Shun-ching in the early eighties. After the Sino-Japanese War, it was reorganized as an official enterprise bearing the name of Tienli Coal Mining Co., with a capital of $120,000 and an annual output of 40,000 tons.

(4) The Naitsushan Coal Mine, covering an area of 50,000 *mou*, was started in the early seventies. In 1909 a man called Li Ming secured a license for its operation, and its yearly output was 3,000 tons. In the year 1928, it was reorganized and called the Naitzushan Coal Mining Co. It increased its shares, and with an additional capital of $1,500,000 new machinery was installed. The Chiao-Nai branch railway was built by the Kirin-Tunhua Railway to provide it with better transport facilities. Its daily output is about 300 tons.

(5) The Huoshihling Coal Mine is divided into two parts. One part covering 1,600 *mou* is under the management of the Yuchi Coal Mining Company. It was capitalized at $300,000 and has a daily output of 50 tons.

The other part covering 2,159 *mou* is under the Yutung Coal Mining Company with a capital of $1,000,000. It turns out 200 tons a day.

(6) The Hokang Coal Mine has an area of 9,058 *mou* and is under the management of the Hokang Coal Mining Company. Its coal is of superior quality and enjoys a good market in Kirin and Heilungkiang. The Company is capitalized at $3,115,327. It owns a branch railway with its own rolling stock.

38. **The various iron works.** There are rich iron deposits in the Three Eastern Provinces. But the Anshan Iron Works under Japanese control and management, the Penhsi Coal and Iron Minig Company, a Sino-Japanese undertaking, and the Kunchangling Iron Mining Company have under their operation more than half of the iron mines. The following table gives the names of the other important iron mines which have been surveyed by experts.

Place	Quantity (in 1000 tons)	Percentage of iron	Proportion per 1000 tons
Kuotishan, Haicheng....	2,000	29.31	600
Wengchengtze, Fuhsien..	300	36.00	100
Kanghsikou, Fengcheng..	120	40.00	48
Chitaokou, Tunhua......	1,200	40.00	480
Hsuchiatun, Kaiping.....	300	33.00	99
Talitzekou, Linkiang.....	13,500	40.00	540
Hsiaoliangchan, Acheng..	10,500	40.00	420

39. **Gold mines richest in China.** The gold deposits in the Three Eastern Provinces are the richest in China. The gold mining business is most successfully and profitably undertaken in Heilungkiang, followed by Kirin and Liaoning. There are seven gold collecting bureaus established in Kirin in addition to the Hsinchu Gold Mining Corporation, a joint Government and commercial enterprise. There are many gold mines in Heilungkiang:

the Fengyuan, Teyuan, Chenhsin, Yupien Yuanli, Kuhsi, Chicheng, Hungyueh, Taching, Hsinan, Kuyuan, Kuanghsin, Yuhsingho, Hsinhua, Taiping, Moho, Sansing, Wutungho, Yenho and Lingchuan gold mines. According to investigations made by the experts, the estimated output of the gold mines in the Provinces is as follows:

Province	Gold District	Output (in kilogram)
Heilungkiang	Aihui	5,000
"	Huma	1,801
"	Moho	338
"	Shihwei and Chikangho	700
"	Nun-kiang	100
"	Hsiaohsinganling	328
"	Upper Sungari River	820
Kirin	Sansing	820
"	Mutankiang and Mulingho	328
"	Suifenho and Tumenkiang	500
	Total output	10,735 km.

40. **Copper mines.** There are no less than thirty places in the Provinces where copper is to be found, but only three copper mines have been opened.

(1) The copper mine in Tsingshihchushan, Panshih district, Kirin.

This mine has copper deposits estimated at approximately 70,000 tons. In 1908, it was started as a Government enterprise, later it passed into commercial control, and now it is run by the Yung-Heng Provincial Bank at Kirin.

(2) The copper mines at Tienpaoshan, Yenchih district, Kirin.

This mine covers an area of sixty square *li*. It also produces silver. The mine was started in the year 1889, turning out 160,000 taels of silver in the first three years. Owing to the Russo-Japanese War, its operation was for a time suspended. In 1916, it was taken over by the Tien-paoshan Silver and Copper Mining Company, and from 1917 to 1920, the total output of copper lumps amounted to 1,320,294 tons, and lead lumps above 100,000 tons.

(3) The Copper Mine at Malukou, Penhsi district, Liaoning.

This mine was first started in 1916, but owing to the depreciation in the prices of copper it was later suspended. In the year 1923, it was taken over by Mr. Wang Pien-tzu. Its anual output is from six to seven hundred tons.

41. **Lead and silver mines.** There are fifty-eight lead and silver mines in Liaoning which have been registered with the Government; thirty-one in Kirin; and seven in Heilungkiang. Among the lead mines now under operation the most successful are that in Tsingchengtze and in Jentzukou, Liaoning and the one in Kuanmachutze, Kirin.

42. **The talc.** The talc is found in large quantities in Liaoning, Hsiuyen and other districts in the Province of Liaoning, especially in the south-east of Haicheng. There are fifty-three such quarries registered with the Government. The talc found at Taling is of the very best quality. The Taling Talc Quarry was started by private interests in 1916, but it was taken over by the Taling Talc Company in 1919 with a daily output of thirty tons.

43. **The magnesite.** The largest magnesite beds known are found in the two districts at Haicheng and Kaiping in Liaoning about thirty-five kilometres in length, and some parts are as deep as 900 metres. These beds are being worked by the Hsinai Company and two other companies. There are eleven such beds now registered with the Government. Their annual output is as follows:

1917	1,800 tons
1920	6,940 "
1921	2,940 "
1922	4,510 "
1923	2,700 "
1924	10,142 "
1925	13,773 "
1926	20,000 "
1927	21,400 "
1928	25,454 "
1929	31,682 "

44. The clay beds. The clay beds so far discovered and registered are forty-nine in number, of which about one-fifth are under operation. The most successful of these enterprises is the one at Wahutsui, Fuhsien, in Liaoning which covers 6,000 *mou* with deposits estimated at about 28,128,000 tons. It had been successively worked upon by different companies known as the Tungyi, Yiho, Tienhocheng, Tatung, Fuyuan, Tahua and Tungholung Companies. Lately, it has been taken on by the Northeastern Mining Company, but pending the settlement of differences between China and Japan, actual work has not been started yet. The following table shows its output during the past seven years from 1923 to 1929:

1923	25,119 tons
1924	38,505 "
1925	25,796 "
1926	34,371 "
1927	38,353 "
1928	53,763 "
1929	59,827 "

45. Other minerals. There are other minerals which have been discovered, such as sulphureted iron, sulphur, and various kinds of stone quarries, rock salt, soda fields, etc., but their areas are not large nor are they developed on a large scale.

CHAPTER V. COMMUNICATIONS.

1. Railways.

46. General view of the railways. Viceroy Li Hung-chang was the first to realize the importance of railways in the development of the Three Eastern Provinces. Under his energetic leadership the Peking-Mukden Railway was completed with the construction of the section outside of the Great Wall. In 1896, an agreement with Russia was entered into for the construction and the joint control of the Chinese Eastern Railway. The southern section of this railway, from Changchun to Dairen, now known as the South Manchuria Railway, was transferred to Japan as a result of the Russo-Japanese War. During the governorship of Hsu Shih-chang and Si Liang, Japan, without any sound legal justification, objected to the proposed construction of the Hsinmintun-Fakumen and Chinchow-Aigun lines. Later on, the Kirin-Changchun and Ssupingkai-Taonan Railways were built with Japanese loans. In the autumn of 1924, Marshal Chang Tso-lin adopted the plan for railway construction in the Provinces submitted by Mr. Wang Yung-kiang, the civil governor of Fengtien (Liaoning). Japan's consent to waive her right of constructing the Kaiyuan-Hailung line having been obtained, steps were immediately taken to raise the necessary funds through popular subscription and Government appropriations for the construction of the Mukden-Hailung Railway. The Tahushan-Tungliao branch line was also built about this time with the surplus from the Peking-Mukden Railway. This was followed by the construction of the Kirin-Hailung Line in Kirin, the Hulan-Hailun and Tsitsihar-Koshan Lines in Heilungkiang, and Taoan-Solun Line in Liaoning. All these lines were financed and built entirely with Chinese capital and by Chinese engineers. The Taonan-Angang-chi and Kirin-Tunhua railways, however, were constructed with Japanese capital advanced by the South Manchuria Railway Company. The present length of Chinese owned railways in the Provinces is 3,000 kilo-metres. They are as follows:—[8]

[8] Prepared by the North-eastern Communications Commission.

Name	Terminal Points	Distance (kilometre)	Year of Construction	Year When Commenced	Nature	Width of Rails
Peining Railway (section outside Shanhaikwan).	From Shanhaikwan to Shenyang (including Ying-Tung, Chin-chao, Hulutao and Peiling lines)	904.08	1894	1907-27	National Government Railway (with foreign capital)	1.435 metre (4.85 ft.)
Ssu-Tao Railway.	From Ssupingkai to Tao-nan; from Chengchiatun to Tungliao	424.91	1916	1923	"	"
Tao-Ang Railway.	From Tao-nan to Nonni River.	224.28	1925	1926	"	"
Ki-Chang Railway.	From Kirin to Changchun.	127.74	1909	1912	"	"
Ki-Tun Railway.	Kirin to Tunhua.	210.43	1926	1928	"	"
Shen-Hai Railway.	From Shenyang to Chaoyangchen; Meiho to Hsi-an.	319.00	1925	1927	Provincial Government Railway	"
Ki-Hai Railway.	From Kirin to Chaoyangchen.	183.40	1927	1929	"	"
Su-Hai Railway.	From Sung-pu to Hailun.	224.50	1925	1928	"	"
Tsi-Ko Railway.	From Nonni River to Koshan.	175.80	1928	1931	"	"
Tao-So Railway.	From Tao-an to Solun.	84.00	1928		"	"
Ho-Kang Railway.	From Lienhuapao to Hokang.	56.00	1926	1928	Private owned railway for the transportation of coal	5 feet
Kai-feng light Railway.	From Kaiyuan to Hsi-feng.	64.00	1925	1926	Private owned railway	1 metre
Tsi-an light Railway.	From Tsitsihar to Nonni River	29.00	1909	1910	Provincial Government railway	"

47. **The Mukden-Hailung line.** Fifty per cent. of China's railways are in the Three Eastern Provinces, where more than two-thirds of all Chinese-owned railways were constructed entirely with Chinese capital. The Sheng-Hai Railway was the first line which was financed entirely with Chinese capital. This enterprise, which extends from the provincial capital of Liaoning to Chaoyangchen in Hailung district, was undertaken by the Liaoning Provincial Government in co-operation with the people. The work for its construction was started in July 1925, and completed in August 1927. It was built at a cost of over $14,000,000 including the purchase of land. It covers a distance of 319 kilometres. The value of this railway together with its property is in excess of $20,900,000.

48. **The Hulan-Hailun line.** The next in order is the Hu-Hai Line which extends from Sungpuchen in Hulan district to Hailun City. It was an undertaking financed by appropriations from the Heilungkiang Provincial Government and by popular subscription. The Company was organized in the provincial capital of Heilungkiang in August 1925, and work was commenced in October of the same year. The whole line was completed and open to traffic on December 15th, 1928. Its trunk and branch lines cover a distance of 224 kilometres. The cost for its construction amounted to $11,088,000.

49. **The Kirin-Hailung line.** The Ki-Hai Railway is another line built by China without foreign capital. It extends from the provincial capital of Kirin to Chaoyangchen. It connects with the Sheng-Hai Railway to form the big trunk line in the eastern section of the Three Eastern Provinces. It was also a joint enterprise between the Provincial Government and the people. The

work for the building of this line, which covers 183 kilometres, was started in May 1927, and completed in June
1929. Its properties are valued at over $9,110,000.

50. **The Tsitsihar-Koshan line.** The Tsi-Ko Railway
is another line built with Chinese capital. It extends
from the Nonni River to Koshan by way of Tsitsihar.
The work for the building of this line was commenced in
October 1928, and by 1931 it was all but completed. It
was the original plan to make Tsitsihar the terminal
point. The necessary funds were provided by Liaoning,
Heilungkiang and the Ministry of Communications, each
advancing the sum of $400,000 making a total of $1,200,-
000. Additional shares were issued when it was decided
to extend the line to Koshan. According to the Tsi-Ko
Railway Administration, the sum of $4,890,000 was raised
for this purpose by the end of 1930.

51. **The Taoan-Solun line.** The Tao-So Railway is
still another line constructed with purely Chinese capital.
It extends from the Taoan station north-westward along
the northern bank of Tao-Erh River till it reaches Solun
on the border of Heilungkiang. It is 170 kilometres in
length. This line was built with the object of opening
up the barren tract of land along the frontier. The work
for its construction was commenced on August 15th,
1929. The Peining Railway advanced $100,000 every
month for its expenses. By February 1931, the section
of Hwai-yang-chen was completed, covering 84 kilometres. The cost for the completion of the whole line
was estimated at $5,000,000. This railway would have
been completed and put into service if it had not been
brought to an abrupt termination by the sudden military
coup dealt by Japan on September 18th, 1931.

52. **The Tahushan-Tungliao line.** The Ta-Tung line

is an important branch of the Peining Railway. It extends from Tahushan to Tungliao district and connects with the Cheng-Tung (Chengchiatun-Tungliao) branch of the Ssu-Tao (Ssupingkai-Taonan) Railway. It is 253 kilometres in length. The work on this line was started in the winter of 1922. The section to Hsinlitun was finished in May 1925, and the entire line was completed by October 1927. The sum of $7,200,000, derived from the surplus of the Peining Railway, was spent on its construction. With the completion of the Ta-Tung line, it was not long before through traffic was effected for the four main lines—the Peining, Ssu-Tao, Tao-Ang, and Tsi-Ko—in the western section, and later extended to the four principal lines in the eastern section—the Peining, Sheng-Hai, Ki-Hai and Ki-Tun. The establishment of close inter-relationships for all these lines has given great impetus to the industry and commerce of this vast but as yet partially developed region. Far from proving detrimental to the interest of the South Manchuria Railway, these Chinese lines have become its most valuable feeders. According to reliable statistics two-thirds of the goods handled by the four western lines, and nine-tenths by the four eastern lines are shipped to the southern terminus of Dairen through the South Manchuria Railway.

53. **The mileage and amount of business on the lines.** The increase in railway mileage from 1900-1930 in the Three Eastern Provinces is as follows:

Year	Increase for the Year (in kilometres)	Total
1900	91.97	91.97
1907	326.95	418.92
1912	123.61	542.53
1914	174.00	666.53
1917	33.37	699.90
1921	113.70	813.60
1923	320.95	1134.55
1924	111.00	1245.55
1925	175.98	1421.53
1926	344.20	1765.70
1927	505.06	2270.76
1928	462.73	2733.49
1929	257.90	2991.39
1930	194.10	3085.49

During recent years the rapid increase in population has greatly stimulated the material development of the Three Eastern Provinces. This is reflected in the marked increase in the earnings of the nine railways. The following are the figures for the year 1930 compiled by the North-eastern Communications Commission.

Name of Railway	Number of Passengers	Passenger Receipts	Freight Tonnage	Freight Receipts	Total Receipts
Peining	6,906,904	15,804,420.00	8,611,243	20,911,332.00	36,716,012.00
Ssu-Tao	962,634	2,052,032.75	954,787	5,315,949.57	7,367,982.32
Tao-An	418,349	729,372.17	317,495	867,019.69	1,596,411.86
Ki-Chang	793,253	927,260.72	784,422	2,040,343.39	2,967,550.11
Ki Tun	366,797	491,960.90	574,424	1,140,786.99	1,632,747.89
Hu-Hai	633,504	952,894.85	684,254	2,969,606.60	3,922,501.45
Tsi-Ko	270,617	398,626.96	319,160	1,155,888.17	1,554,515.13
Sheng-Hai	1,347,855	2,471,165.54	758,155	4,905,772.07	7,376,937.61
Ki-Hai	383,024	817,123.29	323,303	937,854.57	1,754,977.86

The receipts and expenditures of the nine railways for the last three years, from 1928-1930, together with their profits and losses, are as follows:

Name of Railway		Receipts	Expenditures	Profits	Losses
Peiping:	1928	21,821,545	10,958,396	10,863,749	....
	1929	37,105,807	18,512,682	18,593,125	....
	1930	36,716,012	20,416,402	16,299,610	....
Ssu-Tao:	1928	6,063,293	......	......	....
	1929	6,930,405	7,758,156	......	927,751
	1930	7,967,982	......	......	....
Tao-Ang:	1928	1,138,313	1,042,849	95,464	....
	1929	2,080,759	1,653,157	427,638	....
	1930	1,596,412	......	......	....
Ki-Chang:	1928	3,628,480	2,553,015	1,075,465	....
	1929	3,884,751	2,697,007	1,187,744	....
	1930	3,028,352	2,779,906	248,446	....
Ki-Tun:	1928	......	......	......	....
	1929	1,802,086	1,746,479	55,607	....
	1930	1,778,974	1,735,297	43,677	....
Hu-Hai:	1928	4,574,711	2,468,311	2,106,400	....
	1929	4,741,599	2,873,702	1,867,897	....
	1930	3,922,501	2,600,265	1,332,344	....
Tsi-Ko:	1928	......	......	......	....
	1929	1,570,000	......	......	....
	1930	1,554,515	......	......	....
Sheng-Hai:	1928	3,728,086	......	......	....
	1929	5,343,086	3,399,840	1,943,246	....
	1930	7,376,937	4,353,027	3,023,910	....
Ki-Hai:	1928	......	......	......	....
	1929	1,045,460	......	......	....
	1930	1,754,977	......	......	....

54. Compared with the South Manchuria Railway.
According to the figures given out by the South Manchuria Railway Company, its receipts for the year 1930
amounted to 122,103,743 yen. As this railway covers a
distance of 1,128 kilometres, its receipts for this year
were therefore in the neighbourhood of 110,000 yen per
kilometre, which is equivalent to more than $200,000 in
our currency at the rate of exchange as obtained at that
time. The nine Chinese-owned railways in the Three
Eastern Provinces aggregate 2,794 kilometres, and in
the year 1930 their combined earnings totalled $64,889,-
636. Their receipts for this year therefore amounted to
only $23,224 per kilometre ten times less than the rev-

enues per kilometre of the South Manchuria Railway in the same year. This tremendous difference is easily accounted for by the fact that the South Manchuria Railway serves the most densely populated and the most productive districts in the Three Eastern Provinces; whereas, with the exception of the Peining Railway, all the other Chinese lines pass through sparsely populated and undeveloped territory. The Ssu-Tao and Tao-Ang Railways are being actually run at a loss. Far from feeling discouraged our Government is planning to construct two main lines—one from Kirin to Tung-kiang and the other from Na-Ho to Hei-Ho—with the object of reclaiming the vast barren tracts of land. Every new railway built by our Government has materially benefited the South Manchuria Railway, as shown by its steady increase of annual receipts since 1926.

2. Water Transportation.

a. SEA TRANSPORTATION.

55. **The harbours: decline and fall of Yingkow.** Besides Port Arthur and Dairen, the harbours in the Three Eastern Provinces which have been opened to shipping are Yingkow, Antung and Tatungkow. The Hulutao harbour is in the course of construction.

Yingkow became a commercial port in 1858. Its wharves were built on the right bank of the Liao River. It rapidly became the foremost shipping and commercial centre in the Provinces. But it is handicapped by the fact that it is frozen for four months every winter. Furthermore, its harbour is easily silted, thus rendering it difficult of passage by big liners. For these reasons it could not successfully compete with the ice-free port of Dairen, which, after it was opened as a commercial port, soon out-distanced Yinkow as the premier port of the Three

Eastern Provinces. Nevertheless, its shipping and commerce showed steady increase. The dredging work which is being energetically taken in hand by the Liao-Ho Conservancy Bureau gives room for hope that Yingkow will have a great future. We shall give the figures [9] concerning the vessels of various nationalities which entered and cleared the port, together with the registered tonnage, for the past three years.

1928.

Nationality	Number	Registered Tonnage
China	864	691,588
Japan	509	454,969
Great Britain	218	289,933
Norway	39	51,511
Germany	24	25,844
Holland	8	16,520
France	58	20,844
United States	4	18,096
Total	1,724	1,569,305

1929.

Nationality	Number	Registered Tonnage
China	739	616,360
Japan	632	689,292
Great Britain	260	378,868
France	12	2,712
Germany	14	12,684
Holland	6	10,932
Italy	4	2,966
Denmark	2	9,420
Norway	39	67,577
Finland	2	1,848
United States	2	10,870
Total	1,712	1,803,529

[9] *North-eastern Year Book, 1931.*

1930.

Nationality	Number	Registered Tonnage
China	686	583,295
Japan	751	880,504
Great Britain	244	344,090
France	..	18,808
Germany	..	24,866
Holland	..	5,412
Italy	..	4,534
Denmark	..	11,722
Norway	..	5,418
United States	..	17,764
Total		1,879,413

56. **Antung.** Antung became a commercial port in 1903. Its harbour is bounded on one side by Shaokou and on the other by Wutaokou. It has berthing accommodations for 3000-ton vessels. It soon became an important shipping and commercial centre in South Manchuria. Like Yingkow, it is not an ice-free port, being frozen for four months in winter. The figures for its shipping for the last three years are as follows:

Year	Nationality	Number	Registered Tonnage
1928	China	342	166,714
"	Japan	588	299,378
"	Great Britain	62	77,264
"	Norway	4	4,240
	Total	996	547,596
1929	China	294	140,020
"	Japan	548	273,578
"	Great Britain	60	80,134
"	Finland	4	5,822
	Total	906	499,554
1930	China	272	163,744
"	Japan	526	238,022
"	Great Britain	88	114,290
"	Norway	2	3,038
	Total	888	519,094

57. **Tatungkou.** Tatungkou was made a commercial port in 1903. It is situated outside the mouth and along the western bank of the Yalu River. It almost constitutes an outer harbour for Antung. In former times it was the principal trading centre in Liaoning Province, but since Antung was opened up for international trade it rapidly fell into insignificance until finally in 1922 when the Customs House, which was established there in 1907, was abolished and amalgamated with the Customs House in Antung.

58. **The principal shipping companies.** The principal shipping companies operating in the Three Eastern Provinces are the Cheng Chi, Shao Hsing, Yu Ta, Hai Chang, Pei Fang, Chih Tung, Ta Tung, Tung Pei and Jih Chang Companies, while the China Merchants Steamship Navigation Company, the best known and oldest Chinese shipping concern, whose ships ply along the China coast and also on the Yangtze, and the Sanpei Company, have in recent years also been doing their best to extend their operations into the Provinces. Of these companies, Cheng Chi has shown the best results. Organized in the first year of the reign of Emperor Hsuan Tung (1909), this company operates a fleet of ships between Yingkow, Dairen and Chefoo. During the Great War (1914-1918), when many foreign ships were recalled for war service in Europe, Cheng Chi practically monopolized the shipping trade between the Three Eastern Provinces and the coastal provinces of China proper. With the conclusion of the War, foreign ships returned to the China waters and keen competition resulted in considerable losses for the company. The Chinese authorities of the Provinces stepped in and saved the situation by investing $2,000,000 in the company, and strengthened its foundation. Since then it has shown increased profits

every year. The following table [10] shows the number of Chinese shipping companies operating in the Provinces together with their ships and their tonnage:

Name of Company	Number of Ships	Tonnage
Cheng Chi	20	25,983.23
Chih Tung	5	2,626.80
C. M. S. N. Co	16	32,910.33
Nan Hua	2	5,123.88
San Pei	8	13,986.35
Hai Chang	3	5,177.78
Shao Hsing	4	6,523.26
Ning Shao	2	4,992.41
Pei Fang	4	6,383.62
Ho Feng	2	3,797.06
Yu Ta	3	1,728.00
Ta Tung	3	(not available)
China United	3	2,804.56
Yung Ning	2	(not available)
Other Companies	17	17,772.02
Total	94	129,809.19

59. **The Hulutao harbour.** The construction of a harbour at Hulutao represents one of the greatest communication enterprises which the Chinese Government has undertaken. Hulutao is a promontory in the northern part of the Gulf of Pechili. It is located in the Lienshan Bay which lies between the ports of Yingkow and Chinwangtao. Ice-free in winter and typhoon-free in summer, Hulutao is, indeed, an ideal port of the North-eastern Provinces.

The idea of making Hulutao a port dates back to 1908, when Mr. Hsu Shih-chang was still viceroy of the Three Eastern Provinces. Mr. W. R. Hughes, a British engineer, was engaged to make the necessary surveys, and it was finally decided to construct a harbour at Hulutao. Work was commenced in October 1910, and when it was suspended one year later on account of the Chinese Revo-

[10] *Ibid.*

lution, only the seven and a half mile railway between Hulutao and Lienshan, a station on the Peiping-Mukden Railway, had been completed together with the 400 feet of the proposed breakwater and other minor structures. In 1920, there was talk of reviving the project, but no progress was made. On January 24th, 1930, a contract was signed at Tientsin between the Peining (Peiping-Mukden) Railway Administration and the Netherlands Harbour Works Co. of Amsterdam, Holland, providing for the completion of the Hulutao Port project by the latter firm for the sum of G. $6,400,000. Mr. Kao Chi-yi, managing director of the Peiping-Mukden Railway, acting under the instruction of the Ministry of Railways of the National Government signed on behalf of the railway, while the Dutch Company was represented by Mr. Robert de Vos, their general representative for China.

60. **The contract for its construction.** The contract provides that after meeting its British loan obligations, the Peiping-Mukden Railway shall set aside G. $95,000 from its revenues monthly to meet the contract price of G. $6,400,000 and that the harbour work shall be completed within a period of five and half years. It is further stipulated in the agreement that the contractor shall pay to the Chinese railway $1,000 (silver dollars) for every day of delay in the completion and delivery of the works to the Chinese Government within the time-limit stipulated in the agreement.

After the contract was signed, the Peiping-Mukden Railway and the Dutch Company deposited $1,000,000 and $500,000 respectively as a guarantee for the fulfilment of the contract. On July 2nd, 1930, a ceremony was held for the opening of the construction work. The details of the Hulutao scheme are: (1) a breakwater of 5,100 feet; (2) a quay wall of 3,700 feet; (3) retaining dykes of 7,900 feet; (4) dredging of harbour basin and an entrance channel (an area of about 70,000 square feet); (5) reclamation of low grounds and a part of the foreshore.

In addition to these, lighthouses, dockyards, go-downs, etc. are to be completed, while municipal works also are under consideration. When the harbour is completed, Hulutao will play a great rôle in the economic development of the Three Eastern Provinces.

b. INLAND NAVIGATION.

61. **Navigation on the Sungari and the shipping companies.** Of all the rivers in the Provinces, the Sungari is the most important so far as shipping is concerned. Connecting the Ussuri River and the Amur River, the Sungari forms a profitable line of navigation with Harbin as its centre. The Russians used to monopolize the navigation of the three rivers. After the Russian Revolution, Russian ships on the Amur were conspicuous by their absence. In 1918, a shipping company known as the Wu Tung Company was organized and began to run ships on the Sungari, the Amur and the Ussuri. In 1920, the Wu Tung Company was converted into a joint enterprise of the Government and the merchants. In 1925, the company failed and sold all its ships to the Government of the Three Eastern Provinces which established a North-eastern Navigation Bureau to manage them. In 1927, this bureau combined with five private and public shipping concerns to form the North-eastern Government and Commercial Joint Navigation Bureau. This bureau owns 48 ships and 69 tugs. Besides the Sungari and Amur Steamship Navigation Company, the Kwang Hsing Navigation Company and 29 other shipping companies own 53 ships and 71 tugs. Altogether there are

101 ships and 140 tugs plying on the Sungari, the Amur
and the Ussuri, having an aggregate tonnage of 85,000
tons. Moreover, there are 1,843 junks engaged in the
trade. The Customs reports showing the tonnage of
goods carried by ships on the Sungari during the five
years from 1925 to 1929 give the following figures:

Year	Tons
1925	372,400
1926	468,400
1927	580,300
1928	540,600
1929	781,500

According to the statistics published by the Harbin
Navigation Guild the number of passengers carried by
ships plying on the Sungari for the three years of 1927,
1928, and 1929 are as follows:

	1927	1928	1929
Number of passengers from Harbin to other ports	487,309	507,564	310,531
Number of passengers arriving at Harbin.	308,477	344,753	292,030
Total	795,786	852,317	602,561

62. **The Nonni River.** The Nonni River, which has
close connections with the Sungari, and the Hu-lan River
are also navigable, but owing to its shallowness, the
Nonni is navigable by junks only up to the confluence of
the Sungari and from Tsitsihar and Harbin to Hu-lan.

63. **The Liao River.** The Liao River and its tribu-
taries have a combined length of 3,500 *li,* but the Liao
River is navigable by small craft for about 1,428 *li* between Yingkow and Chengchiatun. As regards its tribu-
taries, the Tai Tze Ho is navigable for 405 *li* from Han-
chiatientzu to Sanchaho, and the Hun Ho about 410 *li*
from Chang Tan to Sanchaho. Over 1,000 ships ply on
these rivers, transporting about 1,300,000 tons of rice

and cereals annually and over 30,000 pieces of miscellaneous goods.

64. **The Yalu River.** Shipping on the Yalu River is not so developed as on other rivers, owing to the fact that it is a silt-bearing stream and that it is ice-bound during most of the winter and spring. Small steamships are most adapted for navigation on this river.

65. **Government shipping organs.** The Chinese Government institutions for the development of shipping in the Provinces include (1) The Navigation Bureau at Harbin, which controls all matters pertaining to the navigation of the Sungari, Ussuri and the Amur; (2) The North-eastern Dockyard which since its opening at Harbin in 1928 had turned out 14 steamships, 15 lighters and three dredging boats up to 1930; (3) The Liao River Conservancy Bureau, which is entrusted with the work of dredging the Liao River; (4) The North-eastern Waterways Bureau which looks after the conservancy of the Sungari; (5) The North-eastern Commercial Navigation School and the Navigation Training Institute which exist for the purpose of training the necessary personnel for the administration of the shipping affairs; and (6) The Shipping Guild which is a mutual-aid institution run on the system of mutual insurance.

3. Postal and Telegraph Administration.

66. **The postal administration.** The Three Eastern Provinces are divided into two postal districts, the Liaoning District and the Kirin-Heilungkiang District. In each district there is a postal administration office. Under the two administrative offices for the two districts there are nine first-class post offices, 99 second-class and 140 third-class post offices, 43 branch offices, 574 postal

agencies and 1,776 post boxes. The following statistics [11] for 1927 throw an interesting light on the postal development of the Three Eastern Provinces.

Postal District	Letters	Parcels	Postal Orders	Savings
Liaoning	39,326,900	392,500	$6,097,100	$254,149
Kirin and Heilungkiang	38,474,600	500,100	$9,905,600	$ 89,630

67. **The telegraph administration.** The development of telegraphic communication in the Provinces has been most remarkable in recent years. There are 139 telegraph offices, including 8 first-class, 12 second-class and 48 third-class and 71 other offices, employing 531 operators. The total length of land wires is 23,535 *li* and the cable lines are 28,534 *li*. The volume [12] of telegraphic traffic for the three years of 1928, 1929, and 1930 is as follows:

Name of Province	Telegrams Sent			Telegrams Received		
	1928	1929	1930	1928	1929	1930
Liaoning	163,081	164,407	176,325	146,987	155,947	189,131
Kirin	193,759	181,015	183,162	178,297	173,452	174,189
Heilungkiang .	80,615	76,128	81,462	76,685	81,338	94,351

4. Telephones.

68. **The growth of the telephone.** The telephone was first introduced in a few of the most important cities of the Provinces. When Marshal Chang Tso-lin assumed control, he popularised the use of this modern means of communication by ordering the establishment of telephone exchanges in as many cities as possible. At present there are 132 telephone offices under Government management and 35 under private auspices, making a total of 167. Of these the Mukden Telephone Administration is the largest. First established in 1907, it in-

[11] Figures given in the annual publications of the Chinese Post Office.
[12] Figures given by the North-eastern Telegraph and Radio Administration.

stalled automatic telephones in 1930. The administration is capitalized at $886,000 and has 5,500 subscribers. Its long-distance telephone lines can communicate with Peiping, Tientsin, and all parts of the Three Eastern Provinces where there are telephones.

Next to the Mukden Telephone Administration are the Kirin and Changchun Telephone Companies, each capitalized at over $400,000. Although they have less subscribers than the Mukden company, they handle a large amount of long-distance telephone calls. The telephone administration at Harbin was originally a subsidiary enterprise of the Chinese Eastern Railway, but since coming under Chinese control, it has introduced many reforms with the result that its business is showing a steady improvement.

5. Wireless.

69. **The growth of the wireless.** The North-eastern Central Wireless Station was established in 1923. At first, it was open only for the sending and receiving of official messages. In the following year, a complete transmitting and receiving set was installed which was capable of receiving messages from Europe and America. In the same year the long-wave wireless station at the Northern Barracks was completed. Equipped with an up-to-date sending machine from the German Telefunken Company, the station could communicate direct with the Chinese wireless stations at Yunnan, Tihua and other frontier stations. In 1927, a short-wave wireless station was established outside the Big North Gate of the city of Mukden, thus opening direct communication with Berlin. In fact, this station has the distinction of being the first radio station in China to communicate with Europe direct. Until the opening of the International Wireless Station at Chenju, Shanghai, 1930, the Mukden station

relayed many telegrams to Europe from the Chinese wireless and cable companies in Peiping, Tientsin, Shanghai, Hankow and other cities. With the installation of a new 20 kilowatt short-wave sending machine, it opened direct communication with the United States in the summer of 1931. To facilitate communication with stations in China, it also installed a number of short-wave German and American machines and established branch wireless stations at Harbin, Tsitsihar, Yingkow, Changchun, Hulutao, Fuchin, Manchuli, Kirin, Lopei, Heiho, Moho, Erhpu and Huma. Both the central and branch stations handled a large volume of business. As to broadcasting stations there are two in the Provinces, one at Mukden and one at Harbin.

6. Roads.

70. **Road extension.** The governments of the Three Eastern Provinces always followed an active policy in regard to road building, the district magistrates receiving constant instructions to repair roads and build new ones. But owing to the fact that the wheels of the mule carts used by the farmers for the transportation of their goods and agricultural products are not adapted to the roads, they easily deteriorate, and although the authorities have done their best to encourage the introduction of other vehicles, the result is far from satisfactory. Indeed, the road question has become one of the most difficult facing the Chinese Government. So far, the motor roads are in a fair condition. Owing to Government encouragement the bus service in the Provinces has registered a marked development in recent years. At present there are 65 bus companies operating 260 cars. The total bus lines aggregate 20,000 *li* or 7,000 miles. In winter, many taxis are put into the bus service on the country roads.

CHAPTER VI. TRADE AND COMMERCE.

71. **History of foreign trade.** The foreign trade of the Three Eastern Provinces began in 1860 with the opening of the port of Newchwang. In 1907, Antung, Dairen, Tatungkow and Manchuli were opened to foreign trade and commerce, followed by Suifenho in 1908, Harbin, I-lan and Aigun in 1909 and Hunchun and Lungchingtsun in 1910. Since then the trade of the Provinces has developed by leaps and bounds. The following figures [13] tell an eloquent story of the development of the trade of the Provinces.

Foreign Trade in the Three Eastern Provinces.

(in million Haikwan taels)

Year	Imports	Exports	Total	Balance of Trade
1907	30.6	22.0	52.7	−8.6
1908	53.1	47.5	100.6	−5.5
1909	69.1	83.0	152.1	13.8
1910	81.7	88.9	170.7	7.2
1911	94.7	103.7	198.5	8.9
1912	102.2	100.1	202.3	−2.0
1913	125.6	113.0	238.7	−12.6
1914	112.4	109.3	221.4	−3.0
1915	108.1	130.0	238.1	21.9
1916	129.5	130.8	260.3	1.2
1917	158.5	161.1	319.6	2.5
1918	177.2	166.8	344.0	−10.3
1919	231.3	212.0	443.3	−19.2
1920	205.1	225.9	431.0	20.7
1921	218.1	234.4	452.5	16.2
1922	196.4	274.6	471.0	78.2
1923	207.0	293.9	500.9	86.8
1924	200.6	269.0	469.6	68.3
1925	244.7	312.3	557.0	67.6
1926	276.8	370.7	647.5	93.9
1927	268.9	408.0	676.9	139.1
1928	302.9	434.0	736.9	131.0
1929	329.6	425.6	755.2	96.0

[13] *Second Report on Progress in Manchuria, 1930*, pp. 136-137.

19

When the 1907 figures are compared with the 1929 figures it will be seen that the trade has increased thirteen-fold in 23 years.

One excellent sign is that save for the imports of machinery and railway equipments, the exports frequently exceeded imports, thereby registering a favourable balance of trade. Another point to be noted is that the foreign trade of China Proper in those 23 years increased only threefold, and if we assume that the 1907 index number is 100, then the 1929 index number for the trade of the Three Eastern Provinces will be 938 and that for China Proper is only 279. The rate of increase of the trade in the Three Eastern Provinces is therefore much greater than that of China Proper. Three reasons may be assigned for this remarkable development.

72. **Reasons in development of foreign trade.** In the first place, the population of the Provinces in 1907 was 16,000,000. To-day it has grown to 30,000,000, an increased of 88 per cent. During the same period, the population of China Proper increased only 30 per cent. Secondly, in the period of 23 years the land under cultivation in the Provinces increased 100 per cent, while there has been no corresponding increase in China Proper, because all the available land there has been cultivated. Therefore, the productivity of the land of the Provinces was doubled in 23 years. Thirdly, newly developed districts need new settlers and new settlers need many new things. Moreover, as life in the North-east is comparatively easy, the demand for goods is correspondingly greater. As a result, the consumption of the people in the North-eastern Provinces is greater than that of their fellow countrymen in other parts of China. This same phenomenon can be found in such newly settled countries as Australia and the Argentine.

1. Principal Items of Export and Import.

73. Agriculture the basic factor of development. Agricultural products always form the chief items in the export trade of the North-eastern Provinces. According to the statistics for 1929, beans, bean oil, and beancakes made up 70 per cent of the Provinces' exports, millet constitutes 4 per cent, *kaoliang* 2 per cent, and timber and hides 2 per cent. In short, agricultural products make up 86 per cent of the trade of the Provinces, while mineral, marine and other products constitute only 14 per cent. This shows that the prosperity of the Three Eastern Provinces is built on agriculture, and that the fruit of the labours of our 30,000,000 people is responsible for the remarkable development of the North-east.

74. The imports. As for imports, the 1929 statistics show that cotton and textiles made up 25 per cent; wool products, 4 per cent; clothes, food and other daily necessities, 28 per cent; steel, iron, machinery electrical materials, cars, petroleum, 15 per cent; and other miscellaneous things 28 per cent. This shows that most of the articles imported were either necessities or those necessary for the purpose of developing the country.

75. Advantages of Dairen. Because of its excellent harbour facilities as well as the fact that it is the terminus of the South Manchuria Railway, Dairen has become the leading port of the Provinces. For many years, the trade of Dairen constituted over 55 per cent of the total trade of the North-eastern Provinces. In 1929, this figure rose to 66 per cent which constitutes a new record for that port, but at the same time, the trade of Yingkow, Antung, Harbin and other cities also registered growth as shown by the following figures: [14]

[14] *Ibid.*, p. 143.

	1908	1918	1929
Newchwang	41,676,055	41,711,507	86,564,949
Antung	8,051,353	45,157,412	92,360,810
Harbin		36,098,213	58,014,030
Aigun		11,504,926	680,037

The reason why the trade of Yingkow, Antung, and Harbin has not shown the same rate of growth as the trade of Darien is because the various Chinese railways not only carry the goods entering by the port of Dairen, but they also serve as feeders to the South Manchuria Railway in the transportation of goods intended for export from Dairen. The benefits which Dairen derives from the Chinese Eastern Railway and the Chinese-owned railways are therefore no less than what it receives from the South Manchuria Railway. This may be proved by the following figures: [15]

Exports from Manchuria.

Year	Eastwards to Vladivostok via Pogranitchnaya	Southwards to Dairen via Changchun	Total	Percentage East-ward	South-ward
1924	770,000	1,180,000	1,950,000	0.39	0.61
1925	815,000	1,520,000	2,335,000	0.34	0.65
1926	1,214,000	1,497,000	2,711,000	0.44	0.56
1927	1,477,000	1,547,000	3,024,000	0.48	0.52
1928	1,520,000	1,587,000	3,107,000	0.49	0.51
1929	897,000	2,369,000	3,266,000	0.27	0.73

76. **Japan deriving benefit from the development of the North-east.** Japan holds the first place in the trade of the Three Eastern Provinces. This is due to her control of the Kwantung Leased Territory and the South Manchuria Railway. China Proper is listed second in the trade, followed by Russia, England, Holland and the United States in the order named. During the last 20 years, Japan's trade in the Provinces has increased

[15] *Ibid.*, p. 76.

ninefold while the increase of trade with China Proper
has been only fivefold. This shows that Japan has gained
most from the development of the Provinces. The following figures [16] are interesting as showing the trade
position of the various countries concerned:

	1908	1929
Japan	31,885,665	307,608,645
Russia	17,990,277	56,030,034
British Empire	3,801,230	55,038,868
Holland	244,143	39,182,428
U. S. A	6,775,989	38,089,358
Germany	151,161	9,954,378
Belgium	33,219	5,784,375
Denmark	1,584	41,503
Other Countries	278	50,839,713
China Proper	39,813,611	192,686,058
Total	100,697,157	755,255,360

2. Introduction of Modern Business Methods.

77. Improvement in business methods. With the
phenomenal growth of trade in recent years as revealed
in the foregoing statistics has come an improvement in
the organization of business and commerce. Traditional
methods unsuited to demands of modern business houses
are in evidence in many parts of the Provinces, particularly in the commercial ports. Worth recording here are
the numerous financial institutions, insurance companies,
stock exchanges and import and export firms which have
sprung up in the principal cities.

78. Modern banks. The forerunner of the modern
bank in the Three Eastern Provinces was the *Chien
Chuang* or the money shop. In 1905, the Tung San Sheng
Kuan Yin Hao, or the Provincial Bank of the Three Eastern Provinces was formed. This marked the beginning

[16] *Ibid.*, p. 140.

of modern banks in the Provinces. To-day there are 19 Chinese banks with branches throughout the Three Eastern Provinces. The aggregate capital of these banks is estimated at $131,000,000. Four of these banks have their head offices in Shanghai and Peiping.

79. **Modern insurance.** Modern insurance was introduced in 1908. There are as present nine insurance companies in the Provinces, operating in accordance with the provisional regulations governing insurance companies. As regards exchanges, the Harbin Grain Exchange is the largest from the standpoint of organization and is the most successful. The Anta Grain Exchange, the Shenghai Exchange, and the Tungliao Grain Exchange at Yingkow are also good in business. Of the exporting companies, the Lida Company is the best known. It maintains its head office in Mukden, and has branches at Harbin and Yingkow and agents at New York and London. It deals in hides, leather, grain, bean and other commercial products.

CHAPTER VII. EDUCATION.

80. **Efforts of modernization.** It was not until 1902 that the modern public school system was introduced into the Three Eastern Provinces following the abolition of the time-honored system of competitive literary examination. A commission of education, entrusted with the duty of enforcing modern education system, was appointed at the same time for each of the Three Provinces. Before 1907, there were only about forty schools in the province of Liaoning, but in the following year their number had increased to over two thousand and one

hundred. The number of schools in Kirin in the year 1907 was only forty; it had increased to over one hundred and eighty in the following year. The number of schools in Heilungkiang had increased from thirty in 1907 to over one hundred and fifty in 1908. Since this time modern education has made rapid progress and the educational system has gone through much improvement There are at present an educational department in each province, while in each district and municipality there is a bureau of education. There are also educational associations and scientific and cultural organizations all working for the advancement of modern education.

1. Elementary Education.

81. **Progress in elementary education.** Elementary education includes primary schools and kindergartens. According to investigations made in 1929, there were in this year fourteen kindergartens with a total enrolment of 634 children in Liaoning; in Kirin, two kindergartens with 104 children; and in Harbin, two kindergartens with 126 children.

Since 1902, very marked progress has been made in primary education. There were in the year 1929 12,357 primary schools in the whole of the Three Eastern Provinces, with a total enrolment of 836,770 pupils, and the number of teachers totalled 23,230. The current expenditures for all these schools amounted to $15,329,792.

The detailed figures are as follows:

Province	Number of Schools	Number of Children	Number of Teachers	Expenditures
Liaoning	10,115	666,459	17,469	11,687,380
Kirin	1,575	114,846	4,158	1,557,858
Heilungkiang	601	41,844	1,030	796,490
Harbin	66	13,621	532	287,974
Total	12,357	836,770	23,189	14,329,702

82. Chang Hsueh-liang donating Hsinmin primary schools. One of the most noteworthy features in the progress of elementary education was the donation of a substantial sum by Marshal Chang Hsueh-liang for the establishment of thirty-two Hsinmin primary schools. No tuition is charged in these schools, and poor deserving students are given financial assistance. They are scattered in all the important centres in Liaoning and carry on experiments in education. There are at present seventy-two classes having a total enrolment of 3,449 pupils. The sum of $372,800 has been expended in school buildings, and the annual current expenditures for all these schools total $103,680. Marshal Chang assumes full responsibility for all the expenses. Twenty-eight more of such experimental schools will be established if the original plan is carried out.

2. Secondary Education.

83. Progress in secondary education. In secondary education, the middle schools have made great progress. According to figures [17] compiled for the year 1929, the middle schools totalled 172 with an aggregate enrolment of 29,723 students. The teachers numbered 1919. The annual current expenditure for all these schools for this year totalled $2,825,788. The detailed figures are as follows:

Province	Number of Schools	Number of Students	Number of Teachers	Expenditures
Liaoning	122	22,153	1,306	$1,725,451
Kirin	33	4,975	354	446,577
Heilungkiang .	7	918	95	140,679
Harbin	10	1,677	164	513,081
Total......	172	29,723	1,919	$2,825,788

[17] Figures given in the *North-eastern Year Book, 1931.*

The Liaoning Tung Tsai Middle School, the Liaoning Tung Tsai Girls Middle School, and the Haicheng Tung Tsai Middle School—all private institutions donated and supported by Marshal Chang Hseuh-liang—are the three best-known private middle schools. The Liaoning Tung Tsai Middle School was founded in June 1925; the Liaoning Tung Tsai Girls Middle School in February 1927; and the Haicheng Tung Tsai Middle School in August 1929. All three schools are run along modern lines and have adopted the most up-to-date methods of instruction. They occupy 375 *mou* of land and have an aggregate enrolment of 1,132 students. The sum of $1,361,500 was spent on the buildings for these three schools and their annual current expenditure totals $280,700.

In Liaoning, there are 98 normal schools and teachers' training departments with 638 teachers and a total enrolment of 7,742 students. The anuual current expenditure is $674,778. There are six in Kirin with 103 teachers and 1,222 students. The annual current expenditure totals $193,245. In Heilungkiang there are 14 with 89 teachers and 1,209 students and an annual expenditure of $146,313.

Liaoning has 49 vocational schools with 233 teachers and 2,834 students. Their current annual expenditure aggregates $242,552. Kirin has two such institutions with 17 teachers and 101 students and an annual expenditure of $24,367. Heilungkiang has four vocational schools with 58 teachers and 559 students. The annual expenditure amounts to $77,939.

In the Three Eastern Provinces, there are thus in all 118 normal schools with 830 teachers and a total enrolment of 10,173 students. Their annual current expenditure totals $1,014,336. There are 55 vocational schools with 308 and a total enrolment of 3,494 students. Their annual current expenditure aggregates $344,858. No

554 MEMORANDA PRESENTED TO

554 MEMORANDA PRESENTED TO

data about the vocational and normal schools in the special Administrative Area of Harbin can be given, because they are attached to the middle schools.

3. Higher Education.

84. **Higher education a later development.** Formerly the graduates of middle schools in the Three Eastern Provinces who wished to receive higher education went to Peiping and Tientsin to attend colleges and other technical schools. Many of them were encouraged to do so by their provincial and district governments with the help of allowances, and the facilities of communication were another favourable factor. This accounts for the comparative lateness in the development of higher education in the Three Eastern Provinces.

85. **Higher educational institutions.** Before 1922, the Shenyang Higher Normal School, the Fengtien College of Liberal Arts, the Fengtien Medical College, the Kirin Law College were the only higher educational institutions. In July 1923, the North-eastern University was established by the Liaoning provincial authorities with the financial support of Heilungkiang and the Harbin Special Area. In the year 1926, the Harbin Technical College and the Harbin Medical College were founded. In the following year, Mr. Feng Yung donated the sum of $1,500,000 for the establishment of a University named after him. In the same year, the Ministry of Communcations established the North-eastern Communications University at Chinchow. In 1929, the Kirin Law College was expanded into the Kirin University. In the same year, the North-eastern College of Agriculture and Forestry, the Harbin Institute of Fine Arts and the Harbin Russian Language Normal School successively came into being. At present, there are in the Three Eastern Prov-

inces eleven higher educational institutions with 816 professors and a total enrolment of 5,136 students. Their annual current expenditure aggregates $3,292,000. The detailed figures are as follows:

Name of Institution	Number of Students	Number of Professors	Annual Expenditure
North-eastern University	1,976	234	$1,330,000
Kirin University	322	55	335,000
North-eastern Communications University	203	34	139,000
Harbin Technical College	1,242	186	700,000
Harbin Law College	630	124	150,000
Feng Yung University	373	59	200,000
Liaoning Medical College	91	38	310,000
North-eastern College of Agriculture and Forestry	120	22	20,000
Harbin Medical College	41	19	60,000
Harbin Institute of Fine Arts	46	14	25,000
Harbin Russian Language Normal College	83	31	23,000
Total	5,127	816	$3,292,000

86. **The North-eastern University.** The North-eastern University is the most up-to-date and best-equipped of the higher educational institutions in the Three Eastern Provinces. At present, it comprises six colleges—the College of Arts, the College of Law, the College of Science, the College of Engineering, the College of Agriculture, and the College of Education. It is situated in Peiling, Mukden, covering over 1000 *mou* of land. It has a well-equipped workshop involving an initial expenditure of $1,750,000 and an Experimental Farm of 100 *mou*. Over $3,000,000 was expended on buildings, three-fifths of this sum being donated by Marshal Chang Hsueh-liang. Among the group of buildings the most up-to-date and attractive are the Stadium, the Library and the Chemistry Building, each costing approximately $250,000. The Library has a collection of more than 100,000 volumes of

Chinese and foreign books, valued at over $600,000. The various workshops and laboratories are equipped with machinery and apparatus worth $1,218,000. Since its establishment in 1923, the number of students graduated from the University totals 320.

4. Social Education.

87. **Nature of social education.** Social education in the Three Eastern Provinces comprises the following classifications:

(1) Public Libraries.—There are 55 of these libraries, not including those established by the foreign residents. Their current expenditure exceeds $400,000 a year. The Liaoning Provincial Public Library is the best-equipped among the public libraries, having a collection of 93,976 volumes.

(2) Museums.—The two best-known are the Museum of the Three Eastern Provinces and the Museum established by the Educational Department of the Special Administrative Area of Harbin. Since 1931, scientific expeditions have frequently been sent out by the Museum of the Special Administrative Area to conduct investigations along the border regions with gratifying results. This Museum spends $33,000 annually for its maintenance.

(3) Public Lecture Halls.—There are in all 42 public lecture halls. Those run by the Kirin provincial government have produced the most satisfactory results.

(4) Popular Education Halls.—There are nine such conducted in the interest of the common people. The first Popular Educational Hall established by the Special Administrative Area is the most efficiently conducted and yields the best results.

(5) Public Athletic Fields.—There are in all eleven public athletic fields, the largest being the First Athletic Field in Harbin. The fact that the athletes of the Three Eastern Provinces have captured the championship in the field and track events in the National Meet for the last two years and that they have distinguished themselves in other branches of athletics shows what a powerful stimulus has been given to sports and games by these public athletic grounds.

(6) Mass Education.—The campaign against illiteracy among the adult population is being vigorously pushed in the Three Eastern Provinces, particularly in Liaoning Province where, according to latest investigations, the number of schools established for this purpose totals 1,302 with an aggregate enrolment of 45,716 persons. Most of the primary schools in the Province of Kirin and Heilungkiang and the Special Administrative Area of Harbin have started classes for the illiterate people. The instruction is based on the 1000 foundation characters, and the course takes four months.

(7) The Pursuit of Higher Education in Foreign Countries.—The returned students are playing an increasingly important rôle in all kinds of constructive activities in China Proper, and even more so in the Three Eastern Provinces. In 1902, there were only fourteen students who were sent at Government expense to pursue advanced studies in Japan. Later on, the number of both private and Government students who went abroad steadily increased. In the year 1930, there were 45 private and 71 Government students in Europe and America. The number of students who pursued studies in Japan totalled 470, of whom 170 were Government expense. Preference was given to courses in science and engineering, followed by social sciences.

5. The Han-ching Endowment Fund for Secondary
and Primary Education in Liaoning.

88. Chang Hsueh-liang's interest in educational development. After he succeeded his father in 1928, Marshal Chang Hsueh-liang evinced great interest in the development of education in the Three Eastern Provinces. Besides his magnificent donation which made possible the group of new buildings in the North-eastern University, he founded and supports the thirty-two Hsinmin Primary Schools and the three Tung Tsai Middle Schools for boys and girls. In the year 1928, he again donated $5,000,000 out of his private means to be used as permanent endowment fund for secondary and primary education in Liaoning Province. This fund is entrusted to a Board of Trustees. It is deposited in the Provincial Bank of the Three Eastern Provinces. Beginning from the year 1929, it yields an interest of 12 per cent a month. Out of the annual interest of $720,000 the sum of $430,000 is used for the encouragement of competent and faithful teachers in the middle and primary schools; $50,000 as scholarships to deserving teachers in the primary schools; $70,000 for the upkeep of the Science Memorial Building; $50,000 for the promotion of physical education; $120,000 for various kinds of scholarships in the interest of education.

The Board of Trustees for the Permanent Endowment Fund mapped out the following plans:

(1) To build a Science Memorial Building, estimated at $500,000. The work of construction was to have commenced in the spring of 1932.

(2) The construction of a public recreation ground estimated at $200,000. Work has already commenced and expected to be completed in 1932.

(3) The establishment of a department of physical education. Four physical directors are to be sent abroad for advanced work in physical education.

(4) For the promotion of primary education, each district in Liaoning is required to send one teacher to attend a special class formed for the purpose in Mukden. The course is completed in half a year.

(5) The funds for the encouragement of teachers in the middle and primary schools are divided into four different categories. The sum of $140,000 has been distributed.

(6) Appropriations for summer school sessions. In the year 1930, over 40 places in various districts opened such sessions, and the Board of Trustees had allotted for this purpose the sum of $50,000.

CHAPTER VIII. CONCLUSION.

89. General conclusions. From the foregoing account of China's efforts in the development of the Three Eastern Provinces, we can draw the following conclusions:

(1) The prosperity of the Three Eastern Provinces is founded on agriculture whose annual products exceed, $2,000,000,000—a sum which is equivalent to the total investments made by Japan in this region. This is the fruit of hard work of the 30,000,000 industrious Chinese people, and it has very little to do with outside assistance.

(2) The rapid agricultural development is the direct result of the marked increase in population, notably in North Manchuria, and this is greatly accelerated by the large-scale influx of immigrants from the various provinces in China Proper. The South Manchuria Railway has little to do with it.

(3) The great strides made in industry, mining, forestry and fishery have been made possible only through the promotion and encouragement given by the Chinese authorities, coupled with the enterprising spirit and strenuous efforts of the Chinese people.

(4) The abundant facilities provided for rapid transportation and communications account for the rapid development of industry and commerce in the Three Eastern Provinces. More than one-third of the railways was built with Chinese capital; and China has gone far ahead of Japan in the expansion of shipping, telephonic and telegraphic communications.

(5) The expansion of trade and commerce in the Three Eastern Provinces is intimately related to production and consumption which again depend upon the increase in population.

(6) Keenly aware of the urgent need of educated leaders in all kinds of constructive activities, the Chinese authorities in the Three Eastern Provinces under the leadership of Marshal Chang Hsueh-liang have energetically promoted education. Intellectual progress has much to do with the development of the Provinces.

(7) The favourable geographical position in the Three Eastern Provinces and the energetic efforts made by the Chinese authorities have enabled this region to enjoy peace and order. Tranquillity has prevailed all

along the Chinese-owned railways and the Chinese Eastern Railway. The Japanese guards and troops maintained in the Kwantung Leased Territory and along the South Manchuria Railway have little to do with this peace and order.

90. **China's wish to open the North-east to all the countries.** We do not wish to belittle the part played by the port of Dairen and the South Manchuria Railway. This we acknowledge and we give Japan due credit. There is, however, this important consideration: Whatever Japan undertakes in this region is actuated by selfish motives, and frequently she has not hesitated to use unfair means in her attempt to obtain for herself monopolistic control. For this reason, she has prevented other countries from making investments in this part of China's territory. Because of Japan's opposition, China was constrained to desist from negotiations for an American loan to build the proposed Chinchow-Aigun Railway after the Russo-Japanese War. Again, in 1920, Japan demanded as the condition for her adherence to the terms of the Four-Power Banking Consortium the exclusion of the Three Eastern Provinces and Mongolia from the scope of the Consortium. Only after the Powers were forced to put the South Manchuria Railway and other railways outside the scope of the Consortium that she consented to become a party to it. Japan's attempt to enjoy the exclusive right of making investments for the development of the North-eastern Provinces has done more harm than good. It is against the principles of the Open Door and equal opportunity for trade as laid down in the Nine-Power Treaty. It would indefinitely retard the opening up of the potential riches of this vast region. The Chinese Government and people, fully conscious of China's international obligations, are eager to develop

the unlimited natural resources in the North-eastern Provinces with the help and co-operation of all countries without any discrimination and wish to throw the whole region open to foreign investment and free trade so that not only the Chinese people will be profited, but the whole world will share in the benefit. For the attainment of this great objective, Japan's policy *vis-à-vis* this part of China's territory must undergo a radical change.

Peiping, June 26th 1932.

MEMORANDUM

ON

Japan's Violations of Treaties and Infringements on Chinese Sovereignty: Some Twenty-Seven Representative Groups of Cases

Document No. 18   Peiping, June 1932

MEMORANDUM ON JAPAN'S VIOLATIONS OF TREATIES AND INFRINGEMENTS ON CHINESE SOVEREIGNTY: SOME TWENTY-SEVEN REPRESENTATIVE GROUPS OF CASES.

I. The maintenance of Japanese troops in the area of the South Manchuria Railway gave rise to various law-breaking cases.

II. The manoeuvre of Japanese troops on the Tumen river and at Hunchen.

III. Japanese troops beleaguered the headquarters of the Chinese Volunteer Corps at Tiehling.

IV. Forcible occupation of farms at Linyu Hsien as target ground by Japanese constabulary.

V. Japanese troops stationed in South Manchuria abetted Mongolian bandits.

VI. Kohi and Endo sent by the Japanese Government assisted the bandits in creating disturbances along the border in Kirin Province.

VII. The destruction of a Chinese vessel and the slaughter of Chinese by Japanese warships in the vicinity of Mago.

VIII. The stationing of Japanese consular police.

IX. The stationing of "civil police" in the Railway towns along the South Manchuria Railway.

X. The arbitrary taking-over by Japanese police of smuggled arms and ammunition seized by the Antung customs house.

XI. The Changsha Case.

XII. The maintenance of Japanese post offices in South Manchuria.

XIII. Japan's violation of the agreement relating to the purchase of Tsingtao salt.

XIV. The smuggling and selling of narcotic drugs by Japanese subjects in China.

XV. The Japanese warship "Tanikaze" shelled and killed fishermen at Pingtan Hsien, Fukien.

XVI. The engagement of Japanese trawlers and motor vessels in fishing industry in Chinese territorial waters.

XVII. The smuggling of arms and ammunition by Japanese steamship "Toyo Maru."

XVIII. The damaging of the Branch Offices of the Antung Custom-House by Korean smugglers.

XIX. Japanese subjects in Foochow not observing the procedure regarding the examination and legalization of deeds of lands leased in perpetuity.

XX. The Japanese consulate in Foochow protecting opium dens.

XXI. Issue between China and Japan concerning telegraphic communication in the Three Eastern Provinces.

XXII. The sailing of the Japanese warship "Fuyo" into the inland waters of China.

XXIII. The Japanese Government ignored the damages inflicted upon China by the Japanese troops during the Tsinan incident.

XXIV. The massacre of Chinese by the "Self-Warning Corps" in Japan after the great earthquake.

XXV. The first anti-Chinese riots in Korea. (December, 1927).

XXVI. The Wanpaoshan case.

XXVII. The second anti-Chinese riots in Korea. (July, 1931).

MEMORANDUM ON JAPAN'S VIOLATIONS OF TREATIES AND INFRINGEMENTS ON CHINESE SOVEREIGNTY: SOME TWENTY-SEVEN REPRESENTATIVE GROUPS OF CASES

I. The maintenance of Japanese troops in the area of the South Manchuria Railway gave rise to various law-breaking cases.

The maintenance of troops in the South Manchuria Railway areas by the Japanese Government without the consent or formal approval of the Chinese Government is a clear violation of China's sovereignty. At the Washington Conference the Chinese delegation strongly protested against the stationing of such troops on Chinese soil and requested that the Conference take definite measures to bring such infraction of China's territorial and administrative integrity to an end. But owing to Japan's stubborn objection, nothing was accomplished in that direction. Japan has continued to maintain the troops in the said railway areas. According to investigation made in August 1931 by the authorities of the Three Eastern Provinces, the total number of the Japanese troops stationed in the South Manchuria railway areas is 24,677 men and officers, including 5,400 railway guards, 1,860 aviation men, 1,937 gendarmes, 720 plain-clothes police, and 14,760 regular army men and officers. These troops have continued to interfere with Chinese civil administration, to arouse disorder throughout adjacent districts and to commit malicious acts in various forms against Chinese public functionaries and civilians. Following are a number of typical cases grouped in three categories which occurred in the past five years.

Category A. Cases in which the Japanese troops interfered with the local administration.

Case 1. On August 9th, 1928, one Japanese railway guard, carrying a sword, strolled into Fengchen Hsien, and molested a Chinese woman. The Chinese police interfered. The next day sixty Japanese soldiers beleaguered the office of the District Magistrate and forced him to apologize.

Case. 2. On September 13th, 1928, a contingent of 300 railway guards beleaguered the Chinese police station at Changchun, seized and disarmed 22 Chinese policemen, and took away by force all the arms and ammunition kept in the station. The Chinese authorities duly protested. The Japanese military authorities released the Chinese police but retained the arms and ammunition.

Case 3. On September 23rd, 1928, seven Japanese gendarmes molested a tea shop at Tiehling. The Chinese policeman, Tsui Chen-chi, tried to stop such action of the Japanese soldiers, but the gendarmes would not listen to reason, and wounded him with swords. One hour later fifty railway guards beleaguered the 15th police sub-station in Tiehling Hsien, disarmed the policemen, and burned official documents. The Chinese authorities repeatedly protested but without result.

Case 4. On the night of October 5th, 1928, Chinese policemen of Liaoyang Hsien opened fire upon a band of robbers. On the morning of the next day some Japanese railway guards bursted into the Chinese police station, seized four policemen, and took away the arms and ammunition. Upon the protest of the Chinese authorities, the Japanese military authorities released the policemen, but retained the arms and ammunition.

Case 5. On March 2nd, 1929, four Chinese policemen, carrying permits allowing them to pass through the South Manchuria Railway area at Mukden given by the Japanese Consul-General there, were on their way to Penshihu on an investigation mission. The Japanese railway guards seized and detained them in the Japanese barrack. Upon the protest of the local Chinese authorities, they were released but their mission had to be given up.

Case 6. On April 12th, 1929, Kwo Yung-chun and other employees of the Telephone Office of Mukden, when they had completed the repairing work on the telephone line at Tungling (The East Tombs) outside Mukden on their way back to the office, were beaten by the Japanese railway guards. Five of them were taken to and retained in the Japanese barrack. Upon the protest of the Chinese authorities, they were released.

Case 7. On April 28th, 1931, the Antung City Electric Power Plant sent some workmen to a place north of Pataukow railway for erecting some new wooden poles. While the work was going on, ten Japanese soldiers arrived who kept watch on the workmen and took away all their materials such as ropes, cords, etc.

As soon as the Director of the plant was informed of what had happened, he went with the secretary of the city government to the place in order to give an explanation regarding the matter. Upon arrival he found six hundred Japanese soldiers already there armed to the teeth. They tried in various ways to frighten and oppress the people. The conduct of the Japanese captain was particularly rude and barbarous. The secretary of the city government was compelled to sign a written apology to the Japanese. It was not until the soldiers became tired of their own meanness that they released the work-men.

Category B. Cases in which the Japanese troops disturbed the peace and order of the Chinese territory adjacent to the South Manchuria Railway areas.

Case 1. The Japanese 33rd Regiment carried on a manoeuvre for the capture of Mukden outside the walled city, begininng from August 1st till September 10th, 1928, destroying crops in the farms and scared the inhabitants. Prior to the manoeuvre, the Commissioner of Foreign Affairs negotiated with the Japanese military authorities not to carry out such military demonstration, but his request was disregarded.

Case 2. On April 17th, 1929, more than 30 Japanese railway guards practised a sham battle at Sanchiaotun in Mukden. The Commissioner protested without result.

Case 3. On May 14th, 1929, Japanese troops practised a sham defensive battle in the streets at Toutaokow, at Changchun. Business in the city was suspended during the manoeuvre. The Commissioner of Foreign Affairs protested without result.

Case 4. On February 20, 1929, the Japanese 33rd Regiment again conducted a manoeuvre for the siege of Mukden. The Chinese authorities protested without result.

Case 5. On August 18th, 1929, a battalion of Japanese troops practised a sham battle in the streets at Shenchen Kai, near Huangkutun, Mukden, completely interrupting the traffic. The Chinese authorities protested without result.

Case 6. In August, 1929, one regiment of Japanese troops manoeuvred in the vicinity of Changchun. As a result some 314 acres of farm land owned by Chinese farmers were overrun by the troops, and the total loss of the farm crops which were destroyed was valued at $40,000. The owners of the farms had to sustain the loss.

The Commissioner of Foreign Affairs consequently lodged with the Japanese Consul at the city a protest requesting payment for the damages by the Japanese military authorities concerned to the sufferers. The Japanese authorities agreed to the appointment of a Japanese delegate to make a joint investigation into the matter with a Chinese delegate appointed by the Commissioner. These delegates investigated into the extent of the destruction of the farm of Li Sze-kung and fixed on a sum of only Yen 120 to be paid to the complainant by the Japanese military authorities. However, even that small sum which was jointly agreed upon was not paid. The Japanese authorities finally paid him only Yen 20. When the Commissioner protested, the Japanese Consul stated that by direct negotiation the complainant agreed to receiving Yen 20 with satisfaction. Upon finding that the statement was unfounded, the Commissioner protested again, but without result.

As regards the other complainants, the Japanese authorities flatly refused to consider them with the Commissioner, although the latter repeatedly protested.

Category C. Cases in which the Japanese troops committed atrocities in various forms against Chinese civilians.

Case 1. On May 28th, 1927, the Japanese railway guards stationed at Ssupingkai shot a Chinese farmer named Yang Tehchai to death.

Case 2. On August 20th, 1927, the Japanese railway guards shot a Chinese farmer Li Weng-kwei to death at Lishu Hsien.

Case 3. On November 5th, 1928, the Japanese railway

guards shot a Chinese farmer Chang Chao-yuin to death at Changkiaputze, a village in the district of Fengchen Hsien, and took away 23 villagers who were later released upon the protest of the local Chinese authorities.

Case 4. On June 6th, 1929, four Japanese railway guards bursted into a village called Hungkoutun, seized Chang Teh-sang, a villager. They tortured him practically to death. The Commissioner of Foreign Affairs protested without result.

Case 5. On April 6th, 1928, the Japanese railway guards stationed at Fushan shot a Chinese labourer named Chang Teh-yi to death.

Case 6. On October 30th, 1929, a Japanese soldier shot to death a Chinese farmer named Liu Teh-chai who was passing through under the railway bridge at Antung. The Chinese authorities protested without result.

Case 7. On October 24th, 1929, when a Chinese carpenter named Chang Tsen-kwei was crossing the railway track at Antung, a Japanese railway guard stabbed him with a dagger and wounded him fatally. Later the guard dragged him on the train which was destined for Lien Shang Kwan station. On the way, the guard pushed him down the train and the poor Chinese carpenter was instantly killed under the train. The Chinese authorities protested without result.

Case 8. On March 7th, 1929, the wife of Wu Chin-sen, a Chinese labourer, was raped by a Japanese railway guard at Chyoda Dori, Mukden, while she was walking through that place. She complained to the Japanese police station at Mukden which simply ignored her complaint.

Case 9. On June 2nd, 1930, the Japanese railway guards, taking their posts at a spot some 2000 metres south of the South Manchuria Railway Station at Changchun, shot at all the Chinese pedestrians who walked near the railway track. A Chinese farmer named Nin Pao-chen who happened to be passing through that place to the market to sell vegetables, was shot dead. The local magistrate of Changchun reported the murder to the municipal authorities who subsequently lodged a protest with the Japanese Consul and demanded only payment for the family of the deceased and the punishment of the culprits. In reply, the Japanese Consul charged Nin Pao-chen as a thief. The municipal authorities pointed out in a rejoinder that all the neighbours of Nin Pao-chen testified him to be a *bona fide* farmer who was engaged in lawful pursuits. The said authorities further stated that the case was clearly one of murder, and that the Japanese Government should comply with the demands. But the Japanese Consul has never replied.

II. The Manoeuvre of Japanese troops on the Tumen River and at Hunchun.

The engineering corps stationed at Hueining in Korea planned to manoeuvre across the Tumen River from Changchwan on the Korean border over to Hunchun on the Chinese border by means of a pontoon bridge. The military practice was scheduled to last for three weeks beginning on August 4th, 1931. On August 8th, a Japanese boat for military use appeared on the Chinese side of the river. On August 11th, thirty-four men crossed to the Chinese side and erected two wooden poles with a red flag on the one and a green flag on the other, evidently for the purpose of surveying in the construction of the pontoon bridge. The District Magistrate of Hunchun made a verbal protest to the Japanese Consul against the building of such a bridge and other matters relative to the manoeuvre. The Consul stated in reply that the manoeuvre must be carried out according to the fixed

MEMORANDA PRESENTED TO

schedule and the proposal of the Chinese local authorities for its cessation could not be accepted. The Ministry of Foreign Affairs, on August 14th, sent a note to the Japanese Minister protesting against the unwarranted actions of the Japanese military authorities.

However, preparations for the Japanese manoeuvre were continued. In the meantime the bridge had been completed. At one o'clock p.m. August 15th, the Japanese soldiers discharged twenty-five mines in the river. By 9 o'clock p.m. the same day, some thirty Japanese soldiers carrying with them two machine guns came across the pontoon bridge to the Chinese side and practised firing. At 10 o'clock a.m. August 18th, some one hundred Japanese soldiers at Chin Yuan Ferry on the Korean side and about the same number of Japanese soldiers on the Chinese side fought a sham battle over the river. At 3 o'clock a. m. August 19th, the Japanese soldiers put up a pontoon bridge from the Chin Yuan Ferry across the river to the Chinese side. The manoeuvre ceased at 3 o'clock p.m. August 19th.

On August 26th, the Ministry of Foreign Affairs sent another protest to the Japanese Minister against the manoeuvre of Japanese troops in Chinese territory. But the Japanese legation has never given any reply.

III. Japanese troops beleaguered the Headquarters of the Chinese Volunteer Corps at Tiehling.

On September 30th, 1929, a few Japanese soldiers of the Japanese army stationed at Tiehling had a petty quarrel with some members of the Chinese volunteer corps in Tiehling Hsien, Liaoning Province. The Japanese immediately mustering over one hundred soldiers beleaguered the headquarters of the volunteer corps. The headquarters gate was then shut. The local Commissioner of Foreign Affairs and an officer of the District Office together with the chief officer of the Japanese Police Station came to the spot to investigate the situation. Simultaneously, the Japanese Consul and an officer of the Japanese army also arrived.

While the party was being engaged in consultation, and the local Commissioner of Foreign Affairs was proceeding to call on the chief of the Public Safety Bureau asking him to take measures to maintain peace and order, the Japanese soldiers forcibly broke the gate, rushed into the headquarters, disarmed all the volunteer corps and made everybody kneel down together with a group of merchants, who had been arrested previously in the neighbourhood, and maltreated them in every possible way.

Finally, they took away from the headquarters more than thirty men of the volunteer corps and a large number of rifles and bullets. They treated these captives with all sorts of cruelty and released them one by one after protracted diplomatic negotiations.

The local Commissioner of Foreign Affairs lodged a protest with the Japanese authorities, submitting the following demands:

(1) Punishment of offenders.
(2) Payment for all the losses suffered by the volunteer corps and merchants.
(3) Apology.
(4) Guarantee of the non-recurrence of similar incidents.

However, the case was never satisfactorily settled.

IV. Forcible occupation of farms at Linyu Hsien as target ground by Japanese Constabulary.

The farms, owned by four farmers of Linyu Hsien, Hopei Province, and situated north of Tuchachwang, in the 16th section of the first district of the said city, were a little more than two *li* (one third of a mile) from the quarters of the Japanese constabulary. The constabulary, without consulting the owners of the farms, or their tenants, destroyed all the cereal sprouts, and turned the farms into a target ground. On each side of the ground they dug a trench intended to serve as a boundary line, about 400 *kung* (1200 metres) in length and 50 *kung* (150 metres) in width. The owners of the farms together with their respective tenants and the sheriff of Tuchachwang protested against the occupation of the farms by the Japanese constabulary. But the latter refused to evacuate. In June 1931, the owners of the farms reported the case to the Ministry of Foreign Affairs. The case has not been settled.

V. Japanese troops stationed in South Manchuria abetted Mongolian bandits.[1]

Bapuchapu, the chief of Mongolian bandits, was pro-Japanese during the Russo-Japanese War. Since Outer Mongolia declared its autonomy, he resumed lawless activities and disturbed the peace and order on the border of Eastern Inner Mongolia. In the spring of 1916, the Chinese Government was informed that a rapprochement between Bapuchapu and Japan was re-established. The Chinese Minister at Tokyo inquired at the Japanese Foreign Office about the arrival of the representative of Bapuchapu at Tokyo. The Japanese Government admitted it as a fact. General Chu Chin-lan who was then the Garrison Commander stationed in Tsitsihar reported to the Central Government the rumour that the Japanese Government was ready to supply the Mongolian chieftain and his men with arms and ammunition which were to be transported to Hailar and delivered to them there. The

[1] *Vide* also *Memorandum on Japan's Plots and Schemes Against Unification of China.*

THE LYTTON COMMISSION 577

rumour was confirmed by the fact that these arms and ammunition were once discovered at Harbin by Russian gendarmes when they were on their way to Hailar.

When the menace of the Mongolian bandits grew more serious, the Chinese Government sent punitive expeditions against them. During the first part of August 1916, the Chinese troops defeated them at Tuchuan. The bandits moved eastward, passed through Shinshihchang, and marched into Huaiteh Hsien. Finally they were admitted into the railway town at the Kuokiatien Station on the South Manchuria Railway line. Kuokiatien is situated 430 *li* north of Mukden, and 60 *li* north of Kungtzuling Station where Japan maintained the headquarters of the commander of the railway guards. In the railway town at Kuokiatien, there were one battalion of the railway guards and one Japanese police sub-station. Outside the railway town at Kuokiatien, the district government of Lian Hsien maintained a police sub-station but no troops.

It was on August 15th, 1916, that the Mongolian bandits under the command of Bapuchapu moved to Kuokiatien. Upon their arrival at the place, other bandits and Manchurian imperialists residing in various railway towns on the South Manchuria Railway line flocked there to join them. Arms and ammunition were supplied to them by the Japanese. On August 19th, several hundred bandits and Manchurian imperialists came from Darien to join them by rail, and the next day several carloads of arms and ammunition were transported from Darien and delivered to them.

The Mongolian and other bandits and Manchurian imperialists called themselves the Imperialist Army. Some forty Japanese, including Wakahayashi, Matsumato and Shinota served in the army as military advisers. The Japanese military authorities declared martial law within the section of the South Manchuria Railway zone, from

20

Ssupingkai to Kungtzuling. Chinese public functionaries were denied the right of entrance into this section. If they entered they would immediately be arrested.

The bandits, using the railway town at Kuokiatien as their base of operation, attacked the self-defence volunteer corps of Kuokiatien killing one and wounding ten others. Four Chinese police officers and 18 policemen were wounded in a battle they fought on the side of the volunteer corps against the bandits.

A Regiment of the Bandit Suppression Army under the command of Chang Ching-hui launched an attack upon the bandits and defeated them on August 20th. While the Chinese troops were closing upon them in the neighbourhood of Kuokiatien Station, a Japanese officer of the railway guards appeared on the field waving a Japanese flag to the Chinese troops and demanded the cessation of hostile actions on the part of the Chinese troops under the pretext that peace of the railway area was disturbed and bullets were fired into the area. The Chinese troops were thus forced to stop attacking the bandits.

The Kwantung Government addressed a protest to the Military Governor of Fengtien Province stating that, as the fighting in the vicinity of the South Manchuria Railway stations menaced the peace and order in the railway areas, the railway guards had compelled both parties to stop the fighting, and that the Kwantung Government would ask the Mongolian troops (referring to the bandits) to leave Kuokiatien and to go back to Mongolia, and that during their retreat the Chinese army should not attack them. The Military Governor sent his Japanese adviser Major Kikuchi to negotiate with the Kwantung Government which submitted the following demands: (1) On September 2nd, the Mongolian army would withdraw from Kuokiatien and retreat to Mongolia. For the maintenance of peace and order of the

railway areas, no fighting should take place east of the
region from Yangchiatachentze (Huaiteh Hsien) to Liao-
yuan and west of the South Manchuria Railway line. (2)
The Japanese army in order to carry out the first condition would supervise the actions of the two parties concerned, and would therefore make necessary movements.
(3) In case the Chinese troops should open fire, the Japanese troops would take such action as they deemed fit.
The Military Governor was forced to accept the demands.
The Kwantung Government then organized a mixed brigade out of the troops of the 7th Division stationed in
South Manchuria to escort the bandits in their retreat to
Mongolia. Major General Sato was charged with this
mission.

The bandits under the escort of the Japanese troops
left Kuokiatien on the morning of September 2nd. On
the next day, they arrived at Chaoyangpo (Huaiteh
Hsien). The bandits looted and burned the shops and
homes of the inhabitants. The people of the place fought
a battle with the bandits. The Japanese troops opened
fire upon the former, killing over ten Chinese and wounding many others. The town was practically razed to the
ground. On the 7th of September, the Mongolian bandits
and the Japanese troops attacked Maokiachengtzu (Huaiteh Hsien), killing scores of farmers and wounding many
others. On their way, the bandits passed through Che-
anyu Hsien and murdered Commissioner Hsu Wei-ping
and one of his staff members Ho Sao-huo. On their way
through Lisu, Sangsan, and Changling districts, the bandits and Japanese troops indulged in indiscriminate killing and plundering.

According to later investigations, the loss of lives and
property caused by the bandits and Japanese troops included the following:

Casualties	Property robbed and destroyed
71 killed	2,092 houses burned
105 wounded	$274,977 ready money robbed
10 missing	1,896 cattle robbed
	224 rifles
	64,970 bullets

The total direct loss sustained by private individuals and the public was estimated at $1,139,600.

VI. Kohi and Endo sent by the Japanese Government assisted the bandits in creating disturbances along the border in Kirin Province.

On September 24th, 1923, the Mukden troops captured a Japanese called Kohi at Yu-kia-pu in Kirin Province when they had routed the bandits in the neighbourhood of the place. Kohi was found carrying various kinds of Chinese jewelry wrapped up in a soiled Chinese silk dress and fastened on his waist. The troops sent him to Ngehamuh station where he was tried by a special judge with the help of a Japanese interpreter who was detailed by the Military Governor of the Province.

In a confession written by himself and impressed with his own finger prints, Kohi admitted that he was sent by the Japanese Government to help the bandits to create disturbances along the border so that Japan might have a pretext to acquire further rights and interests in China, that the firearms in the possession of the bandits were supplied to them by his countrymen and by the Japanese Government, that the two machine guns were transported to Toutaokow, Yenki, where they were delivered to them, but were supposed to have been robbed from the Japanese by the bandits, and that he and another Japanese, named Endo, who had been with the bandits, helped them to dig trenches and fire the machine guns. Furthermore, Kohi confessed that the silver ornaments

and bank-notes were booties. On October 18th, he was
turned over together with the booties by the Commissioner for Foreign Affairs at Kirin to the Japanese Consulate-General for due punishment. On the 20th, the
Commissioner lodged a protest with the Japanese Consul-
General.

On November 18th of the same year, the Chinese Foreign Office lodged a protest with the Japanese Minister
against the activities of the Japanese mentioned above
and also gave him to understand that the Chinese Government was in possession of information as regards a
Japanese organization in charge of special military affairs which was secretly helping the bandits to disturb
peace along the Chinese border in order to create pre-
texts which Japan might seize to despatch troops to the
regions thus disturbed. In view of the discovery of Jap-
anese-smuggled arms and ammunition at Harbin and of
the things that were admitted by Kohi, it could not be
denied that the Japanese were aiding and abetting the
bandits along the Chinese border. The Japanese Minister was requested to transmit China's demand that the
Japanese Government punish severely and exercise strict
control over such Japanese, suppress the smuggling of
arms and ammunition into China by Japanese, and withdraw the Japanese police from the Yenki region where
their presence hampered the Chinese authorities in the
exercise of their powers in checking the smuggling of
arms and ammunition by Japanese and in the suppression of bandits. The reply of the Japanese Minister
dated March 28th, 1923 was that there was no such thing
as the Japanese helping the bandits nor was there evidence to testify that Kohi assisted the bandits and supplied firearms to them. In reply, the Japanese Minister
also demanded that the Chinese authorities concerned be
punished because they had made Kohi to write the unin-

telligible statements (referring to the written confession). The Chinese Foreign Office renewed diplomatic representations on July 9th and December 14th, 1924. But no further reply has ever come from the Japanese authorities.

VII. The destruction of a Chinese vessel and the slaughter of Chinese by Japanese warships in the vicinity of Mago.

On June 2nd, 1920, a Chinese fuel vessel belonging to the Chinese Naval Squadron was sighted on the Amur River in the vicinity of Mago by the Japanese Squadron. Thereupon the Chinese vessel stopped and hoisted two Chinese flags. But the Japanese warships fired at the vessel, eight or nine incendiary shots hitting her stern which resulted in thirty-four of her crew being killed and three marines wounded. The vessel was subsequently burned by the Japanese marines.

Prior to this event, Chen Si-yien, captain of the Chinese gunboat *Kiang Hun* of the Chinese Naval Squadron and the Chinese Consul at Nikolaievsk had called the attention of the Japanese naval authorities to the fact that there was a Chinese fuel vessel in the neighbourhood of Mago and the Japanese naval authorities had taken note of the fact. On December 31st, 1920, the Chinese Foreign Office addressed a note to the Japanese Minister presenting four demands for the settlement of this affair:

1. The Japanese Government should tender an apology for the action of the Japanese Naval Squadron.

2. The officers and marines responsible for the shelling and destruction of the Chinese vessel should be duly punished and the Chinese Government should be informed when the punishment is effected.

3. The 34 Chinese killed and the one seriously wounded should be given compensation.

4. The payment of damage for the destroyed vessel and its goods.

The Japanese reply stated that the Chinese vessel was fired upon because it not only refused to obey the order of the Japanese Squadron to stop, but, on the contrary, tried to escape; that it was subsequently burned for fear it might be utilized by enemies; and that the measures taken by the Japanese Naval Squadron were in conformity with Articles 63 and 49 of the Declaration of London of 1909 as well as with Articles 95, 96, 126, and 141 of the Japanese Regulations governing Warfare on the High Seas. The note further asserted that the Japanese Government, for these reasons, was not responsible for what had happened.

The Chinese Foreign Office sent on February 16th, 1922, another note to the Japanese Minister, stating that the Chinese vessel in question neither could nor did offer any resistance; that according to the Declaration of London and the Japanese Regulations governing Warfare on the High Seas, the Japanese Naval Squadron had not even the right to confiscate the vessel, much less any excuse to shell it; and that the measures taken by the said Japanese Naval Squadron were entirely contrary to the provision of Article 49 of the Declaration of London and of Article 126 of the said Japanese Regulations. The Chinese note insisted that the Japanese Government should accept the four demands specified in the note of December 31st, but repeated diplomatic representations produced no effect.

VIII. The stationing of Japanese Consular Police.

The Japanese Government began to station consular police in the Yenki region, comprising Yenki, Wangching,

Hunchun and Holung districts, immediately after the conclusion of the Chientao Agreement between China and Japan on September 4th, 1909. Article II of the said agreement provides only that the Japanese Government may establish Consular Offices or branch offices of consulates in the trading places; viz.: Lung-Ching-Tsun, Chu-Tzu-Chieh, Tou-Tao-Kou and Pai-Tsao-Kou. No provision is made to authorize the Japanese Government to station consular police in these places. But the Japanese Consulate and branch offices in the Yenki region or the so-called Chientao region each maintained one or two policemen under the pretext of protecting the Consulate or branch consular offices.

Since then, the Japanese Government had kept on increasing the number of consular police in that region. By the year 1911, one hundred forty-four such policemen were stationed there. They were distributed in the manner as shown in the following table.

Table of distribution of Japanese Consular Police in Yenki Region, 1911.

District	Localities	Number of Officers	Number of Policemen
Yenki	Er-Tao-Kou	1	11
	Bah-Tao-Kou	1	7
	Tien-Bao-Sang	1	8
	I-Lan-Szu	1	5
	Tung-Fu-Szu	1	8
Hunchun	Hei-Ting-Tzu	1	8
	Tou-Tao-Kou	1	10
Holung	Hsien-Kai	1	8
	Wai-Lo-Tou-Kou	1	13
	Sao-Tao-Kou	1	4
	Bah-Tao-Hou-Tzu	1	7
	Ma-Pai	1	11
Wangching	Liang-Sui-Chaun-Tzu	1	13
	Yiao-Wei-Tzu	1	17
Total of Officers and Police		14	130

In 1920, the Japanese Government despatched and stationed troops in Yenki, Wangching, Hunchun and Holung districts under the pretext of suppressing the Korean revolutionary movement. After lengthy diplomatic negotiations, the Chinese Government succeeded in getting the Japanese Government to agree to the withdrawal of its troops from that region. When the Japanese Government had withdrawn the troops, it stationed in their place some four hundred consular police in the region. The local authorities protested, the Ministry of Foreign Affairs addressed a note to the Japanese Minister, demanding the withdrawal of such police, and the Chinese Minister to Japan was instructed to negotiate with the Japanese Government to the same effect. All the efforts on the part of China failed. The Japanese consular police have continued to be stationed in the region up to the present. According to the report sent to the Foreign Office by the North-eastern authorities in the summer of 1928, the Japanse consular police were distributed in the following manner.

Table of Japanese Consular Police Stations and Sub-stations established in Yenki region in 1928.

Consular Offices and Localities	Consular Police Offices and and Localities	Number of Police Officers	Number of Policemen
Consulate-General at Lou-Tao-Kou, Yenki	Police Station in Consulate	5	78
Branch Office of Consulate at Tou-Tao-Kou, Yenki	Police Station in Consulate	3	32
Branch Office of Consulate at Chu-Tzu-Chieh, Yenki	Police Station in Consulate	3	38
	Police Sub-station at Er-Tao-Kou, Yenki..	1	19
	Police Sub-station at Bah-Tao-Kou, Yenki	1	9

Consular Offices and Localities	Consular Police Offices and and Localities	Number of Police Officers	Number of Policemen
	Police Sub-station at Tien-Bao-Shan, Yenki	1	17
	Police Sub-station at I-Lan-Kou, Yenki...	1	7
	Police Sub-station at Tung-Fu-Si, Yenki..	1	9
Branch Office of Consulate at Hunchun Hsien	Police Station in Brench Office of Consulate...	2	11
	Police Sub-station at Tou-Tao-Kou, Yenki.	1	11
	Police Sub-station at Heh-Tin-Tzu, Hunchun	1	8
	Police Sub-station at Hsien Kia, Holung..	1	6
	Police Sub-station at Foo-Tung, Holung...	1	9
	Police Sub-station at Bah-Tao-Ho Tzu, Holung	1	5
	Police Sub-station at Ti-Mau-Ton, Holung.	1	5
Branch Offic of Consulate at Wangching	Police Station in Branch Office	3	25
	Police Sub-station at Liang - Sui - Ching, Wangching	1	8
	Police Sub-station at Jia-Yia Ho, Wangching	1	9
TOTAL:	5 Police Stations and 13 Police Sub-stations..	29	306

These police stations and sub-stations are under the direction of the Police Inspector who is stationed at the Consulate-General at Lou-Tao-Kou, Yenki, and under the control of the Japanese Foreign Office.

The number of police given in the foregoing table is not a fixed one but varies from time to time. For instance, the number was increased considerably when thirty plain-clothes police were sent and distributed to the stations and sub-stations by the Japanese Foreign Office in July 1929.

Besides, it is not uncommon for the Japanese Foreign Office to send inspectors to inspect the Japanese police administration in that region and to hold conferences of the police officers. For instance, in 1929, Miura Takemi was sent on such a mission. After a tour of inspection throughout that region, he convened at Lung-ching Tsun a conference attended by the Japanese police officers. At the conference, the following decisions were reached: (1) more plain-clothes police should be sent to watch closely the Koreans in that region, (2) Japanese Reservists Associations should be formed to take care of military measures in places where there are consular police stations or sub-stations, and (3) police intelligence corps should be formed to secure news relating to Chinese military and political matters.

In addition to the consular police in the Yenki region, the Japanese Government has continued to maintain such police in the other parts of South Manchuria. Following is a list of such Japanese consular police stations and sub-stations:

Localities of consular police stations	Number of sub-stations or sentry boxes
Police Station of Japanese Consulate at Newchwang	6
" " " " " " Liaoyang	2
" " " " " " Mukden	7
" " " " " " Tiehling	17
" " " " " " Changchun	6
" " " " " " Antung	10
	48

Japanese police officers under the direct control of the Foreign Office at Tokyo are stationed in the branch office of the Mukden Consulate-General at Tunhua, the branch office of Changchun Consulate at Nonang, the branch offices of Tiehling Consulate at Luhtao, and Hailung.

The Japanese Government has continued to station consular police at Harbin. Since the withdrawal of Japanese troops from the city in the autumn of 1922, Japanese consular police have been patrolling the streets and the Harbin station. The Commissioner for Foreign Affairs lodged a protest with the Japanese Consul at Harbin, but the Consul in his reply refused to withdraw them and stated that the Japanese police hereafter would not wear uniforms. In 1925, the Japanese Consulate of Harbin established, in addition to the police station attached to the Consulate, two police sub-stations, police sub-station No. 1 with two officers and nine police at Yichow Street and police sub-station No. 11 with three officers and thirty-four police at Tituan Street. These Japanese police often interfered with the Chinese police administration, especially when Koreans in the city were involved. The local Chinese authorities protested without result.

The Japanese Government has even continued to station consular police at Tsingtao since the restoration of the German Leased Territory to China. They patrol the streets of the city wearing uniforms and carrying swords.

The following are a few typical cases which show in one form or another the unlawful activities of the Japanese consular police.

Case 1. On the night of August 18th, 1925, some sixteen Japanese armed policemen bursted into the house of Chiang Si-huan at Bing-Lung-kow, Yenki, and arrested his brother Shihbih, on the ground that Si-huan was suspected as being a Korean revolutionist.

Case 2. On February 14th, 1929, Japanese police arrested 52 Korean men and 2 Korean women of Chinese

nationality at Siao-Wu-Tao-Kow, Yenki, and on the following day they arrested 27 Koreans of Chinese nationality at Yan-Tai-Hsi- Beh-Kow in the same district.

Case 3. On March 6th, 1929, a Chinese policeman,
while he was settling a quarrel between a Chinese and a
Korean, was arrested by the Japanese police and taken
to the Japanese Consulate at Lung-Ching-Tsun. He was
badly beaten up and made to kneel on the ground for
four hours as punishment. He was released upon repeated
representations from the local Chinese authorities.

Case 4. The arrest of Ching-Ran-san, vice-President
of the Sanyi District Agricultural Association who was
later turned over to the Japanese Consulate by the Japanese police, took place on April 30th, 1929. Prior to
this, similar cases had occurred. On April 13th, more
than twenty students of Lung-Ching-Tsun were taken
prisoners; on April 24th at Loutaokow, a man by the
name of Li Yuan-shih was arrested; and on the same day
at Shaowutaokow and at Peikow, over fifty men including
Kin Cha-chan, teachers and students of a farmer's school
as well as the farmer Yang Tai-shih were all taken into
custody by the Japanese soldiers.

Repeated protests were sent to the Japanese authorities by the Yenki Municipal Government. However, the
Japanese authorities refused to consider the matter and
resorted to subterfuge and prevarication. The authorities of Yenki city then asked the Commissioner for Foreign Affairs in Kirin to refer the matter to the Foreign
Ministry requesting it to send further protest to the Japanese Minister and demand the immediate release of all
the Chinese subjects. This was accordingly done, but no
reply was made by the Japanese.

Case 5. On July 28th, 1930, the 1st Battalion of the 7th
Regiment of the 13th Brigade which was quartered in the

Lung-chin village, Yenki Hsien, discovered that a crowd of Koreans were gambling at Dusanpo, and detailed, for the sake of keeping peace and order in the city, a captain, by the name of Chang Fun-chuan, with four soldiers to the gambling place in order to make arrests. As a result, three gamblers were captured while the rest escaped.

While the soldiers with the arrested gamblers were passing by the gate of the Japanese police sub-station, a number of Japanese policemen rushed out suddenly and took away the prisoners by force. They also beat up the Chinese captain with clubs and fists. The major of the battalion demanded an explanation from the Japanese police authorities. The latter gave an evasive reply. Then a medical examination of the captain was asked for, and it was discovered that the uniform of the officer was torn to pieces and there were wounds all over the body. The victim was immediately conveyed to the hospital, and a paper testifying the seriousness of the wounds was signed and issued by the doctor.

The case was notified to the Japanese Consul by the Yenki Municipal authorities. Two protests were lodged with the Consul demanding acceptance of the following terms: apology to the officer, payment of indemnity for losses sustained by the wounded, punishment of the offenders and withdrawal of the Japanese police. In reply, the Japanese Consul said that the unfortunate incident was due to misunderstanding. Several conversations were then held between the Chinese and Japanese authorities. The latter finally agreed to send the Japanese Vice-Consul to the Headquarters of the Yenki Garrison Commander to offer an apology and make payment of Yen 50 as uniform and medical expenses. Promises were also given as to the punishment of the Japanese police. They would not hold good, however, only if the Chinese authorities waived the right of bringing up the case officially with the Japanese Government. The case remains unsettled.

Case 6. On May 14th, 1932, the officer and some eleven police of the Japanese police sub-station at Tien-Bao-Sang, Yenki, insulted and arrested Chang Bing, the school superintenednt of the Yenki district who, in company with a Chinese policeman and a few Koreans, was on his way to the School Board of the city for the enforcement of Chinese Government Regulations in the schools for the children of Koreans of Chinese nationality. He was detained in the sub-station for more than fifteen hours.

A casual review of the few typical cases as described above shows sufficiently clearly that the Japanese Government has not lived up to the declaration which its delegation solemnly made at the Washington Conference, namely "(1) Such police (consular police) do not interfere with Chinese and other foreign nationals. Their functions are strictly confined to the protection and control of Japanese subjects, and (2) The most important duties with which the Japanese police are charged are, first, to prevent the commission of crimes by Japanese, and second, to find and prosecute Japanese criminals when crimes are committed." This declaration was made only to obviate any insistence China might show for the immediate withdrawal of such police from Chinese soil. Since the conference, facts have continued to prove that the history of Japanese consular police in China has been a record of a series of encroachments upon China's administrative integrity. During the last ten years, the Chinese Government has addressed notes on several occasions to the Japanese Government demanding the withdrawal of such police from Chinese soil. On May 30th, 1929, the Chinese Foreign Office sent a note to the Japanese Chargé d'Affaires demanding the withdrawal of such police from

Manchuria and Tsingtao. On July 16th, 1929, the Japanese Chargé d'Affaires stated in his reply that the Japanese consular police stationed in China were for the purpose of protecting Japanese residents, that the policy of the Japanese Government was to have these police to co-operate with the Chinese police that in order to avoid misunderstanding on the part of the Chinese officials and subjects these police would limit the use of their uniforms except when they were necessary, and that the Chinese Government should order its police to co-operate with these Japanese police. As to their withdrawal from China, no mention was made in the note.

On December 16th, 1929, the Chinese Foreign Office addressed a memorandum to the Japanese Chargé d'Affaires demanding the withdrawal of the Japanese consular police from China on the ground that their presence in China is prejudicial to its administrative integrity and furnishes dangerous possibilities for disputes between China and Japan thus making the relations between the two countries strained more than ever. The memorandum of the Japanese Legation dated March 17th, 1931, acknowledged only the receipt of the said Chinese memorandum.

In February 1930, the Japanese Consul-General at Yenki proposed to the Municipal authorities a set of regulations in six articles regarding co-operation between the Chinese and Japanese police and another set of regulations in ten articles regarding cultivation of good-will between the Chinese and Japanese police. The Municipal authorities refused to accept the proposals and made it known to the Japanese Consul-General that the fundamental thing was that the Japanese Government should withdraw its consular police from the Yenki or so-called Chientao region.

From the foregoing review, one realizes that the Japanese Government is determined to maintain its consular police in China. Small wonder that all the efforts of the Chinese Government in requesting the Japanese Government to withdraw such police have been unsuccessful. Thus the case remains unsettled between the two Governments.

IX. The stationing of " Civil Police " in the railway towns along the South Manchuria Railway.

In addition to the consular police, Japan has continued to maintain, without the authority of any treaty or agreement, another type of police called civil or municipal police in the railway towns along the Japanese controlled railways in South Manchuria. Such police are under the control of the Governor of the Kwantung Government. Following is a list of the stations and sentry boxes of the "civil police."

Localities of Civil Police Station	Number of Sentry box
Civil police station at Wagfantien	13
" " " " Tashihchao	9
" " " " Anshan	14
" " " " Liaoyang	10
" " " " Mukden	20
" " " " Yingkow	4
" " " " Tushun	25
" " " " Penshihu	13
" " " " Tiehling	8
" " " " Kaiyuan	13
" " " " Ssupingkai	12
" " " " Kungchuling	8
" " " " Changchun	19
" " " " Antung	28
Total	196

As to the total number of such civil police, the official statistics of the South Manchuria Railway Company give as approximately 2,500 men and officers. A comparison of this number with the number of such "civil police" which the Chinese delegation submitted at the ninth meeting of the Committee on Far Eastern and Pacific Questions during the Washington Conference shows that the total number of such police has been increased five times that of 1922.

None of the Sino-Japanese treaties sanction the stationing of Japanese police agents, including the so-called civil police, in the railway towns along the Japanese-controlled railways in South Manchuria, nor do any of the Russo-Chinese treaties concerning the Chinese Eastern Railway where the rights were transferred to Japan as a result of the Russo-Japanese War. Since the declaration made by Japan together with the other Powers during the Washington Conference to withdraw these police agents from Chinese soil, the authorities of the Three Eastern Provinces have tried every means at their disposal to protect the lives and property of foreign residents. They have, on the whole, succeeded in giving as adequate and effective protection to foreign residents as to Chinese subjects. In spite of all this, Japan has refused to withdraw such civil police from South Manchuria. Besides, these civil police are not only active within the railway areas but have also repeatedly interfered with the administrative functions of the local Chinese governments outside of the railway areas. The following are a few typical cases.

Case 1. On September 8th, 1913, a police officer, Feng Sao-wu of Lishu Hsien and twenty policemen, while patrolling in the neighbourhood of Ssupingkai, were fired upon by bandits. The Chinese police returned fire and divided themselves into two parties, one of which chased after the retreating bandits, and the other including the officer Feng Sao-wu stationed itself at a spot outside the railway town at Ssupingkai in order to prevent the bandits from escaping into the railway area.

The Japanese police and the railway guards closed on the Chinese police and compelled them to go to the Japanese police station. There they were detained. Upon prolonged negotiations between the Director of the Bureau of Foreign Affairs at Kungtzuling and the Japanese Consul at Changchun, the Chinese police officer and men were finally set free.

Case 2. On March 14th, 1915, the Chinese police of Hwai-teh Hsien arrested eight Chinese gamblers at Tung Chien-ying's house which was situated outside the railway town at Fangchiatun along the South Manchuria Railway. The Japanese police demanded the release of the offenders but the demand was rejected by the Chinese police station. Thereupon the Japanese police officer and some thirty armed railway guards beleaguered the Chinese police station, took away the culprits, the rifles and ammunition from the station. At the same time, they took away two Chinese police officers and seven Chinese policemen as prisoners to the Japanese police sub-station. They were detained there for more than six hours and maltreated with various forms of insult and cruelty. The two officers and four of the Chinese police were later sent to the Japanese police station and detained there for another 24 hours. Finally they were released on giving a bond in which they were made to confess that they had acted unlawfully in making the arrests in the neighbourhood of the railway town.

Case 3. On June 15th, 1929, at 10 : 30 p.m., a Japanese policeman by the name of Higuma made a forcible entrance into the Chinese Post Office at Mukden and wounded the Chinese postman, Li Wan-lin, with his sword. The culprit was arrested by the Chinese police and turned over to the Japanese police station at the provincial capital. The matter was then taken up by the Commissioner of Foreign Affairs with the Japanese Consul, but no settlement was effected.

Case 4. On August 23rd, 1929, a postman named Ho Yu-san while delivering mail within the South Manchuria Railway area at Mukden, was compelled by the Japanese police to go to the Japanese police station. His mail bag was searched and three copies of a newspaper entitled "Awakening the World" were taken away. He was kicked and beaten. The chief of the Chinese Post Office verbally protested to the Japanese Consul and the Japanese police chief demanding punishment of the culprits. They expressed regret for the outrages of the Japanese police and promised immediate investigation into the matter. Later a reply from the Japanese Consul said that what the Chinese postman recounted did not tally with the facts as reported by the Japanese police station. The demand was therefore not accepted. The case was not settled in spite of repeated protests.

Case 5. A Japanese who was the owner of a morphine shop at Funsui Station, Kaiping Hsien, was once assassinated, and the Japanese police made several arbitrary arrests in territory under purely Chinese administration. The local Chinese authorities repeatedly requested the Japanese police to refrain from such actions. On the 23rd of May, 1929, three Japanese policemen arrested a farmer named Chang Yu-tang on the charge that he was the suspected assassin of the Japanese in question. The farmer was frightened and turned to his heels. Thereupon the Japanese police fired at him and captured him. The next day the Japanese police demanded the head of the village to claim him back. On the 25th the poor man died. The local authorities demanded the Japanese police authorities to punish the criminal, to pay an indemnity and to refrain from again making arrests in territory which has nothing to do with the Japanese. But the case was never settled in spite of protracted negotiations.

Cases like these can be readily multiplied. In order not to go into tedious details, however, only one case for each of the last ten years, from 1922 to 1931 inclusive is listed as follows:

Crimes committed by the Japanese civil police against Chinese civilians in South Manchuria (1922-1932).

Date	Case	Criminal	Names of Victims	Place of incident	Remarks
Jan. 17th, 1922	Murder	Japanese police	Yu Lang-kiang	Siao Li Tzu Kow Ling Kian Hsien	Protest filed by Chinese authorities with no result.
Nov. 10th, 1923	"	"	Tsui Yung-teh	Tsuikiatung Chuanho Hsien	"
Jan. 30th, 1924	"	"	Sui Tien-ching	Chilan Hsien	"
Mar. 13th, 1925	"	"	Wang Teh-kung Dong Min-chang Ren Hsia-sai	Shihhokow Chihan Hsien	"
July 16th, 1926	"	"	4 Chinese civilians	Sankia Tang Tze Antu Hsien	"
April 11th, 1927	"	"	Liu Yu-liang	Huangpao Liaoyang	"
Nov. 5th, 1928	"	"	Chang Tso-yung	Chanchiaputze Fengcheng Hsien	"
June 29th, 1929	"	"	Chang Yu-tang	Bahchaokow	"
March 14th, 1930	"	"	Chang Yun-ko	Lihsu Hsien	"
May 21st, 1931	"	"	Mi Shuang-ching	Liaoning	"

X. The arbitrary taking-over by Japanese Police of smuggled arms and ammunition seized by Antung Customs House.

On June 3rd, 1930, the Antung Custom-House seized 69 revolvers, 7,000 bullets, and 138 bullet cases at the Antung railway station. These the Japanese police immediately took away. The Custom-House sent a letter to the Japanese Consul requesting him to issue a receipt for the arms and ammunition taken and to return them to the Custom-House when the case was tried. In reply the Japanese Consul claimed that the articles in question were first seized by the Japanese and should therefore be disposed of by the Japanese authorities concerned.

On July 12th, the Chinese Foreign Office addressed a protest to the Japanese Chargé d'Affaires in China, stating that the seizure of the articles by the Japanese police and the refusal to issue a receipt by the Japanese Consul were contrary to the Agreement regarding the disposal of prohibited goods seized at the Antung station signed in April 1921 by the Custom-House and the Japanese Consul. The Japanese Consul in his reply dated October 6th stated that the smuggler was being detained in Kobe pending a trial and that after a judgment had been rendered the Japanese authorities concerned would instruct him to effect the return of the articles to the Custom-House.

Up to the present, the Chinese Foreign Office has not received any notification from the Japanese Legation as to whether a judgment had been rendered.

XI. The Changsha Case.

When the Japanese steamer *Buria Maru* arrived at Changsha on June 1st, 1923, it happened that a crowd gathered along the shore to listen to the speeches that were being delivered. The Japanese warship *Fushinei* suddenly sent marines ashore to make a demonstration. The local Chinese authorities made every effort to restore order and assured the Japanese Consul that the Japanese residents would be given adequate protection. At the same time they demanded the withdrawal of the Japanese marines. But instead of complying with this demand, over a score of armed Japanese soldiers came ashore. Under direction by their officers, they fired on the crowd, killing two unarmed civilians and seriously wounding twenty others. Since the dead and wounded were all found lying outside the Japanese wharf, the measure taken by the Japanese was not one of self-defence, but was in the nature of hot pursuit.

After this serious incident occurred, the Chinese Ministry of Foreign Affairs, basing upon the report of the Hunan Provincial Government, lodged a protest on the 5th of June with the Japanese Minister and submitted the following demands: (1) The Japanese officers and soldiers responsible for the killing and wounding of the Chinese should be punished according to the Japanese military law. (2) Indemnity for the dead and wounded Chinese. (3) The commander of the Japanese Naval Squadron should tender an apology to the Hunan provincial authorities. (4) The Japanese Government should send a written apology to the Chinese Government. (5) The Japanese Government should guarantee no recurrence of similar incidents. At the same time the Chinese Minister in Tokyo was instructed to take up the matter with the Japanese Government. The Chinese Foreign Office also sent a councillor to Changsha to make an investigation. In spite of repeated diplomatic notes to the Japanese Government urging upon the acceptance of the

five demands referred to above, the Japanese persisted
in the assertion that the measure taken by the marines
was one of self-defence. The case has never been settled.

XII. The maintenance of Japanese Post Offices in South Manchuria.

During the Washington Conference the Chinese delegation purposed the abolition of foreign postal agencies
in China and a Resolution was passed by the four Powers
concerned, including Japan, to the effect that before
January 1st, 1923, all the foreign postal agencies should
be abandoned, "except in leased territories or as otherwise specifically provided by treaty." In July 1922, the
Japanese Minister proposed the appointment of delegates by the two countries to negotiate and conclude
agreements relating to postal matters after the withdrawal of the Japanese postal agencies. On August 18th
of the same year, a conference was held in Peking between the delegates of the two countries. On December
8th, four agreements relating to postal matters were
concluded between China and Japan.

During the conference the Japanese delegation raised
an issue contesting the application of the Resolution
(passed at the Washington Conference) to Japanese
postal agencies in the South Manchuria Railway areas.
Notes were exchanged between China and Japan. The
Chinese Government claimed that the Resolution was
applicable to Japanese postal agencies in the South Manchuria Railway areas, while the Japanese Government
held that Japan agreed to the Resolution with the understanding that the Japanese postal agencies in South
Manchuria Railway areas were to be exempted. In view
of the difference of opinion regarding this matter the
chief delegates of China and Japan agreed and signed on

December 8th, 1922, an appendix to the new Postal Agreements, declaring that "the question of the Japanese Postal Offices in the South Manchuria Railway zone could be made the subject of communications between both Governments."

On September 4th, 1930, the Chinese Foreign Office sent a note to the Japanese Chargé d'Affaires, demanding the abolition of the Japanese postal offices in the South Manchuria Railway areas, but received no reply from the Japanese Legation. The report of the Chinese Postal Administration dated May 2nd, 1928 gives a total of sixty-two Japanese postal agencies in the South Manchuria Railway areas which should be closed up.

XIII. Japan's Violation of the Agreement relating to the purchase of Tsingtao Salt.

It is provided in Paragraph 1, Article 17, Section VI of the Agreement giving details of arrangements for the settlement of outstanding questions in connection with Shantung concluded between China and Japan on December 1st, 1922, that "Japan shall within a period of fifteen years beginning from the 12th year of the Chinese Republic (namely, the 12th year of Taisho) purchase annually Tsingtao salt between the maximum amount of 350,000,000 catties and the minimum amount of 100,000,000 catties. But upon expiration of the above-mentioned period, a further arrangement may be agreed upon." Ever since the conclusion of the Agreement, Japan has never bought annually up to the minimum amount of table salt as stipulated in the Agreement. Moreover Japan even arbitrarily reduced the quantity of table salt ordered annually. For instance, in 1926, out of 90,000,000 catties contracted for, 15,000,000 catties were cancelled; in 1928, out of 80,000,000 catties, 6,000,-

000 were refused; in 1930, out of 100,000,000 catties, 11,-600,000 were rejected. Since the annual amount to be exported as well as the price of the table salt was entirely controlled by the Japanese Salt Monopoly Bureau, the Chinese Salt Exportation Company could not know how much salt to be manufactured or exported annually. Consequently the Company sustained heavy losses.

The Chinese Salt Department, in the past few years, has time and again addressed communications to the Japanese Legation in China protesting against the arbitrary reduction by the Japanese Salt Monopoly Bureau of the annual minimum amount that Japan undertook to purchase. In reply the Japanese Legation stated that the Japanese Salt Monopoly Bureau held that it was authorized to make reduction under the conditions as provided in Article 1, Section VIII of the Appendix to the said Agreement which reads as follows:

"In regard to the quantity of Tsingtao salt to be exported as stipulated in Article 17 of this Agreement, China and Japan need not necessarily be bound by the agreed quantity as stated above and may arrange the quantity to be purchased for that year separately of either the maximum or minimum quantities in case the condition of production or the demand for salt in China and Japan should make it difficult to provide or accept the minimum or maximum quantity referred to above."

The Salt Department in a rejoinder pointed out that in view of the fact that Japan bought annually large quantities of coarse salt from Tsingtao in addition to table salt, the condition arising from the demand for salt did not make it difficult for Japan to accept the minimum amount of table salt, that the Japanese Salt Monopoly Bureau wanted to cut down the price of Tsingtao salt and therefore arbitrarily refused to take the annual minimum amount of table salt as provided in the said Agreement; and that the unilateral decision by the Bureau on the amount of table salt that Japan was to buy without making arrangements with the Chinese Salt Exportation Company was contrary to the provision of Article 1, Section VIII of the said Agreement. The Japanese Legation simply ignored the protest.

The Ministry of Foreign Affairs again took up the matter with the Japanese Legation urging upon the Japanese Government to observe its treaty obligations. But no settlement has been reached.

XIV. The Smuggling and selling of Narcotic Drugs by Japanese subjects in China.

The engagement in the smuggling and selling of narcotic drugs, such as morphine, heroin, cocaine, etc., by Japanese residents in Dairen, Mukden, Kirin, Shantung and other places in China is a fact fortified by numerous evidences. Taking advantage of extraterritoriality, they have been carrying on secretly for years such unlawful pursuits in the treaty ports. Even in the interior of China such illegal activities of Japanese residents have been intensively conducted. The responsibility plainly lies with Japan. There have been innumerable cases where Japanese residents were seriously involved in the sale of such drugs. But when they were taken up diplomatically by the Chinese authorities concerned with the Japanese consular officers or diplomatic representatives, the Japanese have always tried to belittle the matter by making flimsy excuses. They have never taken any effective measures to stop such impossible activities on the part of their nationals. The following are some of the typical cases.

Case 1. Dairen is known as the base of operation of the Japanese tradesmen smuggling and selling narcotic drugs to Tientsin, Mukden, Kirin, Shihchiachwan and other places in North China. This illegal trade was once handled by the manager of the Dairen Commercial Goods Exchange by the name of Harata Koichi and his accomplices. In 1927, large quantities of such drugs worth Yen 4,000,000 were in fact discovered and confiscated by the Japanese authorities. The Japanese local court indicted Shirakawa, Yamamatsu, Kawakami, Kamano and others suspected of being engaged in the sale of such drugs.

On September 5th, 1929, the Ministry of Foreign Affairs sent a communication to the Japanese Legation, stating that in view of the fact that numerous Japanese subjects were engaged in the sale of narcotic drugs at various places in China, the Ministry had already communicated with the Japanese Legation on the 3rd and 27th of June, demanding strict suppression of such trade; that in view of the recent exposure of the Harata Koichi case the Ministry had again requested the Japanese Legation, verbally through Kamimura, the Secretary to the Legation, to the effect that the Japanese Legation should take measures to stop such illegal trade; and that in both cases the Ministry had not been favoured with any reply. The note further stated that having been notified by the Commission for Opium Suppression of the fact that the engagement of the Japanese subjects in the smuggling and selling of narcotic drugs in China was a serious obstacle to the anti-opium movement of the National Government, the Ministry would like again to request the Japanese Legation to suppress completely and effectively such activities of the Japanese residents in China. The Japanese Legation has never replied.

Case 2. The Japanese merchants by the names of Inokari, Omori, Kanena, Ihoma, Tajima, Kyofuru, Nonaka, Yamaura, each maintained firms in Tsinan and manufactured and sold narcotic drugs. On August 21st and 22nd, 1929, a staff member of the Bureau of the Chinese Commissioner for Foreign Affairs, the officers and police of the Bureau of Public Safety of the Tsinan Municipality and a staff member of the Japanese Consulate made a joint investigation into the stores of the said Japanese merchants and discovered large quantities of narcotic drugs as well as raw materials and tools for manufacturing such drugs in every one of the stores, "while pills" being the most numerous among the drugs thus found. The Commissioner sent on the 24th of August a letter to the Japanese Consul, demanding for the punishment of these guilty people. The Japanese Consul in his reply stated that the Japanese subjects in question would be duly punished in accordance with Japanese law, and the drugs and tools confiscated would be burned. The Commissioner further requested the Japanese Consul to notify him when the punishment had been given. But the Japanese Consul has not replied.

Case 3. A great many Japanese subjects have been engaged in the sale of narcotic drugs in Shantung Province. Such cases can be readily multiplied. For instance, in January 1929, the Chinese Post Office at Tsingtao discovered registered parcels of cocaine and heroin, 27 of which were smuggled by Messrs. Sanrin & Co., a Japanese firm in the city, and 74 of which were smuggled by Messrs. Yashioka & Co., another Japanese firm in the city. The Provincial Government of Shantung reported in April 1929, to the Ministry of Foreign Affairs that there were 105 Japanese stores in the port of Tsinan, 49 at Wai Hsien, 6 at Chiao Hsien, 11 at

Huantai Hsien, and 11 at Ito Hsien, engaged in narcotic trade in one form or another. These Japanese stores were nominally engaged in the sale of ordinary Japanese goods but in reality their main business was the sale of such drugs. Basing upon these facts, the Ministry of Foreign Affairs lodged a protest on June 27th, 1929 with the Japanese Legation stating that the Japanese subjects in Shantung Province under the pretext of carrying on lawful commercial pursuits were actually engaged in the sale of narcotic drugs, and that such actions obstructed the anti-opium movement of the National Government. The communication further requested the Japanese Legation to remove such obstacles to China's anti-narcotic measures at the earliest opportunity. But no reply from the Japanese Legation has been received.

Case 4. Nine Japanese merchants in Changli Hsien, Hopei Province, pretended to be medical doctors or apothecaries when in reality they were engaged exclusively in the sale of morphine, cocaine and heroin. They defied the orders of the district authorities prohibiting the sale of such drugs. When the guilty Japanese were arrested, the Japanese troops stationed at Shanhaikwan forcibly took them over and set them free. Sometimes, culprits were arrested and handed over to the Japanese Consul who upon a small fine immediately released them, and they resumed their illicit trade as before. This state of affairs was reported by the Commission for Opium Suppression to the Ministry of Foreign Affairs. The Ministry addressed a memorandum on June 3rd, 1929 to the Japanese Legation, stating that in view of the fact that Changli Hsien was not a treaty port, the Japanese had no right to carry on commercial enterprises there much less to sell narcotic drugs and requesting the Japanese Legation to order the said Japanese to leave the town. The diplomatic representation proved futile.

Case 5. The Japanese shops, called Kyoei, Tenryn, Samukawa, Maruyama, Midashi, Rynsho, Mishima, Kanaoka, and Kaneshiro in Kaomi Hsien, Shantung Province, were engaged in the sale of narcotic drugs. The local authorities ordered the proprietors of the said shops to leave the town on the ground that it was not a treaty port. But they refused to do so, and likewise, turned a deaf ear when they were asked to move out by the owners of the houses in which the said shops were established. Diplomatic negotiations with the Japanese authorities produced no satisfactory result.

Case 6. When the Japanese steamer *Chofu Maru* sailed into Woosung in November 1929, the staff member of the office of the Woosung Forts Garrison Commander searched it and discovered in its hulk twenty-one boxes of opium weighing 300 ounces. The case was referred to the Shanghai Provincial Court for adjudication. The Ministry of Foreign Affairs also instructed the Commissioner for Foreign Affairs at Shanghai to make diplomatic representation to the Japanese Consul-General, demanding that he should order the Japanese steamers bound for the port not to smuggle opium hereafter nor to defy the order of the competent Chinese authorities to search them. The Japanese Consul-General protested saying that the search of Japanese steamers violated the treaty rights of Japan and was not an established practice, and the Japanese Government could not therefore recognize such action. The Commissioner in his rejoinder said that since the smuggling of opium by the Japanese steamer was an action against the Chinese law, the Japanese Consul-General should punish the said steamer and that its search by the competent Chinese authorities was legal. No more reply from the Japanese Consul-General has been received.

Case 7. In November 1928, the Chinese Post Office in Mukden seized over 120 packages of heroin, worth 500 taels each, which were smuggled by a Japanese called Yiiji. The packages were burned before the public. At the same time the Commissioner for Foreign Affairs at Mukden called the attention of the Japanese Consul-General to the fact and requested the latter to punish the offender. In June 1929 the Custom-House in Mukden discovered 239 parcels of heroin smuggled by a Japanese resident in Changchun, Kirin.

In view of the continuous smuggling of narcotic drugs into China by the Japanese, the Ministry of Foreign Affairs again addressed a memorandum on June 18th, 1929, to the Japanese Legation requesting the latter to take measures to suppress such activities of the Japanese residents in China. The diplomatic representation as usual proved futile.

Case 8. A great many Japanese residents in Peiping were engaged in the sale of heroin and other similar narcotics. On December 4th, 1929, a Chinese by the name of Hsu Chung-ling having bought two packages of heroin from a Japanese store called Arita Co. in Peiping was arrested by a police. During 1928 and 1929, one hundred seventy-seven cases of selling narcotic drugs by Japanese residents in the city were dealt with by the local police authorities. In eleven cases, such drugs were found in the houses of the Japanese subjects when they were searched. The culprits were arrested and turned over to the Japanese Legation. In nine cases, Chinese military men, having bought such drugs, were arrested and turned over to the competent authorities for trial. In

157 cases, Chinese civilians, having bought such drugs, were arrested and turned over to the local courts for trial.

Case 9. In November 1930, the Shanghai Custom-House seized 100 boxes of raw opium aboard a German steamer. The bill of lading indicated that they were destined for the Kwantung Opium Monopoly at Dairen. They were seized and confiscated in accordance with the Customs regulations. In May 1931, the Japanese Chargé d'Affaires addressed a note to the Chinese Ministry of Foreign Affairs saying that the Kwantung Monopoly has signed a contract with Persian merchants for the purchase of 100 boxes of opium which were transported by a German steamer and which were reported seized by the Shanghai Custom-House. The note asked for an explanation of the seizure. The Chinese Ministry of Foreign Affairs stated the grounds on which the seizure was made.

XV. The Japanese Warship " Tanikaze " shelled and killed Chinese Fishermen at Pingtan Hsien, Fukien.

Pingtan Hsien is a group of islands situated in the East Sea. On the north of Pingtan lies the Tung Siang Island and between them, the Nan Tai Liu Rock. In the night of February 27th, 1928, a Japanese merchantman *Kinko Maru* ran on the rock when there was a heavy fog and was wrecked. Over thirty Japanese sailors and their belongings were rescued by a Chinese fishing boat owned by Li Ishu. They were taken on board a Japanese warship *Aoi*, which had come to save the Japanese merchantman on the morning of the 28th. When the warship sailed off, the sailors gave Li Ishu Yen 40 in Japanese banknotes as compensation.

By noon of the same day, four Japanese warships in-

21

cluding *Tanikaze,* came to the spot and made investigations into the conditions of the wrecked ship. The marines on board the *Tanikaze* suddenly fired upon the Chinese spectators on the shore of the Tung Siang Island and those in the fishing boats on the sea nearby resulting in the death of twelve Chinese civilians and the wounding of twenty-seven others. Subsequently some sixty armed Japanese marines landed, chased the fleeing civilians and searched every house in the fishing village on the island, but they found nothing which could be taken as pretext for further brutalities against the Chinese.

The Commissioner for Foreign Affairs lodged a protest on March 7th, 1928, with the Japanese Consul at Foochow against the criminal actions of the Japanese marines, at the same time reserving the right to present demands. The Japanese Consul in his reply asserted that on the arrival of the Japanese warships, the Chinese fishing boats were engaged in plundering and that the shelling was for the purpose of driving away the pirates. The Commissioner for Foreign Affairs sent him a rejoinder stating that the Chinese fishing boats were without any doubt engaged in lawful pursuits and demanding him to produce evidences of booties, if there were any, and the manner of the plunder. The notes emphasized the point that in view of the fact that the armed Japanese marines found no booty in the Chinese homes in the fishing village, the allegation that pirates were active on the spot was absolutely groundless. For the slaughter by the Japanese of the innocent Chinese, the note demanded (1) punishment, (2) indemnity, (3) apology, and (4) guarantee of non-recurrence of similar incidents. The Japanese Consul's reply was evasive. Renewed diplomatic representations by Chinese authorities proved futile, and the case has not yet been settled.

XVI. The engagement of Japanese trawlers and motor vessels in Fishing Industry in Chinese Territorial Waters.

During fishing seasons of the last four years Japanese trawlers and motor vessels have been fishing in Chinese territorial waters, breaking the nets of Chinese fishing boats and causing every kind of obstruction, thus inflicting heavy losses upon the Chinese engaged in the fishing industry. The following are a few outstanding cases illustrating the unlawful activities of Japanese fishing vessels.

Case 1. In the fishing season of 1928, a Japanese fleet of fishing vessels were actively engaged in fishing in the inland sea stretching from Lungkow to Yanchiaokou on the western side of the Gulf of Chihli. The Japanese vessels intentionally destroyed the nets of the Chinese fishing boats there, causing in one month a loss of $30,-000. This was reported to the authorities of the North-eastern Fleet.

The authorities sent ten gunboats to investigate into the matter and warned the Japanese fishing vessels to keep off the Gulf of Chihli which is Chinese territorial waters. Thereupon the Kwantung Government despatched the *Ryokai Maru* to Lungkow and lodged a protest with the said authorities to the effect that Chinese gunboats should not interfere with the Japanese vessels fishing in the Gulf. In addition to that Japan despatched a warship *Kuwa* to the spot to give demonstrations. The authorities of the North-eastern Fleet refuted Japan's arguments and simultaneously ordered the Chinese gunboats to perform their duty of protecting the Chinese fishing boats by peaceful measures.

Case 2. On June 1st, 1928, thirteen Japanese motor

vessels while fishing in the sea stretching along the coast of Chinghsien, known as the Singmingtung fishing-ground, on the south of Liaoning province, destroyed the nets of the Chinese fishing boats. As this had been reported to the sub-station of the Bureau for the protection of Commerce and Fishing Industry in Liaoning Province, two gunboats were sent to protect the Chinese fishing boats. On the 4th, the Chinese gunboats discovered two Japanese motor fishing vessels, one of which called the *Daito Maru* was captured by the Chinese gunboats, while the other escaped. The captain of the *Daito Maru* by the name of Yoshimura Kotaro was summoned aboard the Chinese gunboat *Sui Liao* and told that he had no right to fish in Chinese territorial waters. The captain was released upon giving a bond in which he stated that he would not carry on fishing in Chinese waters hereafter.

Case 3. On July 9th, 1928, the gunboats of the same sub-station captured a Japanese by the name of Sato, who fished with a motor vessel at Yankiatachuan on the coast stretching between Chwanho Hsien and Shincheng Tao. Sato was told that he had no right to fish in Chinese territorial waters. He was also released upon giving a bond in which he stated that he would not fish in Chinese waters hereafter.

Case 4. On the 10th, the said sub-station captured another Japanese by the name of Matsuo Junsaku who was engaged in fishing at the Wangkiatao fishing-grounds near Hokow. He was also released upon giving a bond stating that he had fished in Chinese waters in June 1927, and had now broken the promise not to fish in Chinese waters, but swore once more not to commit it again.

Case 5. In June 1928, Japanese motor fishing vessels, engaged in fishery along the coast of Lingyu Hsien, destroyed more than ten sets of fishhooks of a Chinese by the name of Chi Kwang-yun and drove away the fish shoals causing him to suffer heavy losses.

Case 6. In May 1928, eight Japanese motor vessels fished near Fuyung Tao in Laichow Wan, which is Chinese territorial waters, on the south of the Gulf of Chihli. The Japanese Consul at Chefoo communicated in May with the Inspector of the Chefoo Maritime Customs to the effect that the Japanese Government sent *Tobitaka Maru* to protect the Japanese fishing vessels in the Gulf of Chihli, asking for facilities to be accorded to the Japanese steamer upon entry into, or departure from the port daily. This was reported to the Chinese Foreign Office by the Commissioner of Customs at the port. The Foreign Office instructed the authorities concerned to lodge a protest with the Japanese Consul against fishing activities of Japanese vessels in Chinese waters.

Case 7. In October 1929, Japanese motor vessels fished in Chinese waters near Huaniao Shan off Woosung Kow in Kiangsu Province.

Case 8. In January, 1930, nine Japanese motor fishing vessels were engaged in fishing in Chinese territorial waters near Yuling and Yalung harbours along the coast of Eihsien in Kwangtung Province. When Chinese fishing boats drew near, the Japanese threatened to open fire.

Case 9. On January 26th, 1929, a Chinese fishing boat was sunk by the Japanese fishing vessel *Himashima Maru* on the coast near Wenchow in Chekiang Province. The owner of the said boat, Chu Shen-fah, and his men were taken aboard the *Himashima Maru,* but the fishing nets and other things aboard the boat worth about $3,000 and two thousand catties of fish worth $600 were lost in the sea.

In view of the constant invasion of China's territorial waters by Japanese trawlers and motor fishing vessels, and the destruction by them of Chinese fishing boats as well as the outrages perpetrated by Japanese warships, all of which being serious infringements of China's territorial sovereignty, the Chinese Ministry of Foreign Affairs made representations to the Japanese Minister to China on several occasions.

On November 15th, 1929, the Chinese Foreign Office addressed a note to the Japanese Minister to China, demanding that Japanese fishing vessels should not hereafter carry on fishing in Chinese territorial waters near Huaniao Shan off Woosung, in Kiangsu Province. The Japanese Minister stated in his reply that Japanese fishing vessels had never fished in Chinese waters but only on the high seas at a distance of some fifty or sixty maritime miles off the mouth of the Yangtse River. The The Japanese note further stated that reports regarding Japanese fishing might be due to misunderstanding on the part of the Chinese.

On June 3rd, 1930, the Chinese Foreign Office addressed a note to the Japanese Minister requesting that Japanese fishing vessels discontinue fishing in Yuling and Yalung harbours, Eihsien. The Japanese Minister in his reply stated that the Japanese Consul-General at Canton reported that matters regarding fishing and other actions of Japanese vessels in the said harbours were deliberate falsifications in Chinese newspapers.

In view of the repeated refusals of the Japanese authorities to prevent Japanese fishing vessels from being engaged in fishing in Chinese territorial waters and in the use of Chinese ports such as Shanghai, Tsingtao and Antung as their fishing bases, the Chinese Maritime Customs issued two notifications, one restraining, as from the 1st of May, 1931, importation of fish unless imported under a bill of lading by *bona fide* merchant-vessels from a foreign port. The Japanese authorities protested against these notifications and the Chinese authorities rejoined. But no agreement has been reached, and the issue is still unsettled between the two Governments.

XVII. The smuggling of Arms and Ammunition by the Japanese steamship "Toyo Maru."

The Branch Customs Office of the Tunghai Customs House seized on February 22nd, 1929, the Japanese steamship *Toyo Maru,* which smuggled 105 boxes of arms and ammunition, comprising 300 rifles and 60,000 bullets from Dairen to Shihtao in Shantung Province. Several of the Japanese smugglers including Tukuda Tujikichi were arrested on board the steamship. Subsequently the culprits and the said steamship were sent to Chefoo to be dealt with according to law.

Thereupon the Japanese Consul at the port called on the Tunghai Customs House demanding the handing over of the Japanese smugglers to the Japanese Consulate. This was accepted on the 8th of March on the condition that he would be responsible for turning them over to the Chinese authorities whenever they were wanted and that he would be also responsible for not allowing the steamship to leave the port. But the next day the steamship, escorted by the Japanese warship *Kuwa,* sailed out of the harbour of Chefoo and disappeared. The Commissioner of the Tunghai Customs House called on the Japanese Consul and protested. In reply the latter declared that owing to the damages she suffered in loading and unloading the arms and ammunition the steamship was ordered to go back to Dairen for repairs. By a written statement given to the Commissioner, he guaranteed that she would be called back to Chefoo whenever she was wanted by the competent Chinese authorities.

On April 23rd, 1929, the Ministry of Foreign Affairs sent a letter to the Japanese Minister, insisting upon the steamship being called back to Chefoo and the Japanese smugglers being handed to the competent Chinese authorities to be dealt with in accordance with due process of law. In reply the Japanese Minister stated that at the time when the steamship was on her way to Dairen for repairs, the Japanese warship happened to be just sailing back to Port Arthur for a military anniversary, so that the simultaneous sailing out from the harbour created a misunderstanding on the part of the Chinese. Regarding the smugglers in question, he added that the Kwantung Government was trying its best to collect evidences, that the Japanese authorities at Chefoo and Tsingtao were doing the same thing, and that the offenders would have to undergo a severe and impartial trial. The case has not been settled.

XVIII. The damaging of the branch offices of the Antung Custom-House by smugglers.

On May 17th, 1930, the Antung Custom-House caught a number of Koreans smuggling an immense quantity of goods valued approximately at $9,700 (Haikwan gold unit). The next day the infuriated smugglers twice damaged the branch Customs office at Tukiang which was near the Japanese police station. But the Japanese police did not exercise any power in preventing such mob action. Thereupon, the Chinese Foreign Ministry sent a protest to the Japanese Minister, demanding the arrest and punishment of the Korean smugglers and the co-operation on the part of the Japanese in checking smugglers. In reply, the Japanese Minister said that the Japanese authorities concerned were quite willing to co-operate with the Chinese authorities in checking smugglers and that those who committed crimes had been duly punished.

Again on October 5th, the Inspector of the Antung Custom-House, together with a number of the Customs police dressed in uniform, was on duty at the port. The Japanese police came and took away the clubs from the Customs police. Of this illegal action the Inspector complained immediately to the Japanese Consulate. The Consul contended that the carrying of clubs by the Customs police was not authorized. The Chinese Ministry of Foreign Affairs demanded the Japanese Minister that he should instruct the Japanese Consul at Antung to order the Japanese police to strictly refrain from such intervention as stated above.

While the case was pending for settlement, a similar case occurred on October 28th, at the Kiangchow branch office of the Antung Custom-House. A party of three Japanese refused to subject themselves to inspection by the Customs police. A Korean knocked down Customs police No. 11 and one of the three Japanese, by the name of Nozawa, suddenly stabbed the Customs police No. 12 in his right shoulder with a small knife. The victim was found fatally wounded. While the culprits turned to their heels, the Japanese police were standing by, watching with their hands in the pockets. When the other Customs police chased and arrested the two culprits, the Japanese police took them away and set them free. The Japanese Consul went so far as to demand the disarming of the Customs police when the Inspector of the Custom-House protested. On December 18th, the Chinese Foreign Ministry addressed a note to the Japanese Minister demanding the arrest and punishment of the murderers, the payment of reparation, and the punishment of the Japanese police who released the Korean culprits. But the Japanese authorities have not yet replied.

XIX. Japanese subjects in Foochow not observing the procedure regarding the examination and legalization of Deeds of Lands Leased in perpetuity.

Since 1911 it has been a legal procedure for the deeds of lands leased in perpetuity by aliens in Foochow to be submitted to the competent local Chinese authorities for examination after which such deeds would be returned to the lessees with stamps put on if no dispute was involved.

All the lessees of British, American and other nationalities followed the procedure. So did the Japanese Hospital, the Association of Japanese residents and the bank of Taiwan in Foochow. But the other Japanese subjects only registered their leases in the Japanese Consulate at the port, and did not observe the established procedure in submitting such deeds to the competent local Chinese authorities for examination and legalization. This frequently gave rise to disputes over the right of ownership of such lands.

In September and October 1929, the Commissioner of Foreign Affairs at Foochow addressed communications to the Japanese Consul at the port requesting him to notify the Japanese lessees that they should, in accordance with the legal procedure, submit their deeds for examination and legalization, and that if they failed to do so, the Chinese authorities would not recognize such leases in case of dispute. But the Japanese lessees ignored this communication.

On February 12th, 1931, the Chinese Foreign Office took up the matter with the Japanese Minister who in his reply of April 15th, stated that the Japanese Government had never given recognition to such procedure and that the Chinese authorities should not try to apply it to the Japanese lessees.

On the 30th of May, the Chinese Foreign Office again urged the Japanese Minister to notify the Japanese lessees to follow the procedure, and pointed out that it was contradictory to fact to state that the Japanese Government never gave recognition to such procedure, as testified by such Japanese organizations as the Japanese Hospital and others which did observe such procedure. But no reply has been received.

XX. The Japanese Consulate in Foochow protecting opium dens.

That the Japanese subjects were in no way connected with the opium den, Yifa, situated at the Kowcheli No. 5, Foochow, was once declared by the Japanese Consulate. On August 15th, 1930, the den was searched by the local authorities, and the house was sealed up. Thereupon, the Japanese Consul declared that, although there was no connection between the opium den and the Japanese subjects, the Consulate had nevertheless granted permission to a Japanese subject of Taiwan origin, by the name of Hou Yi, who applied for the house to be used as a store for sea products, and the Consul asked for the removal of the seals and the continued residence of Hou Yi in that house for one and a half months. But, while the case was being settled, the Japanese Consul suddenly on October 23rd sent men to tear down the seals from the opium den, and Hou Yi moved in to display all his odds and ends to give the appearance of a regular store.

Again in March 1931, the seals which by order of the local Chinese authorities closed down the opium den on the Houtien 2nd Street, No. 2 were also torn off by the Japanese Consulate. In their place new seal in the name of the Consulate of the Imperial Government of Japan were pasted. The Japanese Consul went on to declare that the den was the property of a Japanese subject Lin Lo-koo. The Chinese authorities collected all the facts bearing on the case and communicated them to the Japanese Minister. But no answer has ever been given to the protest.

XXI. Issue between China and Japan concerning Telegraphic communication in the Three Eastern Provinces.

During the Russo-Japanese War in 1904, Japanese troops took control of Chinese telegraphic communications and established telegraph lines and telephone services to facilitate military intelligence. In the next year when the war was over, the Chinese Government, in defence of its sovereign rights, demanded the Japanese Government to hand over to China all telegraph lines and telegraph offices which Japan had occupied and to demolish all telegraph lines and telephone services which Japan established during the war. After protracted negotiations a Convention of 8 articles was concluded between China and Japan on October 12th, 1908; Japan handed back all the occupied telegraph lines and telegraph offices to China. This was the beginning of treaty relations between China and Japan concerning telegraphic communications in the Three Eastern Provinces. Important contents of the Convention follow:

1. Japan undertakes immediately to hand over to China against the payment of Yen 50,000 all telegraph lines in Manchuria outside the railway territory. Japan is prepared to enter into negotiation with China with a view to coming to a certain arrangement concerning the Japanese telephone service in Manchuria outside the railway territory. Pending the conclusion of such an arrangement, Japan undertakes neither to extend her present telephone system in Manchuria without having first obtained the consent of the Chinese Government, nor to use her telephone lines for the transmission of telegrams in competition with the Chinese telegraph lines.

2. Japan undertakes, under the reserve of most favoured nation treatment for the future, not to lay submarine cables or to construct telegraph or telephone land-lines or to establish any kind of wireless communication in China, outside her leased or railway territories, without in every case first having obtained the consent of the Chinese Government.

3. At open marts or treaty ports in Manchuria, which are in close proximity to the Japanese railway territory, namely at Antung, Newchwang, Liaoyang, Mukden, Tiehling and Changchun, the Chinese Government agrees, for a period of 15 years, to place one or two special telegraph wires from the said open marts or treaty ports to such railway territory at the exclusive disposal of the Japanese Government.

4. A submarine cable will be laid by the Governments of Japan and China between a point in the Kwantung Province and Chefoo. Japan will lay and maintain the section of the submarine cable from Kwantung to within 7½ miles of Chefoo and China will lay and maintain the section of said cable from Chefoo to a point 7½ miles from Chefoo. The cable shall be connected direct to the Japanese Post Office

at Chefoo during such sufficient time each working day as may be agreed upon and such Post Office shall have the right to transmit over the said cable from and to places under the direct control of the Japanese telegraph system terminal Chefoo Japanese Government messages as well as private terminal Chefoo telegrams.

5. The Japanese Government undertakes to pay to the Chinese Government an annual sum of Yen 3,000 as a royalty on all messages forwarded over the Japanese Manchurian telegraph lines.

The two contracting parties on October 7th, 1908 further signed an agreement concerning the working of the Kwantung-Chefoo cable and another agreement concerning the working of the Japanese and Chinese telegraph lines in Manchuria.

In the years following the signing of the Convention and the Agreements, Japan established telegraph and telephone lines, telegraph offices and wireless stations outside the railway territory. These actions were a violation of her treaty obligations as well as an encroachment upon China's sovereign rights as regards telegraphic communication. We shall cite here a few facts:

1. According to Article 1 of the Convention signed October 12th, 1908, it was stipulated that "Japan undertakes, under the reserve of most favoured nation treatment for the future not to land submarine cables or to construct telegraph or telephone land-lines or to establish any kind of wireless communication in China, outside her leased or railway territories, without in every case first having obtained the consent of the Chinese Government." But Japan, during a number of years, constructed telegraph and telephone lines and established telegraph offices in Chinese cities of Yenki, Lungtsingsun,

Hunchun, Towtaokow, etc., without having first obtained
the consent of the Chinese Government. The Japanese
telegraph office in Lungtsingtsun was called a branch of
the Japanese Hueining office which shows how aggressive
the Japanese Government was. Her maintenance of
wireless stations at Chinwangtao, Manchouli, Kunchu-
ling, Lungtsingtsun, Liaoyang, Hunchun, Peiping, Tientsin and Chungchun is not only a deliberate encroachment upon China's sovereign rights but also creates competition with the Chinese wireless stations in the strictly
commercial sense of the word.

2. According to Article 2 of the same Convention, it
was stipulated that "Japan is prepared to enter into
negotiation with China with a view to coming to certain
arrangement concerning the Japanese telephone service
in Manchuria outside the railway territory. Pending the
conclusion of such an arrangement, Japan undertakes
neither to extend her present telephone system in Manchuria without having first obtained the consent of the
Chinese Government, nor to use her telephone lines for
the transmission of telegrams in competition with the
Chinese telegraph lines." But Japan has established
telephone services at Mukden, Changchun, etc. outside
the railway territory without the consent of the Chinese
Government. In spite of protests from the Chinese Government, no result has been obtained.

3. According to Article 4 of the same Convention, it
was stipulated that "the special wire shall be worked
from the Chinese telegraph buildings by Japanese clerks
in the employ of the Japanese Government." The stipu-
lation clearly shows that there should not be separate
Japanese telegraph office, but Japan, regardless of the
Convention, removed her office from the Chinese Ad-

ministration and established an office of her own at Mukden for the purpose of carrying on ordinary business.

In the spring of 1923, the Ministry of Communications at Peking, in view of the fact that Japan had repeatedly violated the Convention and the Agreements of 1908 concerning telegraphic communication, and that the loan of telegraph lines and offices at Antung, Newchwang, Liaoyang, Mukden, Tiehling and Changchun would expire on November 11th, 1923, notified the Japanese Government that the Chinese Government intended to take back the administration of the lines and the offices. Japan demanded to continue the loan of the line and further permit the revision of the Convention and Agreements of 1908. Representatives of the two Governments met in the Ministry of Communications at Peking on March 6th, 1924 to find a possible settlement of these questions. Japan demanded the extension of the loan of the line to a period of 30 years, but the Chinese Government would consent to its extension to the end of 1930 on the following conditions:—

1. China proposes to construct telegraph lines and establish telegraph offices in Dairen and in the railway territory of the South Manchuria Railway for the purpose of establishing regular telegraphic communication.

The reason for the proposal is that the greater part of the population in Dairen and in the railway territory are Chinese. If Japan has demanded for the advantage of her people the extension of the loan of the telegraph lines and offices outside the railway territory, it is only natural that the Chinese Government in a spirit of equality and reciprocity would demand the construction of telegraph lines and the establishment of telegraph offices in Dairen and in the railway territory.

2. The Chefoo side of the Kwantung-Chefoo cable shall be wholly operated under Chinese Administration.

The Japanese telegraph office at Chefoo was established to facilitate the transmission of Government and private messages in the Japanese language. Inasmuch as the Chinese Administration can now handle these messages with equal efficiency, the existence of the Japanese telegraph office at Chefoo is no longer necessary.

3. The Japanese Government shall pay to the Chinese telegraphic administration a royalty of one-third of the charges of telegrams transmitted between the offices of the South Manchuria Railway and those in Japan. Original copies of the telegrams and the accounts shall be open to inspection by both parties.

The reason for this is that telegrams between the offices of the Railway and those in Japan are very numerous. The royalty of Yen 3,000 a year paid to China according to the Convention of 1908 is much too small; it is necessary to calculate the royalty according to the number of words as is done in the Chinese Eastern Railway.

4. Telegrams entirely transmitted by the Japanese telegraph lines shall be charged at the same rate as in the Chinese Administration so as to eliminate competition.

Telegrams transmitted by Japanese telegraph lines of the Railway are charged at a lower rate than in the Chinese Administration. The consequence is that the Chinese Administration incurred a considerable amount of loss. China demanded that in the future telegram charges should be fixed at the same rate so that competition can be eliminated. All foreign telegraph companies which operate telegraph lines on Chinese territory charge the same rate as the Chinese Administration, those of the Chinese Eastern Railway do likewise. There was no reason why the South Manchuria Railway should act differently.

The Japanese representatives reserved their opinion with regard to the 4 above-mentioned proposals, adding that, in view of the importance of these proposals, they would wait for instructions from their Government. The Conference had several meetings, but due to lack of sincerity on the part of Japan to arrive at a settlement, it broke up without any result.

From the time the negotiation between China and Japan concerning telegraphic communications was suspended Japan has not handed back to China the telegraph lines and telegraph offices which she had occupied in the railway territory. The question was daily becoming more serious, because Japan, pending the settlement of the issue, constructed telegraph and telephone lines and established telegraph offices in Yenki and Lungtsingtsun, and erected wireless stations in Changchun and other places. The Ministry of Communications at Nanking, in view of the above facts, asked the Waichiaopu to send a note to the Japanese Minister to China, requesting the latter to ask the Japanese Postal Ministry to appoint representatives to continue the negotiations with China for the settlement of the questions concerning telegraphic communication between the two countries. The negotiation was resumed on September 17th, 1930 when the Ministry of Communications made the following two proposals:

Proposal A: Concerning telegraphic communication in Manchuria.

1. Japan shall hand back to China all telegraph lines and offices in Mukden, Antung, Liaoyang, Tiehling and Changchun.

Reason: The period of the loan expired on October

11th, 1923. Japan should hand them back to China in accordance with the stipulations of the Convention of 1908.

2. Japan shall hand back to China the long-distance telephone service between Mukden and Hsinmintun which Japan loaned from China.

Reason: The term of the loan has expired.

3. Japan shall abolish all telephone services outside the South Manchuria Railway territory, the establishment of which has not had the consent of the Chinese Government.

Reason: As stated in Case No. 2 (p. 59).

4. Japan shall abolish all telegraph and telephone lines and offices at Yenki, Lungtsingtsun, Hunchun, Towtaokow, etc.

Reason: As stated in Case No. 1 (pp. 58-59).

5. China shall construct telegraph and telephone lines, establish telegraph offices, and erect wireless stations in Dairen, Port Arthur and the South Manchuria Railway territory for carrying on regular business.

Reason: As stated in Proposal No. 1 by the Ministry of Communications at Peking (p. 60).

6. In the stations along the South Manchuria Railway where there are no Chinese telegraph offices, all telegrams, which are sent to and from places where there are or not Chinese telegraph offices, shall be charged at the same rate as in the Chinese Administration. If the telegram is sent to places where there are already Chinese telegraph offices or to foreign countries, the station which receives the telegram shall deliver it to the nearest Chinese telegraph office for transmission. If the station is situated in a district where there is already a Chinese telegraph office, the station shall not be allowed to transmit the telegram.

Reason: As stated in Proposal No. 4 by the Ministry of Communications at Peking (p. 61).

7. When the South Manchuria Railway transmits telegrams to and from places where there are no Chinese telegraph offices, the Railway shall pay a royalty of one-third of the charges received from the transmission of these telegrams.

Reason: As stated in Proposal No. 3 of the Ministry of Communications at Peking (pp. 60-61).

Proposal: Concerning the Kwantung-Chefoo Cable.

1. The Chefoo side of the Kwantung-Chefoo Cable shall be entirely operated by China and the Japanese telegraph office at Chefoo shall be abolished.

Reason: As stated in Proposal No. 2 of the Ministry of Communications at Peking (p. 60).

2. All telegrams transmitted by the cable shall be charged with an additional cable charge.

Reason: According to the agreement of 1908, China should pay to Japan 4 cents for every Chinese plain word, 8 cents for every foreign word or Chinese coded word in all domestic messages, and 6 cents for every word in international messages transmitted through the said cable, and the Chinese Administration has thereby incurred heavy losses each year. But for telegrams transmitted by the Great Northern and Great Eastern Companies there is an additional cable charge, and the Chinese Administration need not pay a further cable charge to the Companies. The same rule should be applied to the Kwantung-Chefoo cable.

3. The Agreement of 1908 concerning the operation of the Kwantung-Chefoo cable shall be revised.

Reason: The Agreement was concluded some 20 years ago, and the articles therein are no longer suited to present-day requirements. Revision is necessary to facilitate the working of the cable.

The Japanese representatives, under the pretext of awaiting instructions from the Government, delayed the negotiation and the Conference broke up without arriving at any result.

XXII. The sailing of the Japanese Warship "Fuyo" into the Inland Waters of China.

At 3 o'clock p.m. on May 18th, 1931, the Japanese cruiser *Fuyo* sailed from Kwanhokow, by way of Suankong into Shiangsuikow, Kuanyuin Hsien, Kiangsu province, stopping at various places and taking photographs all along the way. The action attracted a number of spectators who continued to increase. The Japanese marines were compelled to take down their national flag, and finally the Japanese warship sailed away. This was reported by the Kiangsu Provincial Government to the Ministry of Foreign Affairs.

On June 20th, the Ministry of Foreign Affairs addressed a note to the Japanese Chargé d'Affaires, stating that the Japanese cruiser *Fuyo,* without obtaining permission beforehand from the Chinese Government, sailed into the Chinese inland waters and took photographs all along the way, that such actions were contrary to general international practice and in violation of Chinese sovereignty, and that the Japanese Government was requested to instruct Japanese warships hereafter not to penetrate into Chinese inland waters.

In reply, the Japanese Chargé d'Affaires stated that although it was a fact that the Japanese cruiser sailed from Kwanhokow to Shiangsuikow and took photographs all along the way, it was done in a peaceful way and without any hostile intention; and that the picture-taking was done outside of the strategic points, and that since it was merely a sightseeing trip, it should not be considered a departure from general international practice and infringement upon China's sovereignty.

The Ministry of Foreign Affaires sent, on July 21st, another note to the Japanese Legation, emphasizing that in accordance with international practice recognized by all Powers, foreign warships without previous notice to the Government of another country were not entitled to enter into the territory of that country, and that the Japanese Government should instruct its warships to observe this practice strictly.

The Japanese Legation contended in its reply, dated August 18th, that according to treaties between China and other Powers, the entry of foreign warships into any Chinese harbours was permissible, and that the taking of pictures outside the strategic points by the Japanese cruiser did not constitute an action against general international practice.

However, when the case was pending for settlement another similar incident occurred in Hunan. The Provincial Government reported to the Ministry of Foreign Affairs that a Japanese gunboat *Toriwa* sailed to Shiangtan without previous notice to the Government. Thereupon the Ministry of Foreign Affairs addressed on September 5th of the same year a note to the Japanese Legation, emphasizing the points that were previously raised in its note as regards the *Fuyo* case and especially the fact that the right of entrance into Chinese inland waters was denied to foreign warships. The *Toriwa* gunboat case was clearly a repetition within a period of half a year of the violation of Chinese sovereignty. The note also observed that no such provision as alleged by the Japanese Legation in its note dated August 18th that the entry of foreign warships into any harbour of China was permissible could be found even in the expired Sino-Japanese Treaty of Commerce and Navigation of 1896. It urged the Japanese Government to carry out China's demands as presented in the notes dated June 20th and July 21st, 1931.

On the 16th of September, the Japanese Legation in reply maintained the same views as were held in its previous notes, and further observed that the actions of the cruiser *Fuyo* and the gunboat *Toriwa* were permissible under the most favoured nation treatment provided in the treaties between China and the other Powers.

The cases are still unsettled between the two countries.

XXIII. The Japanese Government ignored the damages inflicted upon China by the Japanese troops during the Tsinan incident.

Tsinan, the capital of Shantung province, was captured by the Nationalist army on May 1st, 1928. On the 3rd, the Japanese troops, stationed at Tsinan despite protests from the Nationalist Government, indiscriminately opened fire without the least provocation on the Chinese troops and civilians alike. The Japanese troops resorted to the use of machine guns and heavy guns to bombard Chinese public buildings and residences. A squad of Japanese soldiers invaded the office of the Commissioner for Foreign Affairs and murdered Commissioner Tsai Kung-shih and over ten members of his staff. Foreign Minister Hwang's office was subjected to a systematic search. As a result, tremendous losses were sustained by China.

Damage to public property already estimated amounted to $1,130,000.00.

Damage to private property already estimated amounted to $2,180,000.00.

In addition to these damages, however, more than one thousand people were killed and a still greater number were either wounded or missing.

The investigation into the losses sustained by China and Japan was charged to a Joint-Commission of Investigation composed of an equal number of Chinese and Japanese commissioners provided in a Protocol signed by both parties on March 28th, 1929, when the Tsinan incident was declared as settled. The Chinese Foreign Office in pursuance of the Protocol decided with the Japanese Minister that each country appoint three commissioners for investigation. In June 1929, the Chinese Foreign Office notified the Japanese Minister of its appointments, but received no reply from the latter. The Chinese Government in May 1930, renewed its attempt to ask the Japanese Government to make its appointments but likewise produced no effect.

XXIV. The Massacre of Chinese by the " Self-Warning Corps " in Japan after the Great Earthquake.

Immediately after the great earthquake a large number of Japanese young men and reservists organized themselves into what was called the "Self-Warning Corps" with the object of suppressing illegal activities of the Koreans in Japan. The members of this corps, however, together with soldiers and policemen slaughtered a great many Chinese, most of them being merchants and labourers and also a few students in Tokyo and Yokohama on September 2nd, 3rd and 4th, 1922. A commission of three was sent by the Chinese Government to investigate the massacre on the spot. The report of the commissioners gave the following details:

Some two thousand Chinese lived in the Section (*chome* in Japanese) from I to VIII inclusive on Oshima Street,

Tokyo. On September 3rd, three days after the earthquake, the members of the "Self-Warning Corps" including a few soldiers and policemen compelled a large number of Chinese to hand over all their money and marched them to an open place in Section No. VIII, Oshima Street. There they were mercilessly killed by the Japanese with swords and clubs. These Chinese could not be mistaken for Koreans for they were dressed in Chinese costumes. Their corpses were cremated. The rest of the Chinese not murdered were detained in a barrack and later expatriated to China. The news of the massacre later leaked out and was published in the November 11th issue of a vernacular newspaper of Tokyo, *Yomiuri Shimbun*. The Tokyo authorities, learning the publication of the news, ordered the press to call back all the copies of the paper and to take out that section of the block concerned with this news item before they went to circulation. Fortunately the Chinese Commission found one original copy of the paper containing the news.

Immediately after the earthquake, a Chinese student by the name of Wang Shi-tien was actively engaged in the relief work for the Chinese residents. He was murdered by the gendarmes in Tokyo on September 12th. The Japanese authorities, however, verbally stated to the Chinese commissioners in Tokyo that at 3 o'clock a.m., September 12th, the police station at Kamedo handed over Wang Shi-tien to Captain Sasaki, Captain of the Gendarmerie, to be detained in a barrack, but the Captain set him free on his way to the barrack and that henceforth Wang Shi-tien became missing. One of the surviving Chinese by the name of Chou Min-su who was detained together with Wang at the police station reported that he was an eye-witness to two armed soldiers taking Wang out at 3 o'clock a.m. September 12th. On December 20th,

Count Mutsu Hirokichi and other well-known Japanese held a memorial service for Wang Shi-tien in the Salvation Army Headquarters in Tokyo. One of the commissioners was invited to attend the memorial service.

Besides, seven Chinese were murdered in Yokohama and its vicinity.

Altogether five hundred twenty Chinese were wilfully killed by the members of the "Self-Warning Corps" and soldiers and policemen. This was a case of inhumane wholesale massacre unprecedented in the history of international relations.

The Chinese Minister to Japan filed a protest with the Japanese Government and the Ministry of Foreign Affairs lodged repeated protests with the Japanese Minister to China, showing him the lists of casualties and losses, and demanding indemnity and punishment of the culprits. But Japan has never settled the case with China.

XXV. The First Anti-Chinese Riots in Korea. (December 1927).

From the 7th to the 16th of December 1927, anti-Chinese riots by Korean mobs broke out at various places in Korea, notably at Riri, Sanrei, Tokei, Gunsan, Sanshu, Chojo, Sintaijin, Tenan, Ninsen and other towns, insulting and killing Chinese residents, looting and plundering their property, and beseiging and attacking the Chinese Consulate at Ninsen. As a result two Chinese were killed and forty-eight wounded. The direct losses sustained by the Chinese amounted to Yen 29,763.49.

The continuous mob violence committed by the Korean rioters against the Chinese merchants and labourers engaged in lawful pursuits at the various places in Korea suffices to testify that the local authorities did not exercise due diligence to check rioters in perpetrating crimes against the Chinese for which the Japanese Government should be responsible. The Anti-Chinese movement spread all over Korea and extended to a period of ten days. On the tenth day of the reign of terror, the mob violence had assumed such grave proportions at Ninsen that the Chinese Consulate became threatened and twenty-two Chinese were wounded by the rioters. A situation like this could not have developed if the Japanese Government resorted to every means at its disposal to protect Chinese nationals and consular officials in Korea.

Instead of checking the anti-Chinese movement from the very start or taking effective measures to suppress it completely, the Japanese Government instructed its Minister to China to address a memorandum to the Ministry of Foreign Affairs stating that the ill-feeling of the Koreans towards the Chinese residents in Korea was evoked by the alleged oppressive measures taken by the authorities of the Three Eastern Provinces against the Koreans there.

On December 20th, the Chinese Foreign Office lodged a protest with the Japanese Minister, urging the Japanese Government to take effective measures to protect Chinese Consulates and lives and property of the Chinese in Korea, and at the some time reserving the right to demand indemnity for casualties and damage done to property. On the 24th, the Japanese Minister addressed a memorandum to the Chinese Foreign Office, explaining that the local authorities tried to use all their means to suppress riots and attributing once more the outrages to the alleged oppressive measures of the authorities of the Three Eastern Provinces. On February 4th, 1928, the Chinese Foreign Office addressed a memorandum to the Japanese Minister, stating that the authorities of Mukden and Kirin provinces stated in their replies to the office that protection provided in the treaties between China and Japan had been given to Koreans as usual and no oppressive measure was ever directed against them. On April 2nd, 1928, the Chinese Foreign Office addressed a note to the Japanese Minister inclosing a list of the Chinese killed and wounded in the Korean riots, demanding the payment of Yen 6,000 for the two persons killed and Yen 3,056 as compensation for 48 persons severely wounded. The Japanese Government, however has never agreed to any settlement of the case.

XXVI. The Wanpaoshan Case.

(*Vide Memorandum on. the Wanpaoshan Case*).

XXVII. The Second Anti-Chinese Riots in Korea. (July 1931).

(*Vide Memorandum on The Anti-Chinese Riots in Korea, July, 1931*).

Peiping, June 26th, 1932.

MEMORANDUM

ON

THE CURRENCY IN THE THREE EASTERN PROVINCES AND ITS RELATION TO THE SOYA BEAN

Document No. 19   Peiping, June 1932

MEMORANDUM ON THE CURRENCY IN THE THREE EASTERN PROVINCES AND ITS RELATION TO THE SOYA BEAN.

I. Introduction.
1. The two periods in currency history.

II. Currency and Banking in the Three Eastern Provinces before 1928.
2. Currency upset as result of war.
3. Vicissitudes of the *Fengpiao*.
4. Increase of note issue.
5. The fall of the notes.

III. The Stabilization of the *Fengpiao*.
6. Stabilization ordinance June 25th, 1929.
7. Frontier Bank notes.

IV. Soya Beans and the Bank of Issue.
8. Soya beans and the currency.
9. Three ways where the beans come into the banks.
10. The soya bean pool: its purposes.
11. Aim to defeat unfair buying by Japanese.
12. Buying for its own account.
13. Conclusion.

V. Inflation, or over Issue, in the Provinces by the Japanese.
14. Japanese really responsible for chaotic currency: inflation and confusion of standards.
15. Amount of Japanese issue.
16. Third factor of disturbance by the Japanese.

Memorandum on the Currency in the Three Eastern Provinces and its Relation to the Soya Bean

I. INTRODUCTION.

1. **The two periods in currency history.** The currency history in the Three Eastern Provinces is conveniently divided into two periods, a period of war and chaos and a period of peace and stabilization. The year 1928, in which Marshal Chang Hsueh-liang assumed power and a new regime came into being, marked the division. From 1917 on for ten years, it was a period of civil war. Although there were intervals of rest and the warfare never actually took place in the Provinces, still the currency there was in a state of confusion. Since 1928, the national flag has been flown throughout the Provinces, peace has prevailed, currency has been gaining its equilibrium, and its stability for which people had been longing for many years has become at last a reality, in spite of the fact that its value remains depreciated at a certain point. On June 25th, 1929, when the currency crisis was not entirely over the Chinese authorities issued an order for the stabilization of the Mukden notes, and the currency has become stable ever since. The stability of the Mukden notes since 1929 has been very marked, although it is true that the same cannot be said of the notes issued by the Kirin Provincial Bank and the Provincial Bank of Heilungkiang.

II. CURRENCY AND BANKING IN THE THREE EASTERN PROVINCES BEFORE 1928.

2. **Currency upset as result of war.** As war is always destructive, it upsets the currency system. History is full of instances of this kind. The American currency crisis after the American civil war, the collapse of the German mark after the Great War, of the French franc from 1918 to 1927, of the rouble after the Russian Revolution, and of the pound sterling between 1919 to 1925, are a few of many examples of chaotic currency as a legacy of war. China, therefore, with the many civil wars which have unfortunately befallen the country these many years, is no exception. But happily those times of uncertainty seem to have passed and the conditions of the currency in the Provinces within the last two or three years indicated that it was going through a healthy improvement.

3. **Vicissitudes of the** *Fengpiao*. It is perhaps too involved to trace the history of the various kinds of notes and coins circulating in the Provinces. For our present purposes, we need to concern ourselves with only the most important note issue, which is the *Fengpiao*, or the Mukden notes. The *Fengpiao* is the standard currency in Liaoning Province; it also circulates extensively in Jehol, Kirin, Heilungkiang, and Hopei Provinces. It was first issued in 1906 and was redeemable at par for small silver coins. It was well accepted by the people and remained stable and at par for ten years. In 1916 when Yuan Shih-kai died after having failed in his monarchical schemes there was a wild run on the banks in Peking. When the crisis reached Mukden, the Bank of the Three Eastern Provinces was in difficulty. But it managed to pull through. In 1917 came another run

22

on the bank when it was compelled to stop cash payment. Instead of maintaining a free silver market, the Bank placed an embargo on silver and established a sort of silver exchange standard whereby a bearer of the Mukden notes could not get silver coins with them but a demand draft on Shanghai at the market rate in Mukden.

4. **Increase of note issue.** In July 1918, the Bank of the Three Eastern Provinces began to withdraw its old notes and issued $6,000,000 in exchange notes. As time went on, the issue increased. It rose to $30,000,000 in 1921; $60,000,000 in 1924; $193,995,000 in 1925; and $1,530,622,000 in 1928. The Bank also issued notes through its Harbin branch in Harbin local currency. The following table shows the issue in the two cities from 1925 to 1930:

Notes issued by the Bank of the Three Eastern Provinces (1925-1929).

Year	Issued in Mukden	Issued in Harbin
Jan. 31, 1925	193,995,590	13,287,423
Mar. 31, 1926	207,697,873	15,770,794
Jan. 31, 1927	324,628,869	17,645,321
Jan. 31, 1928	470,461,987	74,594,351
Apr. 30, 1929	1,366,369,692	346,779,880
Dec. 31, 1929	1,530,622,574	339,243,846

5. **The fall of the notes.** The story of the depreciation of the notes is very instructive; for not only does it show how civil wars affect the currency system, but, at the same time, it supplies another instance of the quantity theory of money. The more notes the Bank issued, the more their value depreciated. From 1916 to 1923 the value of the notes was quite stable, and the exchange rate with standard money (silver dollar) was about 1.28 to 1.30. In August 1924, it depreciated to 1.50, and in

December to 2.05. From 1925 onward, the fall became more precipitate until it touched the bottom in May, 1929 with 72 to one dollar which was sixty times lower than its original value.

III. THE STABILIZATION OF THE *FENGPIAO*.

6. **Stabilization ordinance June 25th, 1929.** Seeing the wild depreciation of the Mukden notes at the beginning of 1929, the Provincial Government of Liaoning Province issued an order on June 25th, 1929 by which the notes were stabilized at 60 to 1, that is 60 dollars in Mukden notes is exchangeable for one silver standard coin. That was the beginning of currency stability. Sufficient reserve was kept, and the rate of the notes was strictly maintained. As a further means of stabilization, a Commission on Currency and Foreign Exchange in the Three Eastern Provinces was established in October, 1929, to enquire into the situation and make recommendations for improvement. The Commission submitted its report in November, 1930, and the government began to pursue an intelligent currency policy based on that report. Its recommendations were being put into effect when the crash came on September 18th, 1931.

7. **Frontier Bank notes.** The other important Bank which issues notes is the Frontier Bank. Its notes are in standard silver dollars which circulate throughout the Provinces. Before November, 1928, its issue was less than one million dollars, but since the Mukden notes were stabilized in June, 1929, it has increased its issue. In August, 1931, its notes in circulation were around $20,000,000. These Frontier Bank silver notes have been always at par and stable, and have been gradually replacing the *Fengpiao*. It was the policy of the Chinese

authorities to withdraw the *Fengpiao*, although it had
been stabilized, and the new issue in silver dollars has
been taking its place which was especially so in 1931.
At the beginning of that year the Bank of the Three
Eastern Provinces also issued notes in silver standard
dollars, hoping that the new issue in standard money
would replace the old notes in the shortest possible time.

IV. SOYA BEANS AND THE BANK OF ISSUE.

8. **Soya beans and the currency.** The Bank of the
Three Eastern Provinces has been accused of depre-
ciating the currency in the Provinces through the purchase of soya beans. Let us see how the Bank bought
the beans and in what ways it disposed of them. There
are three ways through which beans came into the Bank.

9. **Three ways where the beans come into the banks.**
In the first place, as the Three Eastern Provinces are
predominantly agricultural and soya beans an important product, the Bank has had to deal with them in one
way or another. In accordance with usual banking
practices, the Bank would often give credit or advance
money to a farmer against his beans. This is technically
known as "advances against agricultural products."
It is part of the ordinary business. Two things follow
however: (1) The advances made to the farmer lead to
a temporary expansion of currency, sometimes known as
"seasonal expansion." (2) Sometimes, however, the
farmer fails to meet his obligations with the Bank. In
that case, the Bank will be compelled to accept the beans
which he has mortgaged to the Bank as security for the
advance made to him. It is thus that beans get into the
hands of the Bank. This is ordinary banking transaction
and is normal.

10. **The soya bean pool: its purposes.** Secondly, beans

came into the bank through the soya bean pool of which it was a member. The purpose of the pool was to dispose of the temporary "over-production" of beans, to help the farmer against forced sale, and to defeat unfair buying by the Japanese. In 1930, the soya bean crop was unusually good, but unfortunately it was a year of world depression, when the prices were low and the market extremely dull in Europe. Under those circumstances the farmer in the Provinces was unable to sell his beans without heavy loss. That reacted on the Banks which naturally could not work smoothly if all the farmers failed. A pool was then organized, and four Banks— the Bank of the Three Eastern Provinces, the Provincial Bank of Kirin, the Provincial Bank of Heilungkiang, and the Frontier Bank,—became its members. They bought over 900,000 tons of beans, which benefited the farmer, although at the end of the year the pool itself had to meet heavy loss. What the American bankers did with over-production of cotton and the Canadian bankers wheat, that the Chinese bankers did in the Provinces for soya beans.

11. **Aim to defeat unfair buying by Japanese.** Another object of the pool was to defeat unfair buying of beans by the Japanese. The situation of the bean market was this: The export trade of the soya beans, with the exception of a small amount bought by the Danish, Dutch, German, and British merchants, was done exclusively by the Japanese under the leadership of two big trading firms, the Mitsui and the Mitsubishi. They had a monopoly of the bean market in the Provinces, because they were secretly granted freight rebates of 10% to 20% from the South Manchuria Railway while the Chinese and other nationals had to pay the freight in full. So long as the Japanese were the only buyers in the market,

the farmer had to accept whatever low price was offered
to him. Therefore, he was forced to sell because no one
else was able to offer a better price for his product. He
was thus pitifully exploited. The organized pool com-
peted with the Japanese in buying the beans and offered
a somewhat higher price for them so that the farmer
could get a fair return for his labour. The pool was
organized in 1930 and was in operation for one year only.
In 1931, before it started buying, the incident of September 18th had already taken place.

12. **Buying for its own account.** Thirdly, the Bank
of the Three Eastern Provinces sometimes bought beans
for its own purposes. But this kind of purchase
amounted to very little. The record year was 1926, when
the Bank bought about 600,000 tons more than in other
years.

13. **Conclusion.** The conclusion we draw from the
above remarks is as follows: It is true that the Mukden
notes passed through a difficult and chaotic time, but that
time has passed. The notes were stabilized on June
25th, 1929, and have remained stable ever since. It is
true that the Bank, for one reason or another, had to
deal with soya beans, but that time too has passed.

V. INFLATION, OR OVER ISSUE, IN THE PROVINCES BY THE JAPANESE.

14. **Japanese really responsible for chaotic currency:
inflation and confusion of standards.** If currency in the
Three Eastern Provinces is to be described chaotic, it
is in considerable measure due to the large issue of notes
in the Three Eastern Provinces by two Japanese banks,
the Bank of Chosen and the Yokohama Specie Bank.
Such issue is not authorized by treaty with Japan or by

Chinese law. The Yokohama Specie Bank issues notes in silver on the one hand, and the Bank of Chosen issues notes in gold yen on the other. Through these unlawful issues, they not only make the Chinese Bank of issue helpless in controlling circulation and credit, but they also interfere with the efforts at reform. The introduction of two foreign units, one in gold and another in silver, confuses the currency. Two important elements are required in good currency, one is stability and the cther, a single standard. The issues of the two Japanese banks in the Provinces defeat both. The gold yen and the silver yen in the Provinces are never stable anyway in the terms of the Chinese currency; and their introduction into the currency system of the Three Eastern Provinces adds to the confusion. The following tables show the amount of note issue of the two Japanese banks.

Notes issued by the Yokohama Specie Bank in the Three Eastern Provinces.

Year	Amount of Silver Yen
1920	1,761,000
1921	1,037,000
1922	1,231,000
1923	1,484,000
1924	1,496,000
1925	3,088,000
1926	3,305,000
1927	5,460,000
1928	9,863,000
1929	5,938,000

Notes issued by the Bank of Chosen in the Three Eastern Provinces.

Year	Total Amount Circulating at the End of the Year	Amount Circulating in the Three Eastern Provinces
1917	Yen 67,364,000	
1918	" 115,523,000	Yen 19,098,000
1919	" 163,600,000	" 37,066,000
1920	" 114,034,000	" 42,324,000
1921	" 134,360,000	" 46,775,000
1922	" 100,544,000	" 34,251,000
1923	" 110,233,000	" 39,147,000
1924	" 129,113,000	" 45,190,000
1925	" 120,540,000	" 42,190,000
1926	" 110,939,000	" 38,829,000
1927	" 124,527,000	" 44,584,000
1928	" 132,778,000	
1929	" 119,034,000	

15. **Amount of Japanese issue.** The above tables are the official figures published by the two Japanese banks. The actual issue, we have been told, is much larger. But taking the figures as they are, the two issues in 1929 amount to 106,000,000 Chinese dollars. That is, the issue of the two Japanese banks are three times more in market value than that of the Bank of the Three Eastern Provinces, which was only $30,000,000.

16. **Third factor of disturbance by the Japanese.** In addition to what the Japanese have done in the Provinces as regards (1) inflation of the currency and (2) paralysis of the currency and credit control, there is a third factor which frequently confuses and disturbs the money market. The gold yen notes issued by the Bank of Chosen are not redeemable for gold coins or bullion,

but for the notes of the Bank of Japan so that any disturbance or crises in Japan will necessarily affect the Chinese in the Provinces. And crisis in Japan are of frequent occurrence. Cases where crisis in Japan has affected the Provinces are too many to be enumerated, three important ones being sufficient for our purpose: (1) the collapse of the yen in 1919, (2) the banking crisis in 1928, and (3) the removal of the embargo on gold in 1930. Whenever a Japanese Prime Minister was assassinated, or a managing director of a big trading firm was murdered, it always reacted seriously on the Chinese market in the Provinces because of the mingling of the yen in the currency.

Peiping, June 26th 1932.

MEMORANDUM

ON

THE DECISIONS TAKEN BY THE CHINESE GOVERNMENT AT THE BEGINNING OF THE SHANGHAI INCIDENT

Document No. 20   Peiping, July 1932

MEMORANDUM ON THE DECISIONS TAKEN BY THE CHINESE GOVERNMENT AT THE BEGIN- NING OF THE SHANGHAI INCIDENT.

1. Conference with the Commission.
2. Order of January 27th, 1932.
3. Political situation in Nanking.
4. Arrival of the Gendarmerie Force at Shanghai.
5. Reasons for delay in withdrawal and replacement.
6. Outbreak of the Shanghai incident.
7. The purpose for which the 19th Route Army was sent sent to Shanghai.
8. Statement alleging lack of confidence in the Army unfounded.

MEMORANDUM ON THE DECISIONS TAKEN BY THE CHINESE GOVERNMENT AT THE BEGINNING OF THE SHANGHAI INCIDENT

1. **Conference with the Commission.** In the course of a Conference with the Commission of Inquiry at Peiping, June 20th, 1932, the Chinese Government represented by Mr. Wang Ching-wei, President of the Executive *Yuan*, Mr. T. V. Soong, Vice-President of the Executive *Yuan* and Minister of Finance, Dr. Lo Wen-kan, Minister of Foreign Affairs, and Dr. V. K. Wellington Koo, the Chinese Assessor, were given to understand that there was a body of opinion in Shanghai to the effect that in connection with the Shanghai incident, January-March, 1932, the stationing of the 19th Route Army at Chapei constituted a menace from which the Japanese forces saved Shanghai. At the same time, the Commission understood that immediately before January 28th, the Chinese Government had contemplated the withdrawal of the said Army and its replacement by a gendarmerie force. The Chinese Government was therefore requested to make a statement and to verify it, if possible, by some documentary evidence so that the Commission might be in a position to clarify the point in its report to the Council of the League.

2. **Order of January 27th, 1932.** The sincere desire of the Chinese Government to settle peaceably the dispute arising out of the attack on a few Japanese monks in January last was fully evidenced by the complete acceptance by the Chinese Mayor of the demands pre-

sented by the Japanese Consul-General at Shanghai. In order to give further effect to its peaceful intentions, the Chinese Government made an important decision to replace the 19th Route Army at Chapei with a regiment from the gendarmerie force, so that the interposition of a non-fighting strength would ensure the avoidance of a clash between the Chinese and Japanese forces. A telegraphic order [1] in that sense was issued on January 27th, 1932, at 1:10 p.m. (Nanking) by General Chu Pei-teh, Chief of General Staff, and General Ho Ying-ching, Minister of War, to General Kuo Chen-lun, Commander of the Gendarmerie Force, General Chen Ming-shu, Commander-in-Chief of the Defence of Nanking and Shanghai Areas, and General Tai Chi, Garrison Commander of Shanghai and Woosung.

The order reads as follows:—

Kuo, Commander of the Gendarmerie Force; Chen, Commander-in-Chief of the Defence of Nanking and Shanghai Areas; Tai, Garrison Commander of Shanghai and Woosung:—
In order to exert every effort to avoid conflict between the Chinese and the Japanese troops, one regiment of Gendarmes shall be immediately despatched to the Chapei area at Shanghai to take over the garrison duty there. This regiment is to be placed under the command of Tai Chi, Garrison Commander of Shanghai and Woosung, with a view to preventing contact and conflict between the two forces. This order shall be immediately carried out and report expected. Chu Pei-teh and Ho Ying-ching. Twenty-seventh, at noon. Seal.

3. **Political situation in Nanking.** In this connection,

[1] A photographic copy of the order together with its draft translation as well as photographic copies of three other related documents were sent to the Commission, June 28th, 1932.

it may not be out of place to say a word about the political situation then prevailing in Nanking. At that time, Mr. Sun Fo, the President of the Executive *Yuan,* was resigning from that office, and the present President, Mr. Wang Ching-wei, was on the point of being elected to succeed him. Pending the formation of a new government, the direction of national affairs was entrusted to the Standing Committee of the Central Political Council, of which General Chiang Kai-shek and Mr. Wang were then and still are members. It was under their joint instructions that Generals Chu and Ho issued the order in question. Mr. Wang was subsequently elected to the presidency of the Executive *Yuan* in the evening of the 28th of January.

4. **Arrival of the Gendarmerie Force at Shanghai.** Upon receipt of the telegraphic order quoted above, General Kuo Chen-lun at once caused to be despatched to Shanghai the 6th regiment of the Gendarmerie force, which boarded the train at Nanking at 8 p.m., January 27th, started for Shanghai at 2 a.m. the following morning and arrived at Chenju about five miles from Shanghai, at noon, January 28th.

5. **Reasons for delay in withdrawal and replacement.** In order to effect the replacement, it was necessary first to withdraw the 19th Route Army from Chapei. While necessary preparations for transportation were being made in the afternoon to bring about the withdrawal and replacement, it was learned that the tense situation was considerably eased by China's acceptance of the Japanese demands. The declaration of the Japanese Consul-General that the settlement of the case was satisfactory gave the Chinese authorities good reason for believing that the Japanese naval commander would not

resort to such drastic measures as he had threatened to take; and that consequently there was less likelihood of an armed clash. The fact that in any case withdrawal and replacement could not possibly be completed within the few hours of daylight that remained persuaded the military authorities to decide to begin the process early in the morning of the 29th.

6. **Outbreak of the Shanghai incident.** All of a sudden, however, at 11:25 p.m. of January 28th, the Japanese naval commander despatched a communication to the Chinese authorities demanding the immediate withdrawal of the Chinese troops stationed at Chapei. About half an hour later, at 11:50 p.m., the Japanese armed detachments, supported by machine guns, proceeded to invade Chapei by opening attack first on the Chinese police and then on the regular Chinese troops. It was under these circumstances that the 6th regiment of the Gendarmerie force, which was originally intended to relieve the 19th Route Army in the work of maintaining peace in Chapei, was compelled by force of circumstances to become a body of reinforcements to the 19th Route Army in their resistance against Japanese aggression.

7. **The purpose for which the 19th Route Army was sent to Shanghai.** It may be pointed out here that the 19th Route Army, which was under the general command of General Chen Ming-shu but in immediate charge of Generals Chiang Kwang-nai, Tsai Ting-kai and Tai Chi, had successfully taken part in several campaigns against the anti-government forces as well as in the campaign for the suppression of communists in the Province of Kiangsi. In October of 1931, this Army was transferred from Kiangsi to Nanking and Shanghai for garrison duty, at a time when the leaders of Nanking and Canton assem-

bled at Shanghai to readjust some internal political problems. It was believed that the presence in Nanking and Shanghai of this Army, well-disciplined and loyal to the cause of internal peace and order, would increase the mutual confidence of both parties and facilitate an understanding between them. It is therefore quite obvious that when the 19th Route Army was despatched to Shanghai in October, 1931, it could hardly have been anticipated that it should subsequently be engaged in operations for defending Shanghai against the advancing Japanese forces. And it is still less comprehensible to allege that the Chinese Government had sent the 19th Route Army to Shanghai to attack Japanese residents there and to threaten the safety of the International Settlement.

On the contrary, that the Chinese troops held themselves strictly on the defensive appears to be best proved by the fact that even at one moment in the course of the fighting, when the Japanese troops were hard pressed and were retreating in the direction of the Settlement, the Chinese troops, out of a desire to respect the safety of the Settlement, refrained from following up their successes by pursuing across its boundaries.

8. **Statement alleging lack of confidence in the Army unfounded.** At one time, another body of opinion gained currency stating that the proposed replacement of the 19th Route Army by a part of the gendarmerie force indicated the lack of confidence on the part of the Government in the Army. This statement was also unfounded, in view of the fact that on several occasions in 1929 and 1930, this Army had fought loyally for the Government against the opposing forces. Besides, if the allegation had been true, then the command of the 6th regiment would not have been entrusted to General Tai

Chi who was a colleague of General Tsai Ting-kai, Commander of the 19th Route Army, and is known to be on friendly terms with him. As has been said above, in making the decision as contained in the telegraphic order of January 27th, the Chinese Government was animated by the sole desire to avoid hostilities and maintain peace.

It may be added in conclusion that as the urgency of the situation at Shanghai often required immediate decisions and orders, most of them were therefore communicated between Nanking and Shanghai over the direct telephone which was in operation until interrupted by the subsequent hostilities. It is believed, however, that the telegraphic order quoted in the present Memorandum would suffice to answer the purpose of the Commission in requesting some documentary evidence from the Chinese government.

Peiping, July 2nd, 1932.

MEMORANDUM

ON

OUTER MONGOLIA

Document No. 21   Peiping, July 1932

MEMORANDUM ON OUTER MONGOLIA.

1. Present *de facto* situation in Outer Mongolia not recognized by China.
2. Outer Mongolia as a dependency. Provisional Constitution of 1912.
3. Inner Mongolia transformed into provinces.
4. Constitution of 1923.
5. Provisional Constitution of 1931.
6. Russian intrigues in Outer Mongolia. Tripartite Agreement, 1915.
7. Cancellation of autonomy, 1919.
8. Russo-Mongol Treaty, 1921.
9. Recognition of China's sovereignty, 1924.
10. Violation of Treaty by Soviet Russia. China's protest.
11. Conclusion.

MEMORANDUM ON OUTER MONGOLIA

1. **Present** *de facto* **situation in Outer Mongolia not recognized by China.** This Memorandum undertakes to show that the Chinese Government has never given its consent to the present *de facto* situation existing in Outer Mongolia.

2. **Outer Mongolia as a dependency. Provisional Constitution of 1912.** For historical, geographical, ethnological and organic reasons, Outer Mongolia, during the last three centuries, has been considered as a part of Chinese territory in the character of a dependency of the Chinese Empire.

When the Republic was proclaimed in 1912, the Provisional Constitution promulgated on March 10th stated expressly in Article 3:

". . . The territory of the Chinese Republic consists of the twenty-two provinces, Inner and Outer Mongolia, Tibet and Chinghai (Kokonor)."

The distinction is here clearly made between the Twenty-two Provinces and Outer Mongolia which is on equal standing with Tibet and Kokonor.

3. **Inner Mongolia transformed into provinces.** As to Inner Mongolia, it must be said that the Government has always distinguished it from Outer Mongolia. Outer Mongolia, being far away from the influences which were working for the modernization of China, retained her old theocratical regime. Inner Mongolia was much nearer.

There was constant intercourse between her plateaux and the plains of Chihli. Numerous Chinese settlers were establishing themselves within her borders, reclaiming the land and putting under cultivation hitherto uninhabited districts. The organization of Inner Mongolia was accordingly brought by successive steps in line with that of China proper. In 1914, the Government divided Inner Mongolia into three separate administrative areas, called the Special Districts of Jehol, Chahar and Suiyuan. In September 1928, the Special Districts were transformed into Provinces with Provincial Governments established in conformity with the provisions of the Provisional Constitution which we shall quote in another paragraph. Officially speaking, Inner Mongolia no longer exists: there are only the three provinces of Jehol, Chahar and Suiyuan.

The population there is mostly Chinese. According to the latest statistics, it numbers:

> in Jehol............ 4,500,000 inhabitants
> in Chahar.......... 1,997,234 ”
> in Suiyuan........:. 2,133,914 ”

The statistics do not show how many of them are Mongols, but since the whole of the Mongol population of Inner Mongolia does not exceed 1,400,000, the percentage of non-Chinese population in the three provinces must be less than twenty per cent.

4. **Constitution of 1923.** Article 135 of the Constitution of October 10th, 1923, provided for a similar distinction between Outer Mongolia and the rest of China. While anticipating the ultimate transformation of Outer Mongolia into Provinces, it added that, for the time being, "its administrative system shall be prescribed by law."

5. Provisional Constitution of 1931. An identical view of the situation was taken by the Provisional Constitution of June 1st, 1931, the first article of which reads:

> ". . . . The territory of the Republic of China consists of the various Provinces and Mongolia (Outer Mongolia), and Tibet."

The expression "various Provinces" includes the three provinces of Inner Mongolia.

Besides, Article 78 of the Provisional Constitution of June 1st, 1931, says:

> ". . . In each Province a Provincial Government shall be established, which shall attend to the administration of Provincial affairs under the direction of the National Government."

while Article 80 adds in connection with Outer Mongolia and Tibet:

> ". . . The system of local Government in Mongolia (Outer Mongolia) and Tibet shall be determined separately by law in the light of the local conditions."

These two articles show that constitutionally by reason of the "local conditions" obtaining in Outer Mongolia, that part of the Chinese territory was entitled to a special status.

6. Russian intrigues in Outer Mongolia. Tripartite Agreement, 1915. The proclamation of the Republic, to which the reactionary spirit of the Urga theocracy was inclined to be little sympathetic, led to an estrangement between Outer Mongolia and China and facilitated the development of Russian intrigues.

In order to forestall possible Russian action, negotiations were opened with the Russian authorities, and on November 5th, 1913, an exchange of notes took place between the Chinese and Russian Governments, by which Russia recognized that Outer Mongolia was under the suzerainty of China and formed part of the territory of China, while China recognized the right of the Outer Mongolians to provide for their internal administration. As regards questions of a political and territorial nature, China would come to an agreement with the Russian Government through negotiations, in which the authorities of Outer Mongolia would take part. Pursuant to that understanding, a tripartite convention was signed at Kiakta on June 7th, 1915, between the representatives of China, Russia and Outer Mongolia, reaffirming the principles embodied in the 1913 exchange of notes and providing more particularly the following:

> "Article III.—Autonomous Mongolia has no right to conclude international treaties with foreign Powers respecting political and territorial questions.
> "Article V.—China and Russia . . . recognize the exclusive right of the autonomous Government of Outer Mongolia to attend to all the affairs of its internal administration and to conclude with foreign Powers international treaties and agreements respecting all questions of a commercial and industrial nature concerning autonomous Mongolia."

7. **Cancellation of autonomy, 1919.** In 1919, the repercussions of the Great War and of the Russian Revolution led the Government of Outer Mongolia to cancel its autonomy and to request the Chinese Government to resume its full authority over the country. By a Mandate of November 22nd, 1919, the Chinese Government proclaimed the restoration of the *status quo ante* in Outer Mongolia and the annulment of the tripartite agreement.

8. **Russo-Mongol Treaty, 1921.** The new regime, however, did not last very long. Following the raids of the Russian adventurer, Baron von Ungern, the Soviet authorities entered Outer Mongolian territory and imposed by force of arms upon the local rulers the treaty of November 5th, 1921, by which the Soviet and the Revolutionary Mongol Government "mutually recognize each other as the only Governments in the territory of Russia and Mongolia."

When the existence of this treaty became known to the Chinese Government, a strong protest was addressed on May 1st, 1922, to the Soviet Representative in Peking, recalling that the Soviet Government had repeatedly declared its intention to refrain from all encroachments upon Chinese territory, and pointing out that the allegation that Outer Mongolia was an independent State when it had long been recognized by Russia as an integral part of China was a breach of faith as well as a violation of principles of international justice.

9. **Recognition of China's sovereignty, 1924.** When negotiations were resumed in 1924 between China and the Soviet Government the Chinese Government maintained the above expressed views adding that the 1921 treaty constituted an unwarranted interference on the part of Russia with Chinese internal affairs since it was intended to modify the nature of the relations which had for more than three centuries existed between China and Outer Mongolia. The result was that in the *Agreement on General Principles for the Settlement of the Questions between the Republic of China and the Union of Soviet Socialist Republics,* signed at Peking on the 31st of May 1924, the following provision was inserted:

"Article V.—The Government of the Union of Soviet Socialist Republics recognizes that Outer

Mongolia is an integral part of the Republic of China and respects China's sovereignty therein.

The Government of the Union of Soviet Socialist Republics declares that as soon as the questions for the withdrawal of all the troops of the Union of Soviet Socialist Republics from Outer Mongolia,— namely as to the time limits of the withdrawal of such troops and the measures adopted in the interests of the safety of the frontiers,—are agreed upon at the Conference as provided in Article II of the present agreement, it will effect the complete withdrawal of all the troops of the Union of Soviet Socialist Republics from Outer Mongolia.''

In a note dated March 6th, 1925, the Soviet Ambassador notified the Waichiaopu that the Soviet Government had proceeded, with the consent of the Outer Mongolian authorities, to the withdrawal of its troops from Outer Mongolia and that the retirement of the Soviet Army from the Outer Mongolian territory had been completed.

10. **Violation of Treaty by Soviet Russia. China's protest.** However, in spite of the Soviet pledges, Outer Mongolia, in recent years, seemed to fall more and more under Soviet influence. In November 1924, a Soviet Constitution was adopted. China has constantly protested against the violation of the stipulations in the May 1924 Agreement in which the Soviet authorities agreed that they would respect China's sovereignty in Outer Mongolia.

11. **Conclusion.** From the above statement of facts it is clear:

1.—That the autonomy of Outer Mongolia is sanctioned by express provisions of the Constitutions which the Chinese Government adopted on its own initiative.

2.—That when such autonomy was recognized and defined as regards foreign countries, this was done by express provisions of treaties agreed to by the Chinese Government in view of the historical status of Outer Mongolia under the Chinese Republic.

3.—That if China has had to content herself for the present with protesting against the irregular actions of Soviet Russia in Outer Mongolia, and has not succeeded in restoring the *status quo ante,* it is because of the interruption of normal diplomatic relations and the lack of progress in the Sino-Soviet Conference at Moscow.

4.—That China has never departed from her original stand that Outer Mongolia is an integral part of her territory and that local autonomy of that part exists and extends only in so far as determined by decisions of the Central Government.

Peiping, July 3rd, 1932.

MEMORANDUM

ON

BANDITRY

Document No. 22   Peiping, July 1932

MEMORANDUM ON BANDITRY.

1. Japanese accusations.
2. Japanese advisers and disturbances in China.
3. Honjo's role as one of these advisers.
4. Japanese newspapers in China also creating dissension.
5. Japanese statement.
6. Bandits and arms smuggling.
7. Arms smuggling illegal.
8. Difficulties in suppressing smuggling in China.
9. Darien an ideal refuge for arms smugglers.
10. Cases of smuggling by Japanese.
11. Difficulties for the Chinese police in Mukden.
12. Latest case of smuggling on big scale.
13. Japanese Government behind the smuggling.
14. Terauchi's confession.
15. Smuggled arms of Japanese origin.
16. Proofs of Japanese encouragement of banditry.
17. *Mounted Bandits in Manchuria.*
18. Extracts from the book.
19. The bandits gain strength through Japanese help.
20. Bandit raids increasing proportionately with increase of Japanese power.
21. The Provinces free from banditry before the Japanese came.
22. Banditry rampant after September 18th, 1931.
23. Japanese and the bandit chief Lin Yin-ching.
24. Japanese supplying arms to bandits.
25. Japanese encouragement to bandits to create disturbance.

23

26. Japanese estimate of bandit raids.
27. Increase of banditry due to Japanese.

APPENDIX:

    A. *The Manchurian Problem: Common Misconceptions.*

    B. Report and Documentary Evidences on Lin Yin-Ching's Activities in the Three Eastern Provinces Under Japanese Instigation.

MEMORANDUM ON BANDITRY

1. **Japanese accusations.** In the many statements which the Japanese Delegation has submitted during the meetings of the League of Nations since the outbreak on September 18th, 1931, frequent reference was made to the presence of large numbers of bandits in the Three Eastern Provinces and the danger which they caused to Japanese lives and property there. Alleging the need of "self-defence" and of the suppression of these bandits, Japan claims to be justified in resorting to drastic military measures. The Japanese assessor likewise in his memorandum *The Present Condition of China* concluded his discourse on the civil wars in China with the statement that "civil war stimulates the activities of bandits." (p. 122) While it is not for us at present either to affirm or to deny the existence of civil warfare or of the prevalence of banditry in the Three Eastern Provinces, it is necessary that we inquire into the circumstances under which these two evils have been able to develop and the intimate relations which they have with Japan herself.

2. **Japanese advisers and disturbances in China.** It is an open secret that the Japanese have never harboured any friendly feelings towards the Chinese within the last half century or so. During that time thousands of students have gone to Japan for higher education. There they were taught revolutionary ideas which eventually brought about the collapse of the Manchu Government. Taking advantage, however, of the intimacy

which the leaders of the new Republican regime had formed with the Japanese, it is interesting to see how these leaders, frequently against their own will, became involved with Japanese advisers. These advisers were, in the main, agents of the Japanese General Staff, and entrusted with secret services inimical, it may be presumed, to the interests of the Chinese and subversive of the peace and security in this country. They participated in all manner of intrigues, and through clever manipulation succeeded in making pawns of the people whom they were supposed to "advise." They could usually furnish advanced knowledge of military combinations which was used to good advantage in the prosecution of civil strife.

3. **Honjo's role as one of these advisers.** The Commander-in-Chief of the Japanese troops in the Three Eastern Provinces, General Honjo, was himself military adviser to Marshal Chang Tso-lin for eight years. Many of the military expeditions which the Marshal sent into China Proper to participate in civil warfare and for which Japan has been heaping the blame on his memory recently was, if not instigated, at least encouraged by his Japanese advisers.

4. **Japanese newspapers in China also creating dissension.** Moreover, Japanese advisers have not been acting single-handedly in creating mutual suspicion among the Chinese military leaders or stirring up ill feeling among them. They have been assisted in their insidious work by large numbers of Japanese newspapers published in China. These journals have the same object in view, that is, to spare no effort in creating a state of restiveness or discontent through the spread of distorted news and information. They give wide pub-

licity to baseless rumours and false news so long as they are likely to create trouble and dissension among the Chinese leaders. Such acts violate Chinese laws. But these journals cannot be interfered with by the local authorities because the Japanese enjoy extraterritorial rights. Formal representations lodged with the Japanese authorities either locally or in Tokyo do not bring any satisfactory results.

5. **Japanese statement.** To come back now to the question of banditry. The Japanese assessor said, "Chinese brigands are of many kinds, but usually they are very brave and determined; they number sometimes as many as several hundreds or several thousands equipped with the modern weapons. The Cantonese and Manchurian bandits especially are in no way inferior to regular soldiers whether from the point of view of organization or discipline." [1]

6. **Bandits and arms smuggling.** But where and how do the bandits usually get their supply of arms? It is a well-known fact that they get it mostly by way of smuggling.

7. **Arms smuggling illegal.** It must be noted at the outset, however, that smuggling or dealing in any way in arms, ammunition and explosives, is a crime punishable by imprisonment according to the Chinese law. The same crime is also punishable in Japan with fine or imprisonment according to the criminal code of that country. Treaties concluded between China and the foreign countries also provide against smuggling of any sort, including that of munitions of war.

8. **Difficulties in suppressing smuggling in China.** Nevertheless, smuggling has ever been a thorn in the

[1] *The Present Condition of China*, p. 122.

side of the Chinese authorities. Under ordinary circumstances, the elusiveness and artifice of the smugglers are already difficult enough to deal with. But in coping with the situation in the face of extraterritorial rights of foreign persons or ships, and in some cases, in territories under foreign administration in China, the difficulty has been increased to an extent unknown in Europe or America.

9. **Dairen an ideal refuge for arms smugglers.** Japanese concessions, the South Manchuria Railway areas, and the Kwantung Leased Territory are found to be especially favourable to smugglers. There they could play the game of hide and seek with the authorities and could usually make good their escape long before the indispensable Japanese authorization could be obtained for their arrest. Besides the Kwantung Leased Territory enjoys the additional special right of importing all kinds of merchandise for use or consumption in its own duty-free area. Smugglers in that territory can, therefore, first land their goods free, and then smuggle them into Chinese-administered territory in a leisurely and unhampered manner. The Commissioner of Customs there and his staff must, according to the Darien Customs Agreement of 1907, be of Japanese nationality, and the Chinese Government has to depend entirely upon them for the prevention of smuggling of goods into the adjacent Chinese-administered territories. But instead of affording that assistance, it has frequently occurred that the Japanese authorities appear to have connived at the illicit trade.

10. **Cases of smuggling by Japanese.** A large number of cases have occurred some of which are worth relating here.

In 1907, the *Tatzu Maru* was searched off the coast of Kwangtung Province and found to be carrying a shipload of arms into Canton.

In June 1912, a party of sixty Japanese, two hundred Chinese, and fifty Mongolians with more than 300 boxes loaded in more than 40 carts, were discovered at Chaoyangpo, twenty-five *li* from Kwanchuling. Upon the demand of the Chinese soldiers to examine the boxes, the smugglers put up an armed resistance, and were only captured after suffering some casualties. They found in their possession smuggled arms and ammunition including 1500 rifles, 300,000 rounds of rifle-shots, 200 pistols, 20,000 rounds of pistol-cartridges, and 300 military swords. These weapons and munitions were destined for the Mongolians who were then being incited by the Japanese in an open rebellion against the Chinese Government.

In June 1915, General Lung, Military Governor of Kwangtung Province, reported that two Japanese warships, anchored off Hoiphoon, were found to have unloaded 11,000 pieces of rifles and 30 pieces of field-guns destined for the forces opposing the Chinese Government.

In January 1923, a Japanese firm in Harbin under the name of Trading Company for Manchuria and Mongolia was known to deal in firearms clandestinely, and as a result of a search, was found to have in its premises forty-two automatic pistols and 372 rounds of shots.

In April 1926, a Japanese was found in Harbin with 34 pistols and 12,000 rounds of cartridges which were ascertained to have been shipped from Darien.

Even as early as 1908, a Japanese named Nagashima was detected in an attempt to smuggle 90 rifles and 10,-000 rounds of cartridges into Kirin. In March of the same year, an examiner of the Maritime Customs who was despatched to Shanhaikwan to prevent arms smuggling, after a survey of the neighbourhood, reported that he saw two Japanese shops in Hsinmintun which displayed arms of all kinds, and from which one could secure any quantity with ease.

11. **Difficulties for the Chinese police in Mukden.** In one year, in 1930, in the city of Mukden alone, there were eleven cases in which Japanese subjects were caught red-handed in supplying arms to bandits. In Mukden there is an area under the exclusive administration of the Japanese and it is usually not easy for the Chinese police to ferret out Japanese offenders. That under such difficult and unfavourable circumstances the Chinese police were actually able to bring to light so many cases of Japanese engaged in this unlawful trade gives reason for believing that there must be many more cases which have escaped detection.

12. **Latest case of smuggling on big scale.** But the most glaring instance of "gun-running" of recent date was that reported by the Tass Agency and transmitted back here by Reuter's correspondent at Moscow. It stated that numerous arrests were continuing (December 1st, 1931) at Dairen and Mukden involving Japanese employees in governmental and semi-governmental institutions—including the South Manchuria Railway and the Dairen Custom-House—on charge of participation in a supply of arms to General Ma Chan-shan, who was at that time engaged in fighting against the Japanese troops. It appeared that three car-loads of arms despatched from Dairen to Tsitsihar for the Chinese forces were detained at Mukden. The report went on to say that the preliminary results of the inquiry showed that

the alleged smugglers' association was backed by prominent Japanese and non-Japanese officials in the Three Eastern Provinces.[2]

13. **Japanese Government behind the smuggling.** It may be pointed out here that in Japan the manufacture of firearms is a government monopoly; anyone infringing that right is punishable with fine or imprisonment. Nor is anyone allowed to deal in arms or ammunition of any sort without Government authorization, and any violation of this ruling is dealt with under the same penalty. Smuggling arms from Japan into China would scarcely be possible without negligence or connivance on the part of the Japanese authorities.

14. **Terauchi's confession.** Furthermore, it has been found that most of the arms captured from the bandits by the Chinese troops were of Japanese manufacture. What more need we say when the Japanese Prime Minister, Mr. Terauchi, in replying to an interpellation in the Diet in January 1917, concerning the question of Taihei Co., openly admitted that the Japanese merchants and the Japanese military were in the habit of supplying arms to the bandits in the Three Eastern Provinces!

15. **Smuggled arms of Japanese origin.** In the *Second Report on the Progress in Manchuria to 1930*, issued by the South Manchuria Railway, the Japanese themselves admitted that of the arms carried by bandits who were made captive, 25 per cent was found to be of Japanese origin and 20 per cent of Russian origin, presumably of the type seized by the Japanese from the Russians during the Russo-Japanese War. (The same kind of arms

[2] For complete report, see *The Leader*, Peiping; *The Peking and Tientsin Times*, Tientsin, and *The China Press*, Shanghai, of December 2nd, 1931.

was also seized in a raid upon a Japanese shop in the Japanese Concession in Tientsin in February 1914, where six Japanese were found to have sold to Chinese, on various occasions, rifles of the Russian 1884 model). A large part of the arms captured from the bandits was therefore officially admitted to have been supplied by the Japanese themselves. It is easy to infer that the actual amount was even larger.

Great credit must, therefore, be given to Japanese arms smuggling for the fact that the Chinese bandits are so well equipped. The statement in the Japanese memorandum that "the Manchurian bandits, compared with others, are superior in discipline military training and weapons,"[3] has been made probably with intimate knowledge of the sources of their supply and strength.

16. **Proofs of Japanese encouragement of banditry.** We wish now to invite attention to two important Japanese publications which make it clear beyond doubt that the Japanese are in intimate contact with the bandits whose activities the Japanese do everything to encourage. The first in Baron Goto's article which has been dealt with in the *Memorandum on Japan's Plots and Schemes against the Unification of China* and which was reproduced *in toto* as an appendix to that memorandum.

17. *Mounted Bandits in Manchuria.* The second is a book under the title of *Mounted Bandit in Manchuria* jointly written by Kokurin Takahashi and Kifun Akama, and published in 1926 by the *Hakuyei Sha* Book Company. The book describes how the Japanese joined the mounted bandits in the Three Eastern Provinces to be their leaders and how they engaged in political and military activities for the overthrow of the constituted gov-

[3] *The Present Condition of China*, p. 127.

ernment in the Provinces. A few extracts from the book are sufficient to show the close relationship that exists between the Japanese agents and the Manchurian bandits against whom the Japanese representatives at the meetings of the League so vehemently fulminated. The extracts follow:

18. **Extracts from the book.** " It is a well-known fact that the imperialists were those who supported Prince Su in an effort to restore him to the Manchu throne and the leader of the imperialist party was Naniwa Kawashima. Kawashima and Prince Su were sworn brothers. The former wishing his sworn brother to re-establish his prestige in the political world attempted first to bring about the independence of Manchuria as a preliminary step to the restoration of the Ching dynasty. Accordingly, the organization of the Manchuria Expeditionary Force was, from 1916, actually formed. But owing to the sudden change of attitude, at a most critical time, of a certain Ministry which had promised to give its full support, and also to a miscalculation of the real strength of Chang Tso-lin's forces, the expeditionary forces were sadly defeated before they ever got to Manchuria. They were unable to rally again; Prince Su passed his sorrowful days in Port Arthur and died there in 1921. The person, although not a member of the Prince's family, who sighed 'Alas, that is the end!' was Naniwa Kawashima. After the demise of Prince Su, Kawashima took over all the Prince's children and kept them in his own house. The eldest son of the Prince, originally named Hsien-cheng who is now serving in an important post in Manchukuo under the name of Chin Pi-tung, was desired by Count Yenkichi Ogi as his son-in-law, but Kawashima refused to have this relationship established because Hsien-cheng was the Prince's heir. Kawashima

served, during the Sino-Japanese War, as an interpreter in the Headquarters of the Commander-in-Chief of the Japanese army, and had rendered service to a Chinese military officer who was then held as a prisoner of war. The Chinese military officer later got into power, and through his intermediary Kawashima became acquainted with Prince Su. This was the basis of Kawashima's activity in Manchuria." (pp. 6-7).

"Bapuchapu, 'uncanny hero' of Mongolia, organized in secret, the Manchuria Expeditionary Army. He led 3,000 able Mongolian troops into Manchuria, starting from Kulun to Chengchiatun in the summer of 1916. It was in the latter place that they engaged the Manchurian forces in many battles and for a while seemed to hold their own. In the early part of the following Autumn, they were defeated and their leader Bapuchapu was killed. They were therefore forced to retreat into the interior of Mongolia.

"It is needless to say that the expedition of Bapuchapu's forces to Manchuria was designed by the imperialists, and was reinforced by the imperialist army under the leader Kawashima. The idea was to annihilate the Manchurian Army in one blow and to occupy the city of Mukden. It is unfortunate that the combined forces of the Mongolians, who are reputed for their ferocity, and the Japanese, who are both resourceful and brave, should, owing to imperfect training, fail in their campaign.

"The Commander of the Detachment of Mongolian Army was Munenosuke Nakagawa who had been editor of the *Asahi Shimbun* before the Russo-Japanese War. The detachment had its headquarters in Dairen where a force of 500 men were first recruited. They were secretly packed into freight cars and transported to

Chengchiatun. At the same time, mounted bandits in various parts of the land were told to raise their standard of revolt. But before the mounted bandits could rise and the detachment get to Chengchiatun, Bapuchapu's main army had already met with a disastrous defeat much to the regret of the imperialists." (pp. 9-10).

"Though the plot to overthrow Chang Tso-lin and to set up Prince Su as concocted by Kwashina . . . failed, for various reasons, to be carried out, the Japanese remained active as bandit-leaders. Among them were Tenki, at present known as Po Yi-san, the most notorious among Japanese bandit-leaders, Shigenabu, originally chief of the Japanese police at Changchun who after his dismissal became a *ronin* or Japanese rowdy in Manchuria, Kohama, originally manager of a certain company in Antung who subsequently became a *ronin,* Tenraku, a Japanese military man whose experience in banditry was even above that of Tenki. With them were several Chinese bandit-leaders, such as Shuan-shan, Chin-tou, Niao-lung, Chang Chiang-hao, Kao-shan, Shuan-lung and Kuei-tou.

"Tenki rose in Hei-lin, Kirin Province, and Kohama rose in the neighborhood of Peng-hsi-hu, Shigenabu who took advantage of former favours shown to a certain Chao, Commander of a cavalry battalion stationed at the time at Pei-cheng-tzu, Mukden, persuaded him to revolt against Chang-Tso-lin and join hands with himself. Accordingly, accompanied by several Japanese, Shigenabu proceeded to Pei-cheng-tzu.

"Shigenabu fell into a pitiable plight. For Major Chao, being informed of the defeat of the Mongolian Army, changed his attitude, arrested Shigenabu and put to death all of his followers. As to Shigenabu, he was put in a lady's sedan chair and conveyed to Kaiyuan where he was liberated.

"Those bandit-bands who took side with the Mongolian Army were known among the imperialist armies under the following classification:

Tenki's troops as the Sixth Brigade.
Shigenabu's troops as the Seventh Brigade.
Tenraku's troops as the Eighth Brigade.
Kohama's troops as the Ninth Brigade." (pp. 33-36).

"The Japanese who joined the bandits would be sinners unpardonable by Heaven, if they should work for their personal pleasure only. If, however, their act was inspired by their undaunted patriotism, then irrespective of its consequences, it should be tolerated by modern moral standards." (p. 38).

"Takamori Saigo Henmi, a famous Japanese general, has a son named Isako Henmi, who was the Commander-in-Chief of the Japanese mounted bandits during and after the Russo-Japanese War.

"After the war, Henmi went to Changchun, and obtained within the railway zone of the South Manchuria Railway the privilege of operating a gambling resort.

"In that gambling establishment, the Chinese flocked like water seeking its lowest level, and would stake all they had in a desire to win. The percentage collectable by the establishment reached an enormous amount. This money Henmi used for the support of his followers. In addition, the police and the Post Offices at Changchun are said to be built with funds from this very source. This is, however, too scandalous to be revealed." (pp. 45-47).

19. **The bandits gain strength through Japanese help.** Is there anything to be wondered at, therefore, that the bandits in the Three Eastern Provinces, particularly

those in the neighbourhood of the South Manchuria Railway, should be "so well-armed, well-disciplined and well-trained"? Having served the purposes of the Japanese, these bandits would naturally continue their original profession of being pests to society, improving, after their schooling under the Japanese, in armament, knowledge and perhaps atrocity.

20. **Bandit raids increasing proportionately with increase of Japanese power.** With regard to bandit raids in the so-called South Manchuria "railway zone," the *Second Report on Progress in Manchuria to 1930,* issued by the railway, gives some interesting statistics. The number of bandit raids within the "zone" is given as 9 in 1906, an as 368 in 1929, an increase of 4,100 per cent! The frequency of the raids is in direct proportion to the increase of Japanese power in that area. The area, it must be remembered, is policed by the Japanese themselves and is zealously guarded against any intrusion on the part either of the police or of any other Chinese Government agency. The more guards and soldiers the Japanese station in the area, the more frequent are the bandit raids. This is the condition in the places where the Japanese authorities have practically complete control as regards the maintenance of peace and order.

21. **The Provinces free from banditry before the Japanese came.** But outside these Japanese controlled areas a different story is told by Dr. Dugald Christie C.M.G. (see Appendix A). According to this writer, "during the twelve years before the first Japanese invasion, one could travel in every direction in the Three Eastern Provinces without escort of any kind. Brigandage did exist mainly in remote mountainous regions, but was kept well in check by the firm hand of the (Chinese) Government.

War always causes disorder, and each of the three wars which devastated the land from 1894 to 1905 brought a great increase of brigandage and a slackness in rule.''

22. **Banditry rampant after September 18th, 1931.** Such was the condition prevailing in the Three Eastern Provinces prior to September 18th, 1931, when the Japanese troops attacked and occupied Mukden and its neighbourhood. But the Japanese intrigue in arming and creating bandits and making use of them for political purposes has greatly increased since that day. One week after the Japanese occupation of Mukden, the section of the Pei-Ning Railway east of Shanhaikwan began to be infested with bandits, an event unheard of before. We may relate one or two of the instances to illustrate the unscrupulous methods which the Japanese authorities have been employing to invite and enlist the services of bandits to serve their military and political ends.

23. **Japanese and the bandit chief Lin Yin-ching.** On October 11th, 1931, the Headquarters of the Kwantung Army despatched Shigetaro Kuraoka, Takumatsu Matsumoto and Gennosuke Michimoto with notes worth Yen 10,000 to buy over the bandit leader Lin Yin-ching who was an old resident in the Japanese controlled area of the South Manchuria Railway at Mukden. His services so purchased consisted in recruiting bandits and organizing them into the so-called ''North-eastern People's Army for Self-Defence,'' with the avowed object of attacking Chinchow then still under Chinese control and driving out the Provincial government provisionally stationed there after the Japanese occupation of Mukden. All the arms, ammunition, and food supply required by the bandits were supplied by the Japanese military authorities. On October 19th, Lin established his head-

quarters in his own house, No. 18 Goyaicho in the Japanese controlled area. He was given an official seal by
the Japanese, bearing the inscription "Seal of the Commander-in-Chief of the North-eastern People's Army for
Self-Defence." His plan of operation was formulated
for him by the Japanese Kuraoka. The bandit chief
started on his expedition from the Chienshan station of
the South Manchuria Railway and proceeded to Taian
recruiting bandits and rabble on his way. This band was
finally defeated and dispersed by the Chinese troops and
many of the men were taken prisoners. (For full particulars and documental evidence, see Appendix B).

Following the defeat of Lin Yin-ching, the Japanese
looked somewhere else for another tool. They utilized
Chang Hsueh-cheng who figured in several unsuccessful
plots against the Chinese authorities. He was employed
by the Japanese and directed by them also to attack Chinchow. But as the Chinchow authorities had received
early warnings of the attempt and had taken precautions
accordingly, the plot fell through, and Chang Hsueh-
cheng himself was captured.

24. **Japanese supplying arms to bandits.** As a result
of the occupation of Mukden by the Japanese, large quantities of military supplies belonging to Chinese authorities fell into their hands. These the Japanese distributed
freely among the bandits. Some of them even found
their way to Tientsin and were given to those bandits
who attacked the native city with the Japanese Concession as their base of operation in the early part of
last November. Several carloads of these were also
sent to Payintala where they were distributed among
the Mongolian bandits so that they could be used to
attack Jehol, and the northern part of Hopei Prov-

ince. Nevertheless, these bandits finding the Japanese oppression unbearable, and remembering that they were Chinese after all, created disturbances in the localities garrisoned by the Japanese troops for the purpose of harassing them, and with the very war weapons which were supplied to them by the Japanese themselves. With the lawless elements of their own creation rampant, the Japanese authorities have found it impossible to maintain peace and order in places under their military occupation.

25. **Japanese encouragement to bandits to create disturbance.** Thus it is seen that the Japanese organized, equipped and trained up bandits originally for the purpose of disturbing the peace and order in the Three Eastern Provinces in order to give them pretext for their military aggressions. But the bandits having no liking for the Japanese and only lured by prospective gains often executed their mission with too much thoroughness; and carried away by their enthusiasm, they devastated all the places they visited. Not infrequently, finding the Japanese too domineering, they turned against them and ran amuck. Thus the Japanese created a situation in order to involve China in difficulties and advance their own nefarious designs, but have suffered injury along with the Chinese.

26. **Japanese estimate of bandit raids.** How much the Japanese policy of utilizing bandits for political and military purposes has succeeded in increasing the bandit menace in the Three Eastern Provinces may be gathered from the statement made by the Japanese Assessor. He says in his memorandum that from September to November 1931, (i e. after the Japanese military occupation of the Three Eastern Provinces) bandit raids in the terri-

tory numbered more than 1,600 involving a total number of 232,500 bandits, causing grave damage to 5 Japanese, 135 Koreans, one foreigner, and 482 Chinese, or a total of 623 persons. From the middle of September of 1931 to the end of October alone, at certain dates and places, banditry, according to him, brought about 370 massacres, 50 cases of rape, 300 houses burned and about 2,000 houses pillaged. In the same period of time, he continues, but on dates unrecorded though almost certain, there were 180 murders, 100 cases of rape, 500 houses burned and about 1,000 houses pillaged.[4]

27. Increase of banditry due to Japanese. The Japanese claim the right of continuing hostilities in the Three Eastern Provinces in order to rid the territory of banditry. But instead of reducing the number of bandit raids, their actions have brought about a marked increase. In less than 3 months in 1931 from September to December, 1,600 cases of bandit raids took place against 368 cases in the entire year of 1929. That banditry should have become more serious in proportion as Japanese control has become more extended in China's north-eastern territory supports China's belief and contention that the sooner the Japanese troops are withdrawn and Japanese control disappears, the quicker will banditry, as understood by the Japanese, cease to be a menace.

Peiping, July 18th 1932.

---

[4] *The Present Condition of China*, pp. 128-129.

APPENDIX.

A. THE MANCHURIAN PROBLEM: COMMON MISCON-CEPTIONS. By Dr. Dugald Christie, C. M. G.[5]

I went to Manchuria in 1882. During the 12 years before the first Japanese invasion, I as well as others travelled in every direction without escort of any kind, and always met with much kindness from officials and people. Brigandage did exist, mainly in remote mountainous regions, but was kept well in check by the firm hand of the Government. War always causes disorder, and each of the three wars which devastated the land from 1894 to 1905 brought a great excess of brigandage and a slackness in rule.

As a whole, Manchuria has been better governed than most of China. The same failings and abuses found in the Government of Shantung or any other province existed there also, but to a less extent, and the position of foreigners was better than perhaps anywhere else. From 1905 onwards she had a succession of enlightened statesmen as viceroys, who did great things in buiding up prosperity, and in the development of education. The civil wars, that have ravaged China in recent years, left Manchuria untouched, largely owing to the determination of those in rule, that they would do nothing to give Japan a handle for interference.

[5] Published in The Scotsman, Edinburgh, and reproduced in the China Weekly Review, 59. 11. 338. February 13th, 1932.

B. REPORT AND DOCUMENTARY EVIDENCES ON LIN YIN-CHING'S ACTIVITIES IN THE THREE EASTERN PROVINCES UNDER JAPANESE INSTIGATION.[6]

I. Agreement between the Japanese military and Lin Yin-ching.

On October 11th, 1931, the Headquarters of the Japanese Commander in the Three Eastern Provinces sent three men, namely, Shigetaro Kuraoka, Tokumatsu Matsumoto, and Gennosuke Michimoto with ten thousand Japanese yen to Mukden and bought up the Japanese-protected bandit chief, Lin Yin-ching, whose service to be rendered to the Japanese for the said sum of money received was to recruit bandits and vagabonds, and organize them into the so-called "North-eastern People's Army for Self-Defence," all of whom were armed by the Japanese military. This Japanese-organized bandit corps later actually attacked Chinchow and the Headquarters of the Provincial Government of Liaoning. Apart from the cash benefit which the bandit chief Lin received from the Japanese, he was further promised a high position in the Government. The contract made between the Japanese military and the bandit chief, Lin Yin-ching, may be summarized as follows:

1. ORGANIZATION.—That Lin Yin-ching was to organize an army to be known as "The North-eastern People's Army for Self-Defence." The army shall have a commander-in-chief; shall establish a bureau of military affairs, a bureau of political affairs, an office for the staff officers and aides-de-camp, offices of military supplies and transportation, army medical office, military law department, and so forth, for seventeen brigades.

2. MILITARY SUPPLIES.—That arms and ammunition shall be supplied by the Japanese and shall be delivered to Lin Yin-ching at suitable places.

3. FINANCIAL SOURCES.—That the Japanese military shall be responsible for three thousand yen to start with, and other expenses shall be raised locally.

4. PLANS.—That the Headquarters of the Japanese Commander shall be responsible for all plans of military operation; that Lin

[6] From a confidential report.

Yin-ching shall carry out all plans formulated by the Japanese Military Headquarters; that the Headquarters of the Japanese Commander shall be responsible for forty or more men to be sent to various Chinese army corps to stir up the Chinese troops to fight; that the warring zones shall be as follows:

(1) The first base of operation shall be the South Manchuria and Antung lines.

(2) The second base of operation shall be Liaoyang, Hai-cheng, Kaiping, Fuhsien, Chwangho, Hsiuyen, Penhai and Feng-cheng districts.

(3) West of Mukden, such as Taian, Panshan, Yingkow, Hei-shan, Chinchow, Yihsien, Suichung and Hsingchen shall be a district for military expansion.

(4) East and North of Mukden shall be the district for the enlistment and concentration of troops.

II. The Japanese responsibility and Lin Yin-ching's army.

On October 19th, after the agreement had been concluded, Lin Yin-ching, assisted by his Japanese military leaders, established in Mukden the Headquarters of the Commander-in-Chief of the " North-eastern People's Army for the defence of Kwantung "— a territory outside the Great Wall. The three Japanese emis-saries, Kuraoka Shigetaro, Tokumatsu Matsumoto, and Gennosuke Michimoto subsequently assisted Lin Yin-ching in all his military activities. Kuraoka was appointed by Lin to be his adviser and interpreter. Matsumoto and Michimoto were appointed by the Japanese Military commander to be special service men to super-vise Lin's activities so that all pre-arranged plans might be carried out.

1. The Unlawful Activities of Lin's Bandit Army.—On October 20th at 7:05 a.m., Lin Yin-ching directed a group of his bandit soldiers to carry out the plans formulated by his Japanese advisers. The bandit troops went aboard the South Manchuria Railway special train, three car-loads altogether, and arrived at Chien Shan Station at 10.30 a.m. where they received three hundred rifles, 80,000 rounds of ammunition, and six machine guns, which were already prepared for them by the Japanese military. These

bandit soldiers, together with twelve cars of people and a large quantity of ammunition, were despatched toward the West, and later established their headquarters at Tengaopu, where they enlisted over 300 bandits. These bandit troops, on October 29th, actually came into conflict with the 19th Brigade of the Chinese North-eastern Frontier Defense Force, and because the bandit troops were assisted by Japanese airplanes they were victorious. The *Sheng Ching Shih Pao,* a Japanese newspaper, reported the incident on October 30th as follows: " In one day Lin Yin-ching's troops have been increased from 500 to 8,000. They have two airplanes, and a number of cannons. They have been victorious along Panshan, Taian, Liaochung, and other districts."

Obviously, the Japanese themselves admitted that the bandit chief Lin attacked the Chinese regular troops with airplanes which could have been obtained only from the Japanese military authorities.

2. THE PREMEDITATED PLAN OF THE JAPANESE.—The bandit soldiers, who were directed and armed by the Japanese, molested the people wherever they went, and, among other things, they burned down houses of civilians, raped the women, and captured whomever they wished. However, the outrages committed by these bandit soldiers, under the protection of the Japanese, aroused great indignation and engendered ill-feeling among the populace. Consequently, the people took drastic action to protect themselves by means of force, and, in the course of their struggle with the bandit soldiers, they killed many bandits and among whom Lin's Japanese adviser, Kuraoka Shigetaro, in whose possession were found the following documents as evidence of Japanese intrigues in Manchuria:

(1) Documents relating to official appointment.

(2) Plans of military operation formulated by Kuraoka Shigetaro.

(3) Notes showing the transportation of arms and ammunition written by Kuraoka Shigetaro.

(4) Maps showing the operation of the railways in time of war.

(5) Principles of the organization and operation of artillery in war.

(6) Plans for the defence line of the First Brigade of Lin's Army.

Apart from these evidences, letters of official appointment bearing the name of the " North-eastern People's Army for Self-Defence " and that of Tokumatsu Matsumoto and Gennosuke Michimoto were also found. All these documents were subsequently turned over to Marshal Chang Hsueh-liang, and, in the interest of truth they are now reproduced here:

(I.) Facsimile of an official letter of appointment by the Japanese
Kwantung Army Headquarters of Kuraoka Shigetaro as
translator and interpreter with a salary of 130
yen a month, dated September 23rd, 1931.

24

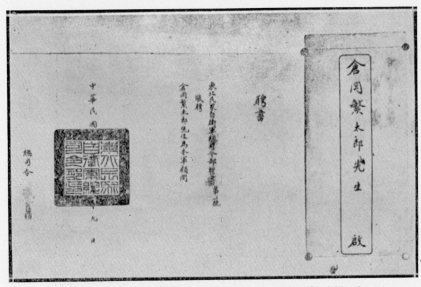

(II.) Facsimile of an official letter of appointment by the "North-eastern
People's Army for Self-Defence" of Kuraoka Shigetaro as adviser
to the said army, dated October 9th, 1931.

(III.) Facsimile of a rough plan of organization of
the bandit army formulated by Kuraoka
Shigetaro in his own handwriting.

III. Organization and military operation plans.

1. PLAN OF ORGANIZATION.—According to the evidence presented above, the plan of organization was briefly as follows:

(a) *Name*—The name of the army shall be known as the Northeastern People's Army for Self-Defence of the Republic of China.

(b) *Aim*—The chief aim of the said army is: (I) Protection, (II) Self-Defence, (III) Self-Government, (IV) Denunciation of the Kuomintang and the National Government in Nanking, and (V) Hoisting of the five colour flag (the flag adopted at the beginning of the Republic in 1912).

(c) *Personnel*—Lin Yin-ching and four others.

(d) *Places for the Concentration of Forces*—Places for the concentration of forces shall be the Liaochung, Taian, and Panshan districts.

(e) *Present Strength*—The present force is 5,000 strong with arms, but ammunition is inadequate.

(f) *Concentration*—The present force shall be concentrated in the stated areas within one week.

(g) *Expenses*—The expenses of operation shall be $50,000.

(h) *Supplies*—The necessary military supplies shall be 2 airplanes, some mountain guns, 200 or more rifles, ammunition, 3 or 4 machine guns.

(i) *Uniforms*—To be made.

(j) *Officials*—All magistrates and chiefs of police shall be changed.

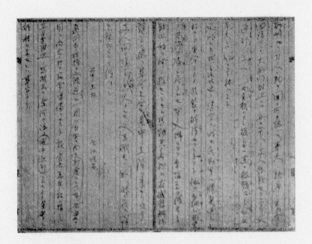

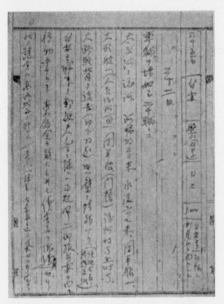

(IV.) Facsimiles of a plan of military operation formulated at Tengaopu headquarters on October 21st, 1931.

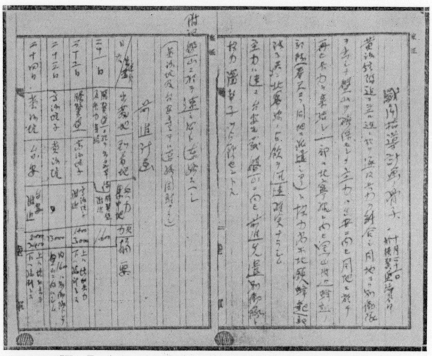

(IV.) Facsimile of a plan of military operation formulated at
Tengaopu headquarters on October 21st, 1931.

(V.) Facsimile of a note found in Kuraoka
Shigetaro's diary showing that a large quantity of arms and ammunition was sent to
Chienshan Station on October 19th — 300
rifles, 80,000 rounds of ammunition, and
6 machine guns.

2. PLAN OF MILITARY OPERATION.—According to the plan drawn up, the five-day programme of military operation may be seen from the chart below:

Date of Operation	Place of Departure	Destination	Place of Concentration	Number of Troops
Oct. 21	Preparation and inspection		Tengaopu	1,600
" 22	Tengaopu	Kao-sha-to-tze	Kao-sha-to-tze	3,000
" 23	Kao-sha-to-tze	Huangsha-to	Panshan	1,400
				1,600
" 24	Huangsha-to	Taian	Taian	3,400 (not including forces at Panshan).
" 25	Taian	Panshan	Panshan	5,400

However, according to the statement found in Kuraoka Shigetaro's diary, this plan was not carried out as originally intended.

(VI.) Facsimile of a letter of appointment by the North-eastern People's Army for Self-Defence of Gennosuke Michimoto as a special service man.

(VII.) Facsimile of a letter of appointment by the North-eastern People's Army for Self-Defence of Tokumatsu Matsumoto as a special service man.

IV. Conclusion.

From the foregoing account of the illegal activities of the Japanese military we cannot help but conclude by saying that (1) the Japanese intrigue in the Three Eastern Provinces is now definitely exposed; (2) the military occupation of the Three Eastern Provinces on the part of Japan under the pretext of fighting bandits therein is contradictory at least in practice, because of the fact that the Japanese military actually has utilized the bandits to disturb peace and order in the Three Eastern Provinces by supplying arms and ammunition to the bandit chief, Lin Yin-ching; (3) the evidence presented above proves that Japan, instead of co-operating with the Chinese authorities in their effort to suppress banditry, has actually, connivingly, and intentionally encouraged the bandits to create disturbances in the Three Eastern Provinces; (4) the act of the three Japanese emissaries Shigetaro, Tokumatsu, and Gennosuke, sent by the Japanese military headquarters in Kwantung to stir up the bandit chief, Lin Yin-ching, to revolt against the 19th Brigade of the Chinese Frontier Defence Force is not only a violation of International Law but is also construed as a criminal offence; (5) the Japanese military authorities have infringed upon China's sovereign right by the use of force, and by utilizing the marauders to create disorder in the Three Eastern Provinces.   Hence, the Japanese authorities in the Three Eastern Provinces have been at least partly, if not entirely, responsible for the banditry and disorder there.

MEMORANDUM

ON

THE SEIZURE OF THE CHINESE MARITIME CUSTOMS IN THE THREE EASTERN PROVINCES

Document No. 23   Peiping, July 1932

MEMORANDUM ON THE SEIZURE OF THE CHINESE MARITIME CUSTOMS IN THE THREE EASTERN PROVINCES.

1. Steps in the control of the Chinese Customs Administration.
2. Ports affected.
3. Lungchingtsun.
4. Antung.
5. Arrest of Customs staff inside "railway zone."
6. Newchwang.
7. Harbin.
8. Dairen.
9. Dismissal of Commissioner Fukumoto for insubordination.
10. Chinese abiding by Dairen Customs Agreement of 1907.
11. Yokohama Specie Bank's refusal to remit funds.
12. Illegal collection of revenue by the so-called "Manchukuo."

MEMORANDUM ON THE SEIZURE OF THE CHINESE MARITIME CUSTOMS IN THE THREE EASTERN PROVINCES

1. Steps in the Chinese control of the Customs Administration. One of the first acts of the " North-eastern Administrative Committee," the controlling body of the so-called "Manchukuo" government which was formally established on February 17th, 1932, was to notify the Superintendents of Customs at the Manchurian treaty ports that the Customs belonged to the "Manchukuo," and would, in future, be under the control of the Committee. At the same time, Superintendents and Commissioners of Customs were instructed to carry on their duties as usual, and were informed that a Japanese Customs Adviser had been appointed for each Manchurian port for the purpose of supervising the general Customs administration. The following brief account shows the steps by which the "Manchukuo" government first immobilized the Customs revenue, then seized the Customs funds accumulated in the several banks of collection and deposit, and finally, by *force majeure,* ejected the lawful Commissioners of Customs and took forcible possession of the Chinese Customs Administration.

2. Ports affected. The ports affected, with the 1931 revenue collected at each, are as follows:—

Lungchingtsun	Hk. Tls.	574,000
Antung	"	3,682,000
Newchwang	"	3,972,000
Harbin	"	5,272,000

The port of Aigun, which is outside the sphere of control of the ''Manchukuo'' government, has not been affected, and is still functioning normally under the control of the Chinese Government. The immobilization of the Chinese Customs revenue at Dairen, and the introduction of a ''Manchukuo'' Customs Administration at that port are dealt with separately and form a special section at the end of this Memorandum.

3. **Lungchingtsun.** During the second week of March, the Superintendent of Customs at Lungchingtsun notified the Commissioner, Mr. A. S. Wallas (British), that the North-eastern Administrative Committee had appointed a Japanese Adviser to the Customs with whom all Customs questions were to be discussed.

Drastic action against the Customs was, however, postponed until late in June when, on the 22nd, the Japanese Adviser ordered the Bank of Chosen—the Customs bank—not to honour cheques drawn by the Commissioner. The Bank of Chosen, being a Japanese institution, and therefore not subject to control of the ''Manchukuo'' authorities, had no excuse in refusing to obey the Commissioner's instructions regarding the disposal of Customs funds.

On June 29th, a party consisting of the Superintendent, the Japanese Adviser, Miyamoto, and Major Inouye, a Japanese Army Intelligence Officer, came to the Custom House. While the Adviser and Major Inouye remained outside, the Superintendent entered the Custom-House accompanied by guards with drawn pistols and demanded the surrender of the Customs. In the face of such *force majeure* the Commissioner had no option but to yield. Whereupon the Superintendent called in the Japanese Adviser and announced that the latter had been appointed Commissioner of Customs.

The last remittance of Customs revenue from Lung-chingtsun was sent on June 22nd, 1932.

4. Antung. The first intimation of interference with the Customs at Antung was given privately by the Japanese Consul to the Commissioner early in March, when the Consul advised the Commissioner, Mr. R. M. Talbot (American), that he must be prepared for a request from the Superintendent to hand over the Customs to "Manchukuo" control. The appointment of a Japanese Customs Adviser followed shortly, but this official took no active steps until the middle of June, when he transmitted definite orders from the "Manchukuo" Ministry of Finance to the Bank of China to the effect that Customs funds were no longer to be remitted to Shanghai. From this time, therefore, the collection of revenue accumulated in the Bank of China until June 16th, when four armed "Manchukuo" policemen accompanied by the Japanese Assistant Superintendent of Police visited the Bank of China and informed the Manager that they had come to "guard the revenue." On June 19th the Bank of China handed over to the Three Eastern Provinces Bank Tls. 783,000 and informed the Commissioner that his action was taken as a result of *force majeure.*

A portion of the Customs revenue at Antung is deposited in the Bank of Chosen, which, being a Japanese institution enjoying extraterritorial status, is not amenable to the jurisdiction of the "Manchukuo" authorities. Nevertheless, the Bank of Chosen declined to remit Customs funds and stated that they had received instructions from their Head Office in Seoul to hand over all Customs funds to the "Manchukuo" government. It was reported to the Commissioner that the Head Office of the Bank of Chosen had referred the question to the Japanese Foreign Office and the Japanese Ministry of Finance.

Having thus seized the Customs revenue, the next step was the seizure of the Customs Administration. On June 26th and 27th, the Japanese Adviser demanded that the Custom-House be handed over to him. The Commissioner refused to hand over, and on the 28th, the Superintendent, the Adviser and ten secretaries, etc., entered the Custom-House and demanded the keys. The Commissioner again refused to comply, and two armed "Manchukuo" policemen (both Japanese subjects) then entered and repeated the demand. The Commissioner once more refused, when four "Manchukuo" policemen (all Japanese subjects) with rifles and fixed bayonets entered and surrounded the Commissioner at his desk. The Commissioner had thus no option but to yield to *force majeure,* and left the Custom-House after a final protest to those concerned in the seizure.

5. **Arrest of Customs staff inside "railway zone."** On June 30th, 27 members of the Antung staff (25 Japanese and 2 Koreans) resigned from the Chinese Customs Service. The Commissioner then withdrew the remaining loyal staff to his house which is situated in the Japanese-controlled "railway zone," and attempted to continue to carry on the work of the Customs.

On the same day, the Japanese Adviser Sakikawa with two armed Japanese in plain clothes entered the Commissioner's house and demanded possession of the Customs archives which the Commissioner had previously brought from the Custom-House for safe keeping, stating that if the Commissioner refused to hand over, he was prepared to take them by force. The Commissioner protested against the forcible entry of armed agents into his house, the residence of an American citizen located in the Japanese Settlement, and asked the Adviser if he was acting with the knowledge and consent of the Japanese Consul. The Adviser replied that he was acting on instructions from Changchun and was prepared to ignore the Japanese Consul. The Commissioner again refused to give up the Customs archives, whereupon three more Japanese in plain clothes entered his house. The Commissioner, however, still declined to surrender his archives, whereupon the Japanese drew their revolvers, and the Commissioner was thus forced at the point of the pistol to surrender the archives which were immediately removed from his residence.

In the meantime, the Commissioner sent a Customs officer of British nationality to the Japanese Consulate which is located next door to the Commissioner's house with a request for assistance. The Consul was out and the Vice-Consul declined to take any action to prevent the forcible removal of the Customs archives.

As 80% of the Antung Customs revenue is collected in the Japanese-controlled South Manchuria "railway zone," the Commissioner attempted to carry on the Customs work there, in the belief that the Japanese authorities would not permit interference therein by the "Manchukuo" police. Unfortunately, such did not prove to be the case, and the "Manchukuo" police entered the 'railway zone," arrested four of the Customs staff and intimidated the remainder. As he was powerless to protect the lives of his staff, the Commissioner was forced to suspend work entirely within the "railway zone."

The last remittance of Customs revenue from Antung was made on April 19th, 1932.

6. *Newchwang.* On March 26th, the Japanese Ad-

viser demanded that the Bank of China hand over the accumulated Customs funds and future collection to the Three Eastern Provinces Bank. The Bank of China yielded to this demand under *force majeure*. Half of the Customs revenue at Newchwang is lodged in the Yokohama Specie Bank, which, being a Japanese extraterritorialized institution, is not subject to the control of the "Manchukuo" authorities. Nevertheless, when the Commissioner, Mr. N. R. M. Shaw (British), instructed the Yokohama Specie Bank to remit the accumulated balances to Shanghai, the Manager of the Bank declined to do so on the ground that the "Manchukuo" government had requested him not to remit. No action was taken against the Customs Administration until June 27th, when the Custom-House was seized by the Superintendent, the Japanese Adviser and a detail of armed policemen. The Japanese staff resigned *en bloc* from the Chinese Customs Service and joined the "Manchukuo" Customs, and Mr. Ehara, formerly Chinese Customs Assistant, was appointed Commissioner of Customs by the local authorities. The Chinese staff were compelled by force to continue to work at the Custom-House and one man who attempted to cease work was arrested and imprisoned.

The last remittance of Customs revenue from Newchang was made on April 16th, 1932.

7. *Harbin.* At the end of March, the "Manchukuo" authorities seized the Customs revenue in the Bank of China at Harbin, and forced the bank to agree to pay over future collections to the Three Eastern Provinces Bank.

For the next two months, the Commissioner, Mr. H. E. Prettejohn (British), and his staff carried on their usual functions, although constant pressure was brought on them to join the "Manchukuo" Customs. The real intentions of the local authorities were disclosed on June 26th when, at midnight, armed "Manchukuo" policemen, led by a Japanese, surrounded and took possession of the Custom-House. The next morning the Commissioner attempted to enter the Custom-House, but found it sealed and guarded. During the course of the day, Japanese in plain clothes (who admitted that they belonged to the Japanese Military Mission) called at the private residences of Chinese and Russian Customs employees and attempted to force them to sign documents promising that they would work for the "Manchukuo" Customs. The Japanese Adviser, accompanied by the police, called on Mr. E. J. Ohrnberger, the Deputy Commissioner (Russian), and offered him the post of Commissioner, *plus* £8,500 in cash, if he would take charge of the Harbin Customs for "Manchukuo." Mr. Ohrnberger refused to be bribed, and a few days later he was arrested and imprisoned for five days. Many other Customs employees were arrested, including Mr. E. T. Schjoth, a Norwegian, who was the Assistant-in-Charge of the Harbin Customs sub-office at Manchouli. The entire Chinese staff was ruthlessly intimidated, and even the Commissioner's house was surrounded by "Manchukuo" police.

The next action of the "Manchukuo" police was the search of the Commissioner's house and the seizure of Customs archives stored therein, while their latest move has been to order the Commissioner and all other Customs employees to vacate their residences.

The last remittance of Customs revenue from Harbin was made on March 28th, 1932.

8. **Dairen.** At Dairen, the Customs function by virtue of a separate Customs Agreement with Japan (1907),

who holds Dairen on lease from China; and, in view
of the fact that the Japanese Government has entire
and sole administrative control of the Leased Territory
(in which Dairen is located), it was naturally not anticipated that there would be any interference with the Chinese Customs Administration there. Such, however, did
not prove to be the case.

Up to June 7th, the Dairen Customs revenue was remitted regularly at intervals of three or four days. No
remittances having been received between June 7th and
14th, the Inspector-General telegraphed to Dairen to
enquire the cause of the delay. In reply, Mr. Fukumoto, the Commissioner, wired that he had hesitated to
remit the revenue as such action would precipitate a
crisis. Mr. Fukumoto added that Mr. Kawai, Chief of
Section for Foreign Affairs of the Japanese Administration of the Leased Territory, had advised him that
the "Manchukuo" government's claims to Manchurian
Customs revenues were well founded.

After a further exchange of telegrams, Mr. Fukumoto
reluctantly prepared to obey the Inspector-General's instructions, and had practically completed arrangements
to remit the revenue to Shanghai, when Mr. Kawai (who,
it must be emphasized, is a Japanese Government official and not an official of the "Manchukuo" government) intervened and insisted that remittances should
be postponed.

9. **Dismissal of Commissioner Fukumoto for insubordination.** The Inspector-General thereupon warned
Mr. Fukumoto on June 22nd that continued failure to
execute instructions would be considered tantamount to
insubordination. Mr. Fukumoto (Chinese Customs Official of Japanese nationality), replied that he had been
cautioned that if he carried out the Inspector-General's

instructions, Japanese interests would be adversely affected, and he therefore declined to remit the revenue—i. e., he carried out the orders of the Japanese authorities and refused to obey the orders of the Inspector-General. Mr. Fukumoto was dismissed for gross insubordination on June 24th.

Following the dismissal of Mr. Fukumoto, the Inspector-General appointed Mr. Nakamura, Deputy Commissioner, to take temporary charge of the Dairen Customs. Mr. Nakamura resigned immediately, and on June 26th all but one of the 62 Japanese members of the Customs Staff at Dairen telegraphed to the Inspector-General that they had severed all connection with the Chinese Maritime Customs.

10. **Chinese abiding by Dairen Customs Agreement of 1907.** The Inspector-General, in accordance with the terms of the Dairen Customs Agreement of 1907 referred to above, then nominated Mr. H. Kishimoto to be Mr. Fukumoto's successor as Commissioner at Dairen, and requested the approval of the Japanese Legation to this appointment on June 25th. Up to the present, four weeks have passed and no reply whatever has been received from the Japanese authorities.

11. **Yokohama Specie Bank's refusal to remit funds.** On June 24th, there was a balance of over Hk. Tls. 500,000.00 Customs revenue [1] on deposit in the Yokohama Specie Bank in Dairen, and the Inspector-General has made repeated demands on the Bank to remit this money to Shanghai, but has been met with a categorical refusal. The Yokohama Specie Bank state that they have been instructed by the Japanese Administration of the Leased Territory to retain the funds in question.

[1] The Dairen Customs Collection for 1931 was Hk. Tls. 12,448,000.

Illegal collection of revenue by the so-called " Manchukuo." After the dismissal of Mr. Fukumoto, the "Manchukuo" government organized a Customs Office in Dairen led by Mr. Fukumoto and staffed with former Japanese employees of the Chinese Customs Service which is now illegally collecting revenue in the Chinese Customs Wharf Service.

The last remittance of Customs revenue from Dairen was made on June 6th, 1932.

Peiping, July 29th, 1932.

MEMORANDUM

ON

COMMUNISM IN CHINA

Document No. 24   Peiping, July 1932

MEMORANDUM ON COMMUNISM IN CHINA.

CHAPTER ONE.—ORIGIN OF THE COMMUNIST MOVEMENT IN CHINA (1919-1924).

1. The Student movement of 1919.
2. The Society for the study of Marxism.
3. The Virtinsky Mission.
4. Formation of the Chinese Communist Party, May 1921.
5. Formation of the Government at Canton.
6. Second Congress of the Chinese Communist Party. Alliance with the Kuomintang rejected by Dr. Sun.
7. Joffe Mission of 1922. Joint Declaration of January, 1923.
8. Karakhan Mission. Pledge not to spread propaganda.
9. Dr. Sun compelled to accept Russian assistance when refused by other Powers.
10. Individual admission of Communists into the Kuomintang.

CHAPTER TWO.—PERIOD OF TOLERATION (1924-1927).

11. Plan of Communist conquest of the Kuomintang.
12. Formation of local Communist groups.
13. First uneasiness of the Kuomintang.
14. Plan of the Communist International.
15. Northern expedition. Communist intrigues.
16. Development of the Communist Party.

CHAPTER THREE. — RUPTURE BETWEEN THE NATIONAL GOVERNMENT AND THE COMMUNIST PARTY. THE PERIOD OF PROSCRIPTION (1927-1932).

CHAPTER FOUR. — COMMUNIST ORGANIZATION IN CHINA.

1. The Communist Party.

39. Connection with the *Comintern*.
40. Central Committee.
41. Regional and provisional Committees.
42. Control of auxiliary organizations.
43. Principal auxiliary organizations.
44. The present situation.

2. The Red Armies.

45. Composition.
46. Higher officers as framework.
47. Auxiliary organizations.
48. Tactics.
49. Technical and political direction.
50. Two bureaus established in 1931.
51. Strength of the forces.
52. Equipment.

3. The Sovietized Areas.

53. Soviet governments. Their organizations.
54. Finance, commerce, banks.
55. Agrarian reform.
56. Agrarian reform in Kiangsi.
57. Organization of the proletariat.
58. Exclusion of well-to-do farmers.
59. Class war in the country. Anti-Bolshevist reactions.
60. Administrative independence of local Soviets.
61. Creation of Soviet Central Government and regional governments.
62. Extension of sovietized areas.

4. The Labour Movement.

CHAPTER FIVE.—CONCLUSION.

APPENDIX:

B2. State of the Red Armies in May, 1931.

B3. States of the Red Armies in January, 1932.

B4. State of the Red Armies in June, 1932.

C. The programme of political and economic rehabilitation
    in connection with the campaign against the Com-
    munists.

Maps showing the provinces with Communist infected
areas.

MEMORANDUM ON COMMUNISM IN CHINA

CHAPTER I. ORIGIN OF THE COMMUNIST MOVE-MENT IN CHINA (1919-1924).

1. **The Student Movement of 1919.** Communism in China, as a political factor, emerged indirectly from a movement organized in 1919 by the students of the colleges in Peking for the regeneration of the country. This movement, both literary and political, was directed against the old traditions of China which the sponsors of the movement believed to be responsible for China's backwardness as compared with the western nations in many fields of human activity. It aimed at the emancipation of the thought of the Chinese people, and for that purpose, it stimulated the publication of a great number of reviews and journals advocating the "rejuvenescence of China" and a deep sense of patriotism for the country.

2. **The Society for the study of Marxism.** One of these periodicals, which did not consider patriotism as being worthy of emphasis in its editorial policy was *The Weekly Critic* founded by a professor of the National University of Peking, Chen Tu-hsiu, a man of some bitterness, violent in his temperament and given to the most radical conceptions. Chen Tu-hsiu felt attracted by the Marxist theories. With Li Ta-chao, he gathered a few young men and formed a society for the study of Marxism. They became fervent partisans of that economic doctrine and formed the first neucleus of Chinese

communism. The group was later joined by some anarchists and trade-unionists, and was organized at Shanghai towards the month of May, 1920. Its organ was the newspaper, *The New Youth*.

3. **The Virtinsky Mission.** The Soviet Government was then watching the evolution of Marxist ideas in China very closely. On July 25th, 1919, it addressed a manifesto to the Chinese Nation as well as to the Chinese Government, renouncing all the advantages, privileges and concessions unjustly extorted from China by the former Czarist regime, and representing the Soviets as "the only allies and brothers of the Chinese in their struggle for freedom." It sent to the Chen Tu-hsiu group a representative of the Far Eastern Secretariat of the Executive Committee of the Comintern, Virtinsky, under whose influence the group eliminated the anarchist and trade-unionist elements and took on a purely communist colour. Two daily newspapers, *The Labour* and *The Employee* were then published at Shanghai and a school of foreign languages was organized from where several students were afterwards sent to the Far Eastern Institute at Moscow, while the others were scattered in the interior of the country as propaganda agents.

4. **Formation of the Chinese Communist Party, May 1921.** In May 1921, the Chen Tu-hsiu group summoned its members to a general conference at Shanghai during which the Chinese Communist Party officially formed. The principal leaders at that time were Chen Tu-hsiu (Shanghai), Li Ta-chao (Peking), Tan Ping-shan (Canton), associated by Tsai Shih-siang and Chang Tai-lai who were then in France. The propaganda was specially organized for the workmen in Shanghai where Soviet syndicates where formed. Chang Tai-lai soon returned

from France in order to devote himself to the organization of the Young Men's Socialist Union, which was afterwards transformed into the League of Chinese Communist Youths.

The party sent a representative to the Congress of the Far Eastern Proletarians convened at Moscow by the Comintern. It was there that the eventual affiliation of the Communist Party with the Kuomintang was for the first time contemplated, an act towards which Moscow was favourably inclined, since it was thought that the development of the nationalist movement directed by Dr. Sun Yat-sen would facilitate the spread of Soviet doctrines among the country people.

5. **Formation of the Government at Canton.** At that moment, a radical split occurred between the North and the South of China, the North continuing in the reactionary and semi-feudalistic politics of Yuan Shih-kai and of those who succeeded him in the Presidency of the Government of Peking, while the South, represented especially by the province of Kwangtung, rallied to the revolutionary programme of the Kuomintang.

In April 1921, with the aid of a number of politicians who shared its ideas without being its official members, the Communist Party in April 1921 elected Dr. Sun the President of the Republic and thus organized a rival Government at Canton which, after a great deal of trouble and many trials among which was the death of the leader which occurred at Peking on May 12th, 1925 where he had come with the hope of winning over the people of the North to his ideas, succeeded in 1927-1928, under the name of the Nationalist Government, in making the whole of China to accept its authority and flag.

6. **Second Congress of the Chinese Communist Party. Alliance with the Kuomintang rejected by Dr. Sun.** At

the second Congress of the Chinese Communist Party held at Shanghai in June 1922,—the party had a little over three hundred members at that time,—a delegate of the Comintern who came from Moscow definitely proposed the alliance with the Kuomintang, in order as he said, to present a "united democratic front."

This proposition was a distinct departure from the proletarian stand which was always strictly followed by the Communist International. The Kuomintang consisted at that time largely of intellectuals, representatives of the liberal professions, officials and students, of what, in Soviet terminology, was the "bourgeois" class against which the "class struggle" is mainly directed.[1] In the view of the pure or irreconcilable elements, however, to combine with the Kuomintang was to covenant with the enemy.

Nevertheless, the proposition was voted upon in spite of the opposition of Chen Tu-hsiu who fought strongly against it, and was passed only as a mark of respect for the assistance which the Comintern had given. But the first overtures made to Dr. Sun Yat-sen as the President of the Kuomintang were rejected by him. It was Dr. Sun's ideal to regenerate China through her entire population and for the benefit of all, without making any distinction between the classes of which the nation is formed. He was opposed to "class struggle" and to the exercise

[1] In October, 1926, after the communists joined the Kuomintang, the proportions of the different elements were very much modified, but the intellectuals continued to be largely represented. The membership of the Kuomintang was then composed of the following:

Labourers	29 %
Professional men	25 %
Soldiers	23 %
Students	10.5%
Farmers	7.5%
Merchants	4.3%

of political power by one class over the others. He had no sympathy for the dictatorship of the proletariat. When, therefore, the communists approached him, his reply was that every Chinese who had belief in the principles of the Kuomintang could join the Party individually, but that the Kuomintang would not allow for the alliance with another party. The proposition of allowing the communists to join the Kuomintang individually was later discussed by the Third Congress of the Communist Party held at Canton in June 1923, without arriving at any decision.

7. **Joffe Mission of 1922. Joint Declaration of January 1923.** Desirous of being officially recognized by the Governments of China and Japan, the Soviet Government, during the autumn of 1922, sent the Joffe Mission to the Far East. In his sonorous declarations, M. Joffe professed the most friendly sentiments of the Union of Soviet Socialist Republics towards the Chinese nation, but when he was pressed by the authorities of the Peking Government to carry out the promises contained in the manifesto of July 25th, 1919, confirmed by a Russian note of October 27th, 1920, especially those concerning Mongolia and the Chinese Eastern Railway, only evasive answers could be elicited from him.

Realizing the indifference which he everywhere met with, M. Joffe went to Shanghai where he was to sail for Japan. It was there that he had a memorable interview with Dr. Sun Yat-sen, and the two authorized the publication of the following declaration on January 26th, 1923:

"Dr. Sun Yat-sen considers that neither the communist organization nor the system of the Soviets can be introduced into China at present because the necessary conditions for the success of the establishment of Communism or Sovietism do not exist there. This opinion is entirely shared by M. Joffe who is of the opinion, further, that the most important and most pressing problem of China is to achieve her national unification and to realize her complete national independence, and for that great task, he has given Dr. Sun Yat-sen the assurance that China has the warmest sympathy of the Russian people and that she could count upon the support of Russia.''

Then followed three paragraphs in which Dr. Sun Yat-sen took note of the pledge made by M. Joffe in the name of the Russian Government to conclude new treaties with China renouncing the former Czarist privileges and to settle the questions of the Chinese Eastern Railway and Outer Mongolia to the satisfaction of China.

The declaration of January 26th, 1923 is particularly important because it defines the political stand *vis-à-vis* the Union of Soviet Socialist Republics from which the National Government has never ceased to follow since it came to power, that is to say, the repudiation of communism and sovietism as suitable, social and political systems for China, although allowing the possibility of the establishment of friendly relations between the two countries, the agreement of M. Joffe to the views expressed by Dr. Sun Yat-sen being held as a formal pledge given by Russia to abstain from all bolshevist propaganda in China.

8. **Karakhan Mission. Pledge not to spread propaganda.** The Joffe Mission did not achieve any practical result, so far as the question of recognition was concerned, and the Soviet Government sent M. Karakhan to China who took a more decided attitude towards the Peking Government than his predecessor. There were

even indications that Russia was then disposed to collaborate with China in order to help her in resisting foreign encroachments and realizing her national aspirations.

However, the Chinese in Peking as well as in Shanghai and Canton were firmly opposed to any extension of the communist doctrines in China, and when the negotiations, which were started by M. Karakhan, concluded with the recognition of the Soviet Government, he was asked, among other conditions, solemnly to confirm the statement made by the Joffe Mission in January 1923. This confirmation was given by Article 6 of the "Agreement on general principles for the settlement of the questions between the Republic of China and the Union of Soviet Socialist Republics" of May 31st, 1924 which reads as follows:

"The Governments of the two Contracting Parties mutually pledge themselves not to permit within their respective territories the existence and/or activities of any organization or groups whose aim is to struggle by acts of violence against the Governments of either Contracting Party.

"The Governments of the two Contracting Parties further pledge themselves not to engage in propaganda directed against the political and social systems of either Contracting Party."

The liberal attiude which was shown by Russia during the negotiations and her renunciation of consular jurisdiction, of a portion of her rights in the Chinese Eastern Railway, of the entire amount of her share of the Boxer Indemnity and of other privileges produced a profound impression on China and won for Russia considerable popularity for some time.

9. **Dr. Sun compelled to accept Russian assistance**

when refused by other Powers. It was not, however, Dr. Sun's idea to rely exclusively on Russia for the realization of his political programme. Soon after his interview with Joffe, he made inquiries through his personal agents in various political and diplomatic quarters in order to find out if he could also rely on their sympathy and support. The answers were not particularly encouraging. There was thus no alternative but to accept, willingly or unwillingly, the offer of assistance made by Moscow. It was then that Borodin and a number of other Russian advisers, both civil and military, came to Canton in the autumn of 1923 and undertook, under the control of Dr. Sun, the internal reorganization of the Kuomintang and the Cantonese army.

10. **Individual admission of Communists into the Kuomintang.** The presence of these representatives of the Comintern and of the Soviet Government gave an immediate impulse to the communist movement in China. Conforming, at least in words, to the pledge made by the Joffe Mission, Borodin assured Dr. Sun that the communists who sympathize with the national movement and admitted within the ranks of the Kuomintang would abstain from working for the proletarian revolution. The principle of the individual acceptance on the part of the communists of the Kuomintang ideology was thus brought up for discussion during the First National Congress of the Kuomintang in March 1924, and favourably voted upon. That was the beginning of the period of toleration for communism in China.

This tactical move consisting in not officially amalgamating the two parties, the Kuomintang and the Communists, involved, however, the disadvantages of allowing the Communist Party with its various committees and groups to subsist as separate organs without being absorbed into the Kuomintang.

At that time, the Communist Party had more than two thousand members and the Red Trade-Unions has about sixty thousand followers. From this it can be seen that the movement was then confined to the intellectuals and the labourers and had not yet reached the country people.

CHAPTER II. PERIOD OF TOLERATION
(1924-1927).

11. Plan of Communist conquest of the Kuomintang. After being admitted into the ranks of the Kuomintang, and supported by Russian advisers and stimulated by the instructions which they received from the Comintern, the Communists attempted the conquest of the Kuomintang Party which had welcomed them. Chen Tu-hsiu thereupon decided on the following plan:

a) To win over to the communist doctrine the largest possible number of Kuomintang members.

b) To weaken the Kuomintang by carefully cultivating doubt as regards the efficacy of its doctrines, and by provoking conflict among its members.

c) To work especially among the lower ranks of the Kuomintang and control the central committees.

12. Formation of local Communist groups. From the original centres of Shanghai and Canton, the Communist propaganda had now been extended to the whole country so that numerous groups were soon formed, divided into three regions consisting of central, northern and southern China. The central group was composed of six sub-divisions; the north, four; and the south, six. Some of the groups included members of the same political formation or origin (the group of the old comrades, directed by Chen Tu-hsiu and Chang Kuo-tao, the group of French returned comrades whose leaders were Li Li-san and Chang Pei-keng, the group of Russian returned comrades, etc.). Others were purely local (the Chekiang and Hunan-Hupeh groups). Still others corresponded to affinities of ideas, of classes or of professions (the group of extremists, of trade-unionists, of militarists, of farmers, and of officials).

Regional organization remained very loose and the groups themselves could not agree either upon a common programme or upon a method to be followed. They were divided and quarrelled on many questions as regards principles and personnel. Nevertheless, certain groups exerted considerable influence, as, for instance, the extremists of the south, whose leader, Chang Yimien, Secretary-General of the Kwangtung and Kwangsi regions, was supported by the all-powerful Borodin.[2]

13. **First uneasiness of the Kuomintang.** The importance the Communists had attained in the councils of the Government in which they tried to propagate their ideas and develop their organization did not take long to cause uneasiness to the Kuomintang. At the Second National Congress of the Party, held at Canton from January 1st to 19th, 1926, it was recalled that in conformity with the instructions of Dr. Sun Yat-sen the Communists could be admitted into the Party only as assistants and not as leaders, since the Party was socialist and not communist. Consequently, in the committees and coun-

[2] The documents seized by the British Government in the search effected in the office of the commercial representative of the Soviet Union at London (Arcos House) and published, in translation, on May 26th, 1927, in the White Paper do not leave any doubt as to the fact that Borodin was a regular agent of the Soviet Government to which he was responsible for all his actions.

cils, the number of communist members did not exceed one-third of the total figure.

14. Plan of the Communist International. The Communist International of Moscow, on its side, however, in order to complete its plans of substituting itself for the Kuomintang after having sowed seeds of internal dissension within the ranks of that Party, made the following proposals to the Central Executive Committee towards the end of 1926:

1. to decide that the nationalization of land should be effected by right and not in virtue of laws or decrees taken specifically for each individual case,

2. to reorganize the Kuomintang on a new basis (a report by Tan Ping-shan informed the Comintern that the strong organization of the Kuomintang hardly left any liberty of action to the communists),

3. to dismiss military leaders hostile to communism,

4. to arm 20,000 communists and 50,000 workers and farmers,

5. not to nationalize the land belonging to workers, farmers, and soldiers.

This attempt brought no success, the demands of the International being for the most part contrary to the principles of the Kuomintang.

15. Northern expedition. Communist intrigues. In the meantime, the campaign conducted by Canton against the Northern militarists was being prepared. The Communists did what they could to delay the campaign. They felt that the success of the enterprise would reinforce the already powerful position of the Kuomintang and delay their own progress. The expedition was however already in full swing, and they tried to hinder it. When the Nationalist Army arrived at the Yangtse Valley, occupied Hankow, Wuchang and Hanyang, and marched towards the east for the occupation of Shanghai in order to join hands with the other revolutionary forces coming directly from the south, the Communists insisted from Canton that it "should not advance too rapidly, and that it 'should slow down its too rapid progress.' " They went as far as to suspend the work in the arsenal at Canton in order to create a crisis by a shortage of munitions. However, when the seat of the Nationalist Government was eventually established at Wuhan, they came in great numbers trying to exercise some preponderant influence over the new regime while the Generalissimo, Chiang Kai-shek, and the other personalities whom the Communists had been in the habit of defying, left Wuhan for Nanchang where they led the operations which soon ended in the capture of Nanking and the Shanghai region. In order not to compromise the success of that campaign, the Kuomintang protagonists were obliged to leave a sufficient amount of freedom of action to the Communist leaders of Hunan and Hupeh. The majority of whom took advantage of the situation and adopted a series of measures of a purely Bolshevist character altogether contrary to the instructions of Dr. Sun. The Nationalist Revolution threatened to turn to Sovietism with all its excesses.

16. **Development of the Communist party.** All these circumstances which we have just described gave an opportunity to the Communist Party to develop itself in considerable proportions in the early days of 1927. It was said to have then 90,000 followers. The Party of Communist Youths contained more than 60,000 members. The number of bolshevistically inclined trade-unionists was even estimated at 3,000,000 and the membership of the farmers' union at 10,000,000.

26

CHAPTER III. RUPTURE BETWEEN THE NATIONAL GOVERNMENT AND THE COMMUNIST PARTY. THE PERIOD OR PROSCRIPTION (1927-1932).

17. **Rupture with the Communists.** As soon as it found itself firmly established in the Yangtse Valley, the National Government deemed it necessary to put an end to communist conspiracies which threatened to undermine its authority and counteract the results of the successful military campaign. There was ample evidence that the Communists admitted into the Party were not observing Kuomintang discipline and insisted upon having their doctrines dominate the Government. It was equally clear that in spite of the formal engagements made by Joffe and the assurances from Moscow, the Russian advisers, who had in other respects rendered useful service, were working under the direction of the Comintern for the spread of Leninist ideas and the organization of a strong Communist Party within the ranks of the Kuomintang which would one day serve as the framework of a Soviet Government.

The members of the Kuomintang also realized the danger of the spread of Communist ideas in China. In April 1927, one veteran member, Mr. Wu Tse-hui, addressed to the Central Executive Committee a petition in which he vigorously denounced the Communist Party along with its Russian advisers and the Committees of Wuhan. His action was supported by 119 similar petitions emanating from organized associations of Shanghai including all the trade-unions. At an extraordinary meeting of the Central Executive Committee the decision to expel the Communists was reached.

18. **Purification of the army and the civil service.**
That decision was soon put into execution. The National
Government was established at Nanking on April 18th,
1927. A proclamation was immediately issued condemn-
ing communism and ordering the immedate "purification" of the army and the civil service. A series of mani-
festoes on that subject were addressed to the workers,
the revolutionary army, the people and the members of
the Kuomintang. The following extracts taken from the
manifesto issued to the people show clearly the position
of the Nationalist Government and the continuity of its
views:

"1. The Revolutionary Party wishes to emanci-
pate the Chinese people as a whole, that is to say, all
classes, including farmers, workers, merchants and
soldiers. It does not wish, therefore, that only one
class should dominate. Especially it does not desire the dictatorship of the proletariat.

"2. The Revolutionary Party wishes to assure
every Chinese of his entire liberty of thought and
action. It will not therefore admit a super-govern-
ment under Borodin. . . . It only admits a government of a liberated China enjoying a full measure of
freedom.

"3. The Revolutionary Party wishes to assure the
welfare and the progress of the entire nation. It can
not therefore allow 390 millions of Chinese citizens
to be treated at will by 10 millions of Communists
(supposing that here are as many as that). Dr.
Sun admitted the Communists into the Party as col-
laborators and the Russians as friends. If the Communists wish to dominate and the Russians desire
to ill-treat us that means the end of their activity."

19. **The Communist try to maintain themselves in the
Kuomintang.** On July 15th, the majority of the members

of the Central Executive Committee of the Kuomintang, who had remained until then at Wuhan, passed a resolution excluding from the Party all the Communists and sending Borodin and the other Russian advisers back to Russia. Some notorious Communists were arrested. The Party found itself again in unity which soon brought about the union of the elements remaining at Wuhan with those at Nanking. The National Government was thus definitely established at Nanking.

It was curious, however, that the Communists who were thus expelled did not wish to admit that they had ceased to be members of the Kuomintang. At the 8th Plenary Conference of the Executive Committee of the Comintern which took place from May 19th to 30th, 1927, the following resolution was adopted:

"The Executive Committee is of the opinion that the policy of uniting the Chinese Communist Party with the Chinese national bourgeoisie is a proper step to take. The independence of the Communist Party cannot be attained by being isolated from the non-proletarian working classes, particularly the farming class. Consequently, the Executive Committee resolutely rejects the idea of the separation of the Chinese Communist Party from the Kuomintang, or any policy which calculates to establish that eventuality." [3]

Consequently, on July 13th, 1927, the Central Committee of the Chinese Communist Party issued a manifesto in which it declared that it had withdrawn its representatives from the National Government, but would continue

[3] In a very curious letter written from Prinkipo, February 9th, 1931, and published by the *Nouvelle Revue Francaise*, April 1st, L. Trotsky, speaking of the action of Borodin and of the Russian advisers of Canton, reproaches the leaders of Moscow of having "hanged" the revolution of the Chinese proletariat in compelling them to come to terms with the bourgeoisie of the Kuomintang.

to collaborate with the truly revolutionary elements of the Kuomintang. The May 1927 resolution was confirmed and amplified by the Executive Committee of the Comintern in a long document dated July 14th, in which the Government of Wuhan was denounced for having, in spite of the reiterated advice of the Comintern, betrayed the cause of the agrarian revolution and "sabotaged" the campaign against the Government of Nanking represented as the great enemy of Chinese communism.[4]

The official separation of the two parties took place only after the *coup d'etat* of Canton and the rupture of relations between the National Government and the U.S.S.R. in December, 1927. (see paragraph 22).

20. **Some units of the army won over to Communist doctrines.** But the effective struggle of the Communists against their former allies who were now their adversaries, soon broke out. The continued efforts exerted by Borodin and by the Communist elements during the days of their ascendancy had unfortunately left traces in the army. As it was the army upon which the Comintern relied for the realization of its policy, it took special care to influence it so that many of the units were won over to Soviet doctrines. Those units consisted of doubtful elements in different parts of the country which it was impossible to disband for lack of funds.

The Communist International saw at once the opportunity of utilizing the army in order to create difficulties for the Government which had openly committed itself against communism. Secret agents were sent to China who established relations with Li-Li-shan, Chu En-lai, Chang Kuo-tao, etc. who constituted a Provisional Cen-

[4] An English translation of the document is found in the appendix of Yakhontoff's book—*Russia and the Soviet Union in the Far East*, New York, 1931, p. 410.

tral Political Bureau. This bureau immediately decided to begin direct action against the Government and to co-ordinate the strength of the red elements among the army ranks.

21. **Revolt of Nanchang.** The " doubtful " elements of whom we have spoken above were placed in the rear during the march from Canton to the Yangtse. The leaders were concentrated in Kiangsi between Kiukiang and Nanchang. In the latter city were the troops of General Yeh Ting who had been infected with communist ideas and the 20th Army with ideas equally radical commanded by General Ho Lung. On July 30th, 1927, these troops revolted together with the soldiers of Chu Teh, summoned for the assistance of the "doubtful" elements of the region, usurped the powers of the provincial government, and plundered, burned and killed the innocent population. Their leaders then proceeded to hold with the representatives of the communist groups of other provinces a kind of plenary conference where they attempted to arrive at a general plan of action; but before they could agree, the Government forces surprised and dispersed them so that they were obliged to flee towards the south.

Taking refuge in the region east of the Province of Kwangtung, they attempted vainly to steal a march upon Swatow in the expectation of finding an outlet to the sea where they would be able to receive aid from the Comintern.

22. *Coup d'Etat* **of Canton.** It was about this time that the Communists began attempting the establishment of local soviet governments in the different parts of the country. They cast their eyes first on Canton where they thought they could count upon the support of the working class. They formed soviet groups at Haifong and Lo-

fong,[5] and convened at Haifong on November 7th, 1927 the first "Congress of Soviet Workers, Farmers, Soldiers and Urban Proletarians." This Congress decided upon the creation of a "Soviet Government of Hailofong" which was soon established with the support of the communist groups of Canton and of Hassis, U.S.S.R. Consul in that city.

The organization under the direction of Heinz Neumann, a delegate of the Comintern and member of the German Communist Party, of Hassis, and of a member of the Chinese Communist Party, Wang Ping, previously Secretary-General of the Pan-Chinese Trade-Unionist Federation, prepared an insurrection which broke out on December 11th and made themselves masters of the city of Canton within a few hours. A soviet government was at once established and during three days Canton went through an orgy of massacre and plunder. The approach of the Government forces compelled the forces of disorder to a precipitate retreat. The city was reoccupied by the regular forces on the 13th. But the insurrection had created 15,000 victims and inflicted upon the population material losses estimated at more than 50 millions of dollars. The Russian Consul Hassis was killed during the course of the suppression, authentic documents were found on the spot showing the part taken in the affair by the official agents of the Soviet Government. A decree was therefore issued by the National Government on December 14th cancelling the exequaturs of all the Russian Consuls throughout the country.[6]

[5] These soviets, directed by Peng Pai, have acquired notoriety through the atrocities which they inflicted without reason upon the population of that region.

[6] The Government at Peking also complained of the interference of Russia in the internal affairs of China, forbidden by the declaration of May 31st, 1924, which we have referred to above. A search conducted in

A subsequent offensive taken by the authorities of Canton and Swatow in February 1928, drove the Communists from Haifong and Lofong and put an end to the existence of the "Government of Hailofong." The excesses at Canton and Hailofong produced a deep sense of repulsion in the population against the Communist Party so much so that some of the Communists themselves, such as Tan Ping-shan and Chang Pei-yung, became disgusted and retired.

23. **Communistic change of the policy.** During the conference of the Comintern held in February 1928, the Moscow leaders after criticizing the faults committed by the Chinese Communist Party appointed Shang Chung-fa Secretary-General of the Chinese Central Committee and Li Li-san its permanent member. The experience of Canton having proved that the Party could not seize political power through revolutionary methods in the form of armed insurrection, it was decided to abandon the policy of force and to confine all the effort in the future to the organization of the working and farming classes.

This change of policy was approved by the 6th World Congress of the Communist International held at Moscow from August 17th to September 1st, 1928. In an appeal addressed to the "Workers and all Labouring People of China," after having praised the heroism of the comrades who had fallen in the Canton *coup d'etat*, the Congress added: "under the cross fire of the Imperialist artillery and the mad terror of the Chinese Government, you are reorganizing your ranks, mobilizing forces, en-

the localities adjacent to the Russian Embassy at Peking on April 6th, 1927, resulted in the discovery of documents irrefutably establishing the proof of aid in money and munitions given by the Government of the Soviet to certain Chinese political parties. Whereupon the Soviet Government by way of protest recalled the entire staff of the Embassy at Peking, leaving in China only the consular agents.

listing new elements for the preparation of the forthcoming onslaught upon the positions still in the hands of the enemy:" [7]

In the detailed resolutions, the Congress instructed the Communist Party to sever relations immediately with the feudal and bourgeois elements. It condemned the Kuomintang, whose ideas were considered anti-revolutionary. It emphasized that the communist movement had developed in an irregular manner "in different provinces of China and amidst various vicissitudes." "It is necessary," it added, "to fight energetically against the *putschisme* of certain sections of the working class, against unorganized and unprepared activities in the cities and countries, against the game with insurrection." It concluded: "The Executive Committee of the Comintern considers that the principal object of the Party and of the sovietized districts is to start an agrarian revolution and to organize the red detachments which will be transformed gradually into a Red National Army."

24. **New programme of the Chinese Communist Party.** The 6th Congress of the Communist Party of China, which was held almost at the same time at Moscow under the auspices of the Third International, soon decided upon the following programme consisting of ten articles:

1. To destroy the power of the Imperialists.

2. To confiscate the capital of the banks and foreign enterprises.

3. To overthrow the Government established by the Kuomintang.

4. To unify China but leave to the population the right of self-determination.

5. To organize the soviet workers, farmers and soldiers.

[7] Yakhontoff: *Russia and the Soviet Union in the Far East,* p. 422.

6. To establish the 8-hour working day and to institute a system of social insurance.

7. To confiscate land belonging to the land proprietors.

8. To improve the living conditions of the soldier.

9. To replace the existing taxes by a special progressive tax.

10. To become allies of the proletariat of the whole world and of the U.S.S.R.

25. **Development of the Party in the cities.** At that time there was a renewal of internal dissension in China, and Li Li-san and Shang Chung-fa were enabled, through one year of continuous effort, once more to establish the influence of the Communist Party to organize a considerable red army to sovietize extensive areas.

The activity of the Communists in the industrial and administrative centres, though by no means to be ignored, did not produce the same effect as in the interior. The Party knew well enough how to gain influence among the intellectuals and the student elements. But it could not, in spite of repeated efforts, bring the working masses under its control because of preventive or repressive measures enforced by the authorities, and also because of the resistance of the trade-unions which had been organized under the guidance of the Kuomintang.

26. **Development in the country.** In the interior of the country, the success of the Communists was much more pronounced. It will perhaps be irksome to go into the details of describing a whole series of local military operations and political events which have marked that success. We shall in the next chapter describe some of its characteristics and what it generally accomplished.

27. **Schism of Li Li-san.** The success was, however,

not sustained. After bringing certain provincial militia under its influence and extending the sovietized areas, some of the leaders of the Communist Party, with Li Li-san at their head, thought that the moment had come for the overthrow of the National Government by a series of organized uprisings and armed insurrections in the cities as a prelude to a general offensive of the Red Armies. The situation called for active revolutionary measures and propaganda work in the professional unions became less necessary. The question was therefore no longer the instruction of the masses but how to enlist them in active service.

This view was altogether contrary to that of the Third International. The "game with insurrection" was precisely what it strongly condemned during the 6th Congress (paragraph 23). But Li Li-san was then in the headquarters of the red armies stationed in the interior, and more or less out of touch with the Central Committee of the Chinese Communist Party which sat at Shanghai and which was the faithful executive organ of the Third International. He thought that he was strong enough to act alone. The Central Committee protested. Li responded to these protests by creating at Wuhan a dissenting "Central Committee of Action." When Moscow intervened, it was too late. Reports concerning the plans of Li Li-san and his followers were pouring into the National Government. It was easier to suppress insurrectionary tendencies because they were more tangible than pure propaganda and the Government without delay adopted necessary measures to cope with the situation. These measures found the Communist Party disorganized as a result of the dissenting views of Li Li-san, and the movement started by him in Wuhan was arrested.

28. **Purification of the Communist Party.** Shang Chung-fa, Secretary-General of the Party, was then sent to Hupeh to unify the Party. Li Li-san was summoned to Moscow to answer for his conduct; and in conformity with the instructions from the Comintern, the Central Committee of Shanghai proceeded, in the winter of 1930, with the "purification" of all its organs.

After expelling some 25% of the total number of the followers of Li Li-san,—the others having accepted the "general line of conduct" of the Comintern,—and numerous influential members suspected of having reached an understanding with the reactionaries of all types, the orthodox members of the Central Committee on January 15th, 1931, convened the 4th Plenary Conference which severely condemned the policy of Li Li-san and proceeded with the reorganization of the Party and its auxiliary organizations based on the instructions of the Third International.

29. **Resumption of the struggle against the Communist armies.** The National Government at that time had just published the Organic Law on October 4th, 1928, and was devoting its energy to the consolidation of its political and administrative organization. Militarily speaking, some months had to be spent in order to readjust the national forces whose strength and equipment after the campaign against the Communists in 1927 and whose weariness as a result of the march upon Peking in 1928 had to be reinforced and replenished. Other internal political complications also presented themselves in the autumn of 1929 and prolonged into the early months of the following year so that it was not until the later months that the Government could seriously undertake the resumption of the struggle against communism. In the 4th Plenary Conference of the Kuomintang held at

Nanking from November 12th to 18th, 1930, it was unanimously decided to suppress the Communists and bandits completely and to despatch the Government forces against the Red Army in order to exterminate it and to reoccupy the sovietized areas.

30. **First Campaign.** The first expedition however ended in failure. General Chang Hui-tsan, who commanded the 18th division, after having achieved success in Kiangsi, was unwise enough to leave his bases far behind and was surrounded by the Red Army. He paid with his life for the mistake he had made. The 50th division which followed him withdrew only after having sustained considerable loss.

31. **Second Campaign.** In February 1931, the Minister of War Ho Yin-ching, took command of three divisions and went to the mountainous regions of Kiangsi for the Red Army. The configuration of the territory which afforded excellent natural defence, and the clever strategy employed by the Red Army which we shall describe later in paragraph 48, prevented him from obtaining any real success. The situation remained unchanged.

32. **Third Campaign.** At last, in the beginning of June, the Commander-in-Chief of China's land, sea, and air forces, General Chiang Kai-shek, himself assumed the direction of the operations. He appointed General Ho Yin-ching to the command of the armies in the front, and the Chairman of Kiangsi Province, Lu Ti-ping, to the command of the reserves. He organized at the same time a political committee to reorganize and rehabilitate the areas devastated by the Soviets as they became conquered.

The efforts were crowned with success. After a series of desperate battles in which the new famous 19th Route

Army distinguished itself, he drove the Soviets back to their political centre at Tunku, encircled them, and on July 17th, captured the city. All the communist establishments, including their military schools, banks, and bureaus were destroyed. Three days after, he occupied another city under Soviet control, namely, Shih-cheng. The Communists fled into the mountains or retreated towards Fukien and Juichin.

33. **Defeat of the Communists. The events of September 1931, stopped the campaign.** After an interval of some weeks, the campaign was resumed in September. The neighborhood of Tunku was cleared. The 3rd, 4th, 5th, 7th, 8th, and 12th corps of the Red Army tried to reach Yufu by way of Shengkuo, the seat of the Soviet government of the province. The 19th Route Army delivered a severe blow to them at Kaochinchow where they lost more than 2,000 men and 3 generals. The left wing of the Government forces arrived at the suburbs of Huichang, in the south-eastern extremity of Kiangsi, while the 18th Route Army on September 13th entered Juichin, an important centre under the rule of the Communists.

Seeking refuge in the out-of-way region between Shengkuo and Huichang, around the Taking mountains, the Communist forces were on the verge of being encircled and annihilated when the events of the Three Eastern Provinces took place. The Government was obliged to recall its troops to other localities in order to face eventualities which might happen and which indeed did happen. The reds, thus made bold, launched a counter-offensive. The conquered regions had to be evacuated and the gains realized in the course of the campaign were almost completely lost.

34. **Lesson from the campaign.** A lesson was however learned: that with well-organized forces carefully conducted, it is possible to reach communist dens even in the most inaccessible parts of the interior. In other words, it was shown that well co-ordinated military action encircling the centres of the Communists, if sustained for a considerable length of time, could have ended in the defeat and annihilation of the red armies.

35. **Communist organizations dispersed.** Simultaneously with the military operations, the Government undertook a campaign of search and the suppression of active communist elements in the rest of the country. Numerous secret organizations were discovered and disbanded, their members arrested to answer for their activities in accordance with the provisional law of March 7th, 1928, dealing with the suppression of counter-revolutionary activities. (This law was revised on March 1st, 1931. Appendix A.)

36. **Shanghai.** At Shanghai, Koo Chen-chang, member of the Central Committee, and Shang Chung-fa, Secretary-General of the Communist Party, were arrested by the authorities on June 3rd and 22nd, 1931. They were tried and executed. The party was thus considerably weakened. It was Koo Chen-chang's duty to move the communist leaders about so as to escape the attention of the police. His death made that part of communist activities less efficient and less sure, and seriously diminished the mobility of the leaders. With the death of Shang Chung-fa, the Party lost one of its most active organizers.

The arrest by the police at Singapore of an agent from the Comintern who was proceeding on an inspection tour of the communist organizations of the Far

East, and an examination of the documents found in his possession enabled the authorities of Shanghai to discover in that city on June 15th, the Far Eastern Bureau of the Comintern and the Bureau of the Secretariat of the Pan-Pacific Labour Union which directed all the Communist movement of the Far East and through the intermediary of which the red organizations in the various colonies of the Pacific, etc., maintained contact with the Executive Committee of the Communist International at Moscow. At the head of that bureau was a person of uncertain civil status and of unknown nationality, who, after having assumed several different names, called himself Noulens, and who was arrested together with his wife and delivered under that name to the Chinese authorities. His case is in course of investigation before the courts.

Owing to this sudden turn of events, the majority of the members of the Central Committee of the Communist Party left Shanghai to seek refuge either in the interior or at Canton. The members of the Special Committee of Shanghai were also dispersed. After the discovery of secret printing offices and a large amount of subversive literature, the propaganda section of the Provincial Committee of Kiangsu ceased all work of agitation.

By July, 1931, it may be said that not only the three organs of which we have spoken had been rendered impotent but also several district committees and the various auxiliary organizations and the Pan-Chinese Trade-Unionist Federation.

37. **Other centres.** At Tientsin, in the month of July, the police succeeded in laying hands upon about twenty influential Communist agents among whom were the

Secretary-General of the Committee for Hopei Province, the members of the Central Committee of the railwaymen of the Tientsin-Pukow Railway, etc.

At Hankow, an attempt on the part of the Communists to capture the city by surprise with a flotilla of junks failed, the plot having been discovered in time (September 2nd, 1931). Numerous arrests were made.

38. Number of arrests. In all, 1,549 arrests were effected in 1930, of which 572 were at Shanghai, 426 in Chekiang and 158 in Kiangsu; and there were 964 arrests in 1931 of which 345 were at Shanghai, and 320 at Hankow. The disorganization of the local committees of the Party manifested itself during the "red days" in the months which followed. These days usually marked by parades and demonstrations passed off in absolute quiet.

CHAPTER IV. COMMUNIST ORGANIZATION IN CHINA.

---

1. The Communist Party.

39. Connection with the Comintern. The Communist Party of the Far East is placed under the control of the Oriental Secretariat of the Third International at Moscow through the intermediary of the Far Eastern Bureau whose seat was at Shanghai at the time when the Noulens couple was arrested (see paragraph 36).

The Party is represented in the Comintern by six delegates. The Comintern is in constant touch with the Communist Party of the Far East through the constant coming and going of the members who thus establish a close relationship between China and Moscow. Since

1920 about one hundred influential agents of the Comintern have passed through Shanghai, including Borodin, Earl Bronder, Serge Dalny, Jacques Doriot, Tom Mann, Musso, Heinz Neumann, Roy, etc.

The Communist Party in China is directed by a Central Committee which co-ordinates the following four branches of activity:

1. Political activity (determining the cause of action of the Party).

2. Military activity (red armies).

3. Administrative activity (government of the sovietized areas).

4. Trade-Unionist activity (labour movement).

40. Central Committee. The Central Committee is divided into twelve departments, namely:

1. The Political Bureau, the directing organ of the Party.

2. The Secretariat, technical executive organs for the instruction of the Political Bureau.

3 and 4. The Departments of Organization of the Party and Propaganda.

5. Information and Counter-spy Service.

6. Department of Sovietized Districts.

7. Military Department.

8. Department of the Labour Movement, which supervises the activity of the Pan-Chinese Trade-Unionist Federation and its secret organs.

9. Department of Communist Youths.

10. Department of Feminine Movement.

11. Department of Peasant Movement.

12. Committee of Control, which has the power of controlling and censuring the activity of the individual members of the Party.

41. **Regional and provincial Committees.** Under the Central Committee are placed the Regional Committees, of which there are five:

1. Manchuria
2. North China
3. The Yangtse Valley
4. South China
5. Kiangnan

sitting respectively at Harbin, Tientsin, Wuhan, Canton, and Shanghai.

In principle, each Regional Committee has under it as many Provincial Committees as there are provinces of which the region is composed. Under the Provincial Committees are the District Committees, etc. as well as communist section organized in the factories, schools, camps, etc. The most important Regional Committees are those of Kiangnan and the Yangtse Valley. The Committee of Kiangnan has under its direct control the Provincial Committees of Kiangsu, Chekiang, and Anhui, and four special committees for:

Northern Anhui,
Southern Anhui,
The Region of Pengpu-Hsuchow (the Tientsin-Pukow Railway), and
The City of Shanghai.

42. **Control of auxiliary organizations.** Dependent also on the Central Committee are the "Communist Sections" organized within the Chinese branches of the international revolutionary organizations affiliated to the Third International, such as the International Red Relief, the League against Imperialism and for Colonial Independence, the International Workers' Relief, etc. It

is through the intermedairy of these sections that the Central Committee of the Party controls the activity of these auxiliary organizations.

43. **Principal auxiliary organizations.** Among the auxiliary organizations, the Communist Youths, the Alliance of Leftist Authors, the League against Imperialism deserve special mention:

The Communist Youths. Chang Tai-lai, who perished in 1927 in the course of the Canton insurrection, organized the Union of Young Socialists, which became afterwards the League of Chinese Communist Youths. Hsiao Tsou-mi founded in 1923 a Union of Marxist Youths meant for the study of the doctrines of Karl Marx. In 1926 this Union was affiliated with the League of Chinese Communist Youths. The League is an independent organ of the Communist Party, but placed under its political tutelage. Its activity, limited at the beginning among the students, has to-day extended to all the young workers. It has eight big centres: Shanghai, Tientsin, Peiping, Tangshan, Canton, Hongkong, Hankow and Wuchang. It encourages the formation of societies of young people. Its members, however, are housed in booksellers' houses or simply shops which serve as refuge to communist members when the police search them.

Alliance of Leftist Authors. In the beginning of 1930, the Communists launched in China what they called the movement for proletarian literature. This literature came to China from Russia by way of Japan where a well-known novelist, with extremist tendencies, Kuo Moh-roh, who left Canton after the failure of the *coup d'etat* of December 1927, found it in a most flourishing state. Kuo Moh-roh introduced the proletarian literature into China and with about fifty of his countrymen founded in March 1930 the Alliance of Leftist Authors aimed at the spread of red propaganda in literature and art. The alliance has been rapidly developing and consists of numerous divisions. It publishes three reviews.

The League against Imperialism. The Chinese section of the League is a transformation of the former Revolutionary Association of China. It participated last year in the Exposition of Oppressed Peoples organized at the same time with the Colonial Exposition of Paris and in the same city.

44. **The present situation.** The outlines described above in paragraphs 39, 40 and 41 deal with the organization of the Party in theory. The measures of suppression taken by the Government on the one hand, and the lack of experienced and tried Communist agents on the other hand, have not allowed for the complete realization of these theories. The actual situation at present appears to be as follows:

Province of Kiangsu. The Communists attach the greatest importance to that Province, because it is the most industrialized part of China, consisting of two-thirds of the total number of Chinese workers. Shanghai and the International Settlement are attractive to the leaders, because in the midst of the moving population of the port (the third in the world by its annual tonnage), it is easy for them to pass unnoticed. The majority of the Communist organs have their centres in that city.

Since the arrest of Shang Chung-fa (see paragraph 36), the Provincial Committee of Kiangsu appears to have disappeared. The Special Committee of Shanghai which was dissolved was reformed into eight subsections consisting of about 220 members. There are also committees at Soochow, Nantung, Wusih, Liao-chiang. Chu Eng-lai, an important member of the Party, was appointed in August 1931, its Secretary-General replacing Shang Chung-fa.

Province of Chekiang. The Provincial Committee was dissolved in 1929. Since then there has been only one agency at Hangchow with two District Committees at Hangchow and Wenchow.

Province of Hupeh. The Wuhan region is most coveted by the Comunists, because it gives them mastery over the middle course of the Yangtse, providing the possibility of threatening Nanking and controlling the vast hinterland whose trade concentrates at Shanghai. That explains the desperate efforts, which the Red Armies have never ceased to exert, to cut the Peiping-Hankow Railway and to seize Wuchang, Hankow and Hanyang.

The Northern Provinces. In 1929 there existed in Peiping a Regional Committee for the nine northern Provinces. It was transformed into the Provincial Committee of Hopei. The Committee of the Metropolitan District of Peiping, dissolved in 1930, was reorganized after the events of September 18th, 1931. The Committee at Tientsin was dissolved last year, so also that at Tangshan which had organized the strike among the miners of the Kailan Mining Administration. There are other important communist centres at Paotingfu in Hopei, and at Tsinan in Shantung.

Province of Kwangtung. In spite of the measures of suppression taken after the Canton insurrection, the Communists for Kwangtung Province still retain their Committee.

Province of Szechuan.   Chungking had been at one time an important centre of propaganda.   But in 1931 the local authorities inforced firm measures of control and arrested about forty ring-leaders thirty of whom were publicly fined.   At Chengtu at the news of the Canton insurrection, the governor imprisoned all the Communists.   As yet, there remain some scattered elements in the districts of Changchu, Pali, etc.

Province of Yunnan.   The centre of activity of the Communists is at Kwen Nien.   They have tried to spread propaganda among the workers in the railway which connects the Province with French Indo-China.   But the arrest of their leader, Li Kuo-chou, has put an end to their agitations.

2. The Red Armies.

45. **Composition.**   The Red Army in China is not organized along strictly communist principles.   It is not, like the army of the U.S.S.R., an army of the proletariat, drawn from among the classes which it desires to set free, organize and protect.   As we have indicated above, its nucleus consists of former Government soldiers or those who were associated with them.   Those detachments with extremist tendencies rallied under the red flag in groups together with their commanders after the rupture of the Kuomintang and the Nationalist Government with the Communist Party.   The number increased as individual deserters joined their ranks.   The leaders might have definite revolutionary ideas.   But the mass of the troops have only vague impressions rather than convictions.   The majority of the soldiers under the command of Ho Lung and Chu Teh have on the whole good military discipline.   With them are the former bandits, who have been attracted there by the

bait of comparatively regular pay and of plunder after successful expedition. Then there are the miserable, ruined peasants, victims of civil war, or drought and floods. Lastly came those who are enroleld and recruited on the spot who, one can be certain, do not enter service out of any conviction. All these different elements join the same ranks, and no wonder they are so heterogeneous.

46. **Higher officers as framework.** The higher officers are perhaps better organized because a good number of them have received and continue to receive technical training in the different military schools of the U.S.S.R. One may find among them non-Chinese elements (Koreans, Formosans, Annamites, Mongolians, Bouriates, etc.).

47. **Auxiliary organizations.** Side by side with the regular army are the auxiliary organizations: the Red Militia, the Young Vanguards, and the Boy Scouts.

The Red Militia is recruited in principle from able-bodied men from 18 to 45 years of age. It is divided, always theoretically however, into the active and the territorial groups. The men of the active group are treated like soldiers, but have no arms. Those of the territorial group are the reservists who are called to serve under the flag in case of necessity.

The Young Vanguards are composed of young men from 16 to 18 years. They are in fact the crack troops who occupy the front ranks in the attack and whose duty it is to "sweep" the conquered localities.

The Boy Scouts are employed as scouts, distributors of published materials and propaganda agents.

48. **Tactics.** The well-known tactics of the Red

Armies is described in their manuals of military instructions. It consists of the following features:

1. Attack the Government forces in the sovietized regions, or in the regions where there are thick forests or wild mountains, and lead them to an ambush.

2. Separate these troops in making them pursue you, then turn around and strike them at their flank or their rear.

3. When the Government forces are concentrated, avoid them by dispersing; when they are in an inferior position, converge the attacks upon them or surround them.

4. Utilize the population of the sovietized districts to harass and frighten the Government forces (for example, by planting red flags on the hills which surround them or by increasing the sound of the trumpets) or place the peasants in the vanguard and do not attack with the main body of the Red Army until the enemy should be tired or be on the point of exhausting his munitions.

5. Do not attack the works of permanent defence, do not deliver yourselves up to arranged battles. Avoid fighting in the regions where the population is not yet sovietized.

6. Undermine the morale of the Government forces by the propaganda agents, farmers, workers and women.

The Communist armies conform themselves very precisely to these prescriptions so that it is rather difficult to join and destroy them. As soon as the Government troops arrive in any great number, the Communist detachments which do not have uniforms disperse, hide their arms and assume the appearance of innocent workers, who would combine again to attack the regular forces as soon as the latter, fooled by the quiet appearance of the country, are no longer on their guard. Furthermore, the Communist armies operate only in the mountainous and woody regions which are difficult of access and deprived of means of communication.

The Communist armies go in for pitched battles only for the possession of cities which they need, because it is from these cities that they raise a portion of their taxes and obtain their supplies. Besides, these cities serve as centres of assemblage and points of strategic support. When these are threatened by the regular army, there will be left detachments to protect them, and these detachments would assume the responsibility of fighting.

49. Technical and political direction. The Red Armies are naturally raised from the Communist Party. Nevertheless, the Military Department of the Central Committee concerns itself only with the propaganda among the militarists and with the establishment of *liaison* with communist sections which exist in all the regiments.

The technical centralized military organ of the Red Armies is the "Committee for Military Affairs," under the Central Committee. It is this Committee which deals with questions of organization and recruitment. Questions relating to operation fall within the competence of the military revolutionary council and of the General Staff of the Red Armies.

There is one department, the General Political Department, which controls the political life of the Red Armies. With the General Staff of each Red Army is a Political Department; each division, each regiment, has a political chairman. The political chairman of the regiment directs the political life of that unit and controls the activity of the communist sections in the companies.

50. **Two bureaus established in 1931.** In the course of the operations during 1931, the Committee for Military Affairs established two bureaus for the Yangtse Valley and for South China. The first of these bureaus was established in the neighborhood of Hankow and the other in the south of Kiangsi. It is the duty of these bureaus to maintain the connections between the Committee for Military Affairs with the regions of operation, and to receive arms and munitions transported from the central supply to the "red" districts.

51. **Strength of the forces.** Nothing is more difficult than to ascertain the strength of the Red Armies. Even their composition, which has been described in paragraph 44, is subject to constant variation. As a portion of them are recruited from the local farmers, they swell when the sovietized areas extend and diminish as soon as certain regions are evacuated.

Then also the figure varies according as certain auxiliary formations are included or excluded. In the appendix are to be found estimates taken from different but, generally speaking, well-informed sources for the year 1930, for May 1931, for January 1932, and for what obtains at present. The estimates of January 1932 give the strength of the communist armed forces, in round figures, at 200,000 men with 150,000 rifles. They are manifestly more than the actual number. The figures for 1930, May 1931 and the spring of 1932 generally agree and approach the real strength of the forces. The figures for January 1932 include some interesting details on the technical grouping of the communist units and their geographical divisions. The campaign which the

Government has seen fit to conduct against the Red Armies at present in order to reoccupy the sovietized areas does not permit the disclosure of the latest information received concerning the position and strength of the Red Armies.

52. **Equipment.** As the tables in the appendix indicate, the red forces are badly armed. Not every soldier is even supplied with a rifle. The bullets are still fewer. The Communists are not in control of any sea-port, and so cannot import any munitions or arms. As far as one can judge, 30% of their arms has been supplied to them by the Government detachments which joined the Communist ranks in 1927 and by the bandits incorporated into the Red Armies; 25% of it was purchased in foreign concessions; 20% forms confiscations and requisitions; 10% is of local manufacture; 15% of other sources.

3. The Sovietized Areas.

53. **Soviet governments. Their organizations.** The occupation of a district by the Red Army, when it appears to last long, is followed by the sovietization of the country around. After the first violence which accompanies the seizure of possessions, killing, plundering, burning, and which has for its object the terrorization of the population and breaking down all possible resistance, the Communists would proceed with the creation of a "Soviet Government" for the district and call an assembly of soldiers, workers and farmers. The local gentry, the property classes are excluded from that assembly, composed entirely of proletarians, who would then elect a Committee composed of a certain number of "People's Commissars." Each "Soviet Government" is generally composed of:

1. A Commissariat for the Interior.

2. A Commissariat for fighting against the anti-revolutionaries (G.P.U.)

3. A Commissariat of Finance.

4. A Committee for Military Affairs.

5. A Commissariat of Rural Economy.

6. A Commissariat of Education.

7. A Commissariat of Hygiene.

8. A Commissariat of Post and Telegraph.

9. A Commissariat of Communications.

10. Committee of Labor and Peasant Control.

It is only in the Soviet districts already stabilized that all the departments indicated above function. But even then the backward conditions of the population of the more distant centres do not allow the functioning of the entire machinery.

The selection of Commissars is, in practice, a duty imposed upon the assemblies by the Intelligence Service of the Party. The control of the new organs is assured by the sections which are introduced in such a manner that the Soviet governments are off-shoots of the Party rather than the representatives or mandatories of the population which has elected them. As soon as they are drawn up, the Soviet puts into force the rules dictated by the Communist Party with regard to finance and agrarian reforms.

54. **Finance, commerce, banks.** According to the principles promulgated in 1928 (see paragraph 24) all the existing taxes should be abolished and replaced by a special and progressive duty drawn from the revenue of the soil. The pecuniary difficulties of the rural population in the sovietized regions hardly permits them to pay the taxes in specie. They are paid in kind, each

producer placing at the disposition of the Soviet a fixed proportion of his harvest.

This financial resource was found to be inadequate and the Soviet has imposed other levies in kind or "fines" on the gentry, bourgeois, proprietors, business men, who have thus been reduced to misery. The small craftsmen, the retailers are not spared and they become gradually itinerant merchants, who are tolerated because of their democratic character.

The Soviets in China would like to follow the example of the U.S.S.R., and nationalize commerce and industry, but without possessing the necessary means for organizing the monopoly, the policy has not in practice been carried out. The "capitalist" banks have been replaced in certain regions by the labour and agricultural banks, which issue "Communist" notes with the effigy of Lenin and Karl Marx.

55. **Agrarian reform.** Agrarian reforms introduced in conformity to the eight general rules formulated in 1930 by the Party. The rules are:

1. To overthrow the political power of the gentry of the country [8] and of the official class, to disarm the counter-revolutionary forces and to furnish the farmers with weapons so that they may uphold the political power of the Soviets in the villages.

2. To confiscate all the lands and properties of the gentry and of big proprietors and to place them at the disposition of the local soviets in order that they may be divided among the peasants who do not

---

[8] The Communists include under this category big and middle class land-owners whose families have established themselves for a long time in the country and exercised a semi-feudal, semi-patriarchal influence. It can be called the small landed nobility if the notion of nobility as understood by European society of 18th century is sufficiently clear.

possess lands or who do not possess them in sufficient quantity.

3. To deliver to the local Soviets with a view to eventual distribution the immovable property of the ancestral temples of the monasteries, churches and other places of worship as well as all the immovable property of a public nature.

4. To reserve in each district a certain quantity of land to be distributed to the soldiers of the Soviet army, farmers and workers in order to assure their subsistence.

5. To declare null and void all contracts bearing a high interest as a result of borrowing on security, etc.

6. To destroy or declare null all title-deeds of land property and lease.

7. To improve agriculture by the reconstruction of farms, the development of irrigation, the adoption of measures for the prevention of droughts and floods by emigration, the establishment of agrarian banks and other co-operative enterprises giving credits at reasonable interest.

56. **Agrarian reform in Kiangsi.** This programme has been applied in Kaingsi under the following conditions:

1. All the lands in the territory, all the property belonging to the ancestral temples and other places of worship, the landed property of the gentry have been confiscated without reserve or exception: the land register, title-deeds and leases kept in the archives of the local administration have been burned. The boundaries have been removed so as to eliminate all traces of the rights of the original proprietors.

2. The local soviets then re-divide the land among all the able-bodied inhabitants without distinction of sex.

3. Children under 16 years of age, the aged and the invalid have no claim to the land, but the family or the house which takes care of them can claim a portion of the land corresponding to their needs. This portion must not exceed one quarter of the amount of land which the family or the house nominally has the right to claim. (This proposition is calculated to reduce, by elimination, the number of persons who constitute a burden to others and who, from the point of view of the Red Armies, are useless individuals.)

4. When a region is over-populated, the excess of the population is to be transported to districts less densely populated.

5. The land assigned to the families of the Red Army is cultivated by other families under the control of the local soviets.

57. **Organization of the proletariat.** The Communist Party, through the execution of its agrarian programme, hopes to obtain the support of the mass. It is especially interested in organizing the poor farmers, i.e. the agricultural labourers because they constitute the reserve from which can be drawn the necessary elements for organizing armed insurrections. With that aim in view, the Soviets often forbid the exportation of rice and other food products in order to lower their prices. This measure is naturally very popular with the urban proletariat. It is not appreciated by the producers whose profits are thereby reduced. The disparity between the price of rice in the sovietized regions and the normal, higher prices obtaining in the rest of the country affords the communist agitators an argument which they have made the best use of in attacking the Government.

A class war is thus organized in the sovietized regions where the Communist Party makes use of the lessons gained through the experience of the Russian Revolution in the villages. The farmers in moderate means are tolerated. But the well-to-do farmers are exposed to all kinds of attack. They are excluded from the civil or military organizations, for fear they might plot against the poor farmers for whose benefit they have been ousted and might thus create in the farming class internal dissensions which would weaken its force and deprive the Revolution of its principal support.

58. **Exclusion of well-to-do farmers.** The policy of excluding the well-to-do farmers who form the gentry of the country has been adopted by the Chinese Communist Party not without some difficulty. On account of the unique organization of the Chinese family, the local gentry is not like the Russian *kulak* a proprietor who has extended his land through his own work or the exploitation of the farmers less active than himself and who employs a proletariat of agricultural labourers. He is the chief of the family, the chief of the clan. He administers for the benefit of the members of the clan or the family the undivided patrimonial property which has been transmitted from generation to generation since time immemorial, and of which he considers himself as the trustee rather than as the proprietor. The hands which work under him for the common benefit are very often those of the descendants, subordinates or relatives who live in his household. Now it is from among the last class that the Red Militia or the Communist Youths are recruited, and tradition gives the gentry a patriarchal authority over them. Thus, it can be observed that even the military element of the Chinese Communist Party has hesitated to break up the ancient bond

27

which has been the foundation of the social structure of China and which many of them would not hesitate to support.

59. Class war in the country. Anti-Bolshevist reactions. Without taking note of these considerations, the propaganda for class war in the country,—necessary for co-ordinating the communist movement in the cities and villages,—has had as a result the formation of an opposition force which bears the name of the anti-Bolshevik Party under the direction especially of the well-to-do farmers who have been ruined by the economic and administrative measures adopted by the Soviet authorities. In certain regions this opposition has manifested itself in anti-bolshevist propaganda. In others, the dissatisfaction of a part of the rural population is transformed into an armed conflict against the Communists in the interior of the districts already sovietized, in which it was sometimes aided by the red troops themselves. These, as we have mentioned elsewhere, contain elements which are Bolshevik only in name and which are inclined to maintain the old traditional rural economy.

Thus, in December 1930, the soldiers of the 20th Red Army, fighting in southern Kiangsi, revolted against their commander Mao Tse-tung. They released the members of the Provincial Committee of the Communist Party, who, owing to their sympathy for the Anti-Bolshevik Party, had been arrested by order of the Political Committee of the army. They arrested at the same time the instructor of the Central Committee of the Chinese Communist Party, disarmed the cadets of the Military School and a part of the 12th Red Army. The Political Bureau of the Party and the Military Revolutionary Council had to employ big forces to suppress the rebellion.

60. **Administrative independence of local soviets.** Until then, the sovietized districts, all politically under the control of the Department for the sovietized areas of the Central Committee of the Party, were administratively independent of one another. They have no common or superior governmental organ. The arrangement has been frequently found to be inadequate, and so it was decided to remedy the situation at the conference of the representatives of the sovietized areas held in May 1930, where they agreed to raise the question before an All-China Congress of the Soviets meeting on November 7th, 1930, the anniversary of the Russian Revolution.

Being unable to complete the necessary preparations in time, the opening of the Congress was postponed first to December 11th, the commemoration day of the Revolution of Canton, then to February 11th, 1931. Then came the question of the elimination of Li Li-san and the campaign of suppression launched by Nanking. The Congress was adjourned on November 7th. It met again on the same day at Juichen.

61. **Creation of Soviet Central Government and regional governments.** The Congress voted upon the constitution of a provisional Central Soviet Government of China, with Mao Tse-tung as President and Shang Ying as Vice-President. Mao Tse-tung was formerly a student in the University of Peking, being in 1919 a member of the group for the study of Marxism. He organized the trade-union of coal-mine workers of Pinghsiang which was the centre of communist activity in Kiangsi and Hunan. He has assumed the political control of the

Red Armies of Hunan, Kiangsi and Fukien for a long time. He is an orthodox Communist, carrying out strictly the orders of the International, and opposed to all ideas of coalition of the Communist Party with any other Chinese political party.

With the formation of the Central Government, the Conference of Juichen has created six sectional or regional governments for the following regions:

1. South-west of Kiangsi.
2. The border districts of Fukien, Kiangsi and Kwangtung.
3. North-east of Kiangsi.
4. The border districts of Hupeh, Hunan and Anhui.
5. The border districts of Hunan, Hupeh and Kiangsi.
6. The border districts of Hunan and Hupeh.

The distribution of these regions indicates that the Communists know how to take advantage of the difficulty with which the provincial militia and the provincial governments combine their efforts of suppression. The border regions between two provinces, and especially between three provinces, are those where the police is the least effective.

The sub-divisions of the local soviets in the six regional governments are not known. Furthermore, it is not certain if the decisions of the Conference have been already put into force or if the Central and regional governments have been effectively organized with their branches and proper resources.

62. **Extension of sovietized areas.** In 1930, at the time when the sovietized areas were most extensive, it was estimated that 181 districts (sub-prefects) in the

interior were under Soviet administration. One hundred of these districts, the equivalent of nearly two provinces, were then outside of the control of the National Government. Those 181 districts were distributed as follows:

Kiangsi.	57
Hupeh.	39
Hunan.	22
Fukien.	14
Kwangtung.	24
Kwangsi.	12
Szechuen.	6
Honan.	3
Anhui.	4

The number has diminished since then, particularly after the campaign of 1931. It does not seem at the present moment that there are more than 80 districts where the local soviets have their influence.

The charts annexed here give the situation which existed at the moment when the punitive campaign of 1931 ended on the whole unsuccessfully, that is, at a time when the red influence was more extensive than at the present moment. A careful study shows that the bolshevized regions, though occupying a considerable area, are not so vast or compact as is often described in the press.

4. The Labour Movement.

63. **Labour unions. Pan-Chinese Federation.** The first labour unions of China were organized in Canton in 1917. These unions fell under the influence of the Communists in 1922 after the first conference of labour organizations which took place at Canton in the month of May of that year attended by 160 delegates representing 300,000 trade-unionists.

The second trade-union conference, composed of 250 delegates representing 570,000 trade-unionists, took place in May 1925, also at Canton. The conference created the Pan-Chinese Trade-Union Federation as the supreme organ of labour organizations, the direction and control of which was entrusted to the Chinese Communist Party. Since that time the influence of the Party on the trade-unions has been growing from day to day reaching its zenith in February 1927, on the verge of the capture of Shanghai by the Nationalists. Shanghai at that time had 289,000 trade-union workers. At the head of their professional organizations was the General Union which, desiring to forestall the action of the Government troops, put to flight the northern troops and tried to organize a local government. That attempt, the success of which would have placed the whole of Shanghai into the hands of the Communists, was frustrated by the Nationalist Government. The local government was dissolved, its leaders, all influential members of the Communist Party, were either executed or disappeared; the General Union was suppressed, and the trade-unions were re-organized with the expulsion of communist elements.

That re-organization was effected in conformity with labour laws promulgated by the Nationalist Government. The "purified" or reorganized labour unions were registered and recognized by the competent authorities. These alone have a legal existence.

64. **Red trade-unions.** The majority of the communist leaders of the labour movement having been expelled from the labour organizations, the Party was obliged to create red trade-unions which were not recognized by law and were consequently secret organizations or to bring spies secretly into the organized trade-unions. The first red trade-unions were formed at the beginning of 1928

and, from that time on, played an important part in the strikes and other labour movements which have occurred at Shanghai.

According to official statistics of the Party, the number of unionist communists at Shanghai was increased at the end of 1929 to 60,000 out of a total of 262,000. The figures for the red unionists in other industrial centres of China are not known, but it is surmised that they vary between 15% and 20% of the total number of unionist workers.

65. Diminution of activity. The policy of Li Li-shan, who aimed at transforming the red trade-unions into committees of action, had from June of 1930 a disastrous influence on the work and even the existence of the red trade-unions. Engaged in questions of a purely political nature, these trade-unions ceased to occupy themselves with the organization and education of labour groups, which caused them to lose the sympathy of the masses and diminish their strength considerably.

66. Technical organization of red trade-unions. From the technical point of view, the red labour movement in China is directed by the Pan-Chinese Trade-Union Federation, which, though under the orders of the Secretariat of the Red Labour International of Moscow, co-ordinates its activity with the Labour Movement Department of the Central Committee of the Chinese Communist Party.

The red labour movement in China, as in all other countries of the world where it has been started, is based on the "industrial" principle according to which all workers working in any enterprise or industry whatever must form a union for that enterprise, irrespective of their real profession, and without taking into consideration the kind of occupation ("corporative" principle) to which they belong. Thus the mechanics of the mills, factories, tramways, etc., do not form a corporative union of mechanics. They are divided among the industrial trade-unions of mills, factories, municipal employees, etc. The trade-unions of the different enterprises forming part of the same industrial branch compose the General Federation of Trade-Unions of the industry in question.

From the administrative point of view, the red trade-unions are based upon the territorial principle, that is, all the labour unions of a province, of a city, of a district, etc., are controlled by the councils of the province, city, district, etc.

67. Shanghai. At Shanghai, which is the most important labour centre, the red trade-unions are divided into 4 principal groups:

1. General trade-union of workers of metallurgical factories.

2. General trade-union of mill workers.

3. General trade-union of workers of maritime transportation.

4. General trade-union of municipal employees.

68. Action in the recognized unions. As to the unions recognize by law, the Communists exercise their influence over them through the intermediary of secret groups or bodies. All the members of the red unions are affiliated with the official unions, and that facilitates the activity of the Chinese Communist Party within the ranks of the latter.

69. Actual state of the movement. All the organization, which we have mentioned above, has undergone changes as a result of the schism of Li Li-shan and of the Government's punitive campaign of 1931.

The Pan-Chinese Trade-Union Federation does not consist, according to the latest communist statistics, of more than 34,380 members of red unionists, about 25,000 of whom are in the Sovietized areas where they are mingled with the organized local soviets. In May 1931, the Secretariat of the Pan-Pacific Union estimated the number of red unionist workers at Shanghai at 2,492. In each of the twelve principal Chinese railways, there is a red union of railwaymen. The most important was that of the Peiping-Mukden line, consisting of seven local unions with more than 500 members. The recent events in Manchuria probably have dissolved them. Next comes the union of the Peiping-Hankow line, one of the earliest and the most active, with about 400 members. The union of the Tientsin-Pukow line does not contain more than 70 members. In all, the railwaymen unions may have 2,000 members.

The Federation of Labour Unions of Maritime Transportation consists of five unions, Shanghai, Tientsin, Hongkong, Canton, Hankow, with about 400 members. As the sailors are for the most part on the sea, they are not particularly active.

70. **Retrogression.** The figures given above agree again with the remarks we have made in paragraph 44 as regards the present conditions of the Communist Party, and show that labour activities have decreased for the last year, indicating that the red labour movement in China is subsiding.

CHAPTER V.   CONCLUSION.

71. Particular form of Communist danger in China. The Communist danger in China assumes a special form. The Communists here are not like those in countries outside of Soviet Russia who simply form a political party, spreading propaganda, seeking to increase their membership, presenting candidates for the elections, succeeding sometimes to have a majority in the municipal council of a city or community, but, with a few exceptions, confining their activity within the limits fixed by the legislation of the country, and seeking, if only for the moment, to realize their policy only by constitutional methods.

In China, the Communist Party is in open rebellion against the constitution, against the laws, against the National Government and against the constituted provincial authorities. It has its own army or armies, which oppose the regular forces, and sometimes even baffle them. It has its own government, its own administration organized in conformity with its own principles; it has its own laws, formulated after those of the U.S.S.R. In the regions brought within its authority, it puts into practice at least a part of its socialistic theories. It is in these respects that the Chinese Communist Party differs from that in the rest of the world and is altogether unique.

72. Tide of new ideas. Its development has been due to the particular conditions through which China has been passing for some twenty years. On the one hand, the growing consciousness in the mind of the Chinese people of their technical inferiority as compared with the western nations has caused them to overthrow a part of the venerable tradition upon which their social structure is founded. A stream of new ideas has spread in the country. Ideas of emancipation, liberty, democracy, often ill-understood and ill-digested by the mass, have grown with great rapidity. The reactions of the Great War, the famous 14 Points of President Wilson have raised great hopes. At the same time, there was Dr. Sun Yat-sen and the Kuomintang Party popularizing the triple idea of national independence, democratic government, and social organization. The result is an enthusiasm, an ardent desire, to reform, to reconstruct, and to revolutionize. The Chinese Communists utilized this psychological moment for the spread of extremist ideas.

73. **Political upheavals.** On the other hand, the march of political events has not fulfilled the expectations of the masses. The Manchu Dynasty fell because it failed in its mission; its political conceptions and administrative machinery could no longer answer the new requirements. Unfortunately most of the Governments at Peking established after the formation of the Republic, tried to govern by the same old and feudal methods, allowing the cupidity of the military governors of the provinces to become unbounded. Then came a series of civil wars which have ruined and devastated the country during the past ten years. The Nationalist Government has been able to give the Three Principles of Dr. Sun Yat-sen a fair trial, but recalcitrance on the part of what remains of militarism and differences of opinion within the Party itself have resulted in further armed conflicts, and the state of upheaval in the country has been prolonged. That furnishes to the Communists unexpected opportunities for propaganda and action. Besides, they have been profited

and aided by the counsels, agents and subsidies of the Third International.

74. Ravages of Communism. Massacres. Ruins. Fortunately, from the practical point of view, the Chinese have not been slow in perceiving that the millennium which the communists promise to usher in is a mirage. If the soviet governments of certain regions had sometimes adopted measures which were welcomed by the population, these advantages cannot be compared with the ruin caused by the soviet dispensation, by its various military activities and the establishment of soviet administrations.

In a report presented to the People's Convention on May 5th, 1931, the Government made the following estimate of the damages inflicted by the communists upon the population of Kiangsi:

Individuals massacred..........	186,000
Those obliged to flee and take refuge in the non-sovietized regions.....................	2,100,000
Loss of personal property.......	$630,000,000
Houses burned.................	100,000

and on that of Honan:

Individuals massacred..........	72,000
Houses burned.................	120,000
Loss of personal property.......	$300,000,000

The Provincial Government of Kiangsi has recently given out information to the effect that there are at the present moment in the province more than 500,000 "refugees of war", in other words, more than 500,000 persons who have fled from the sovietized regions.

One can easily imagine what the effect of that exodus is upon the population. In a general manner, the Chinese farmer can hardly distinguish the communist from the ordinary bandit, the communist being often a former bandit and behaving as such.

75. Diminution of the power of production and consumption. If the new distribution of land helped in certain respects to solve an acute agrarian problem, it has on the other hand, through the persecution of the well-to-do farmers, deprived the country of its best elements. The area of cultivation has diminished, the general output has been considerably reduced, the power of production and consumption of the farmer class has decreased. The exportation and importation figures of the regions, published by the Maritime Customs, give enlightening proof of these statements.[9]

76. Chinese common sense detests Communism. But other more profound causes account for the Chinese aversion to Communism. At first, Communism has a certain mystical halo around it. It is a belief, and for some of its followers, a religion. But, the Chinese, brought up in the positivist and pragmatic philosophy of Confucius, are not mystical at all. The human element always ultimately triumphs over the speculative element. Mysticism is an innate spiritual disposition. It cannot be created in a milieu which is unfavourable to it. Even when the Chinese are carried away by a fit of passion, his strong common sense comes back to him after a period of mental unequilibrium, and he again lives in his traditional concepts.

What is more, the Chinese is very individualistic in his opinions. It is necessary to appeal to his reason in order to make him change them. He is not inclined to follow

[9] Full extracts and discussion of these figures, with comparisons from year to year, would require amplification out of proportion with the size of the present memorandum.

the ways of others by simple discipline, but that and the
subordination of the faculty of individual criticism to dic-
tation by the Party are precisely the essential characteristics of Communism.

**77. The Chinese family opposes to communist indi-
vidualism.** Communism considers society as being
formed of individuals grouped according to their social
functions, but not according to their personal sentiments
or affections. This idea is alien to the Chinese who regard family duties as being of great importance. Communism tends to destroy the family by the relaxation of
the conjugal bonds by entrusting the State with the care
and education of children and by the abolition of private
property. But tradition and the respect for ancestors
are important Chinese social characteristics. It is the
family which for the Chinese is at the bottom of social
structure. Even in the most modern cities like Shanghai,
many of the great Chinese enterprises, corporations,
banks, etc. are either in the possession of or managed by
families or groups of families. Participation in a business on a joint-stock basis or the meeting of shareholders
who are not conjugally related for starting a business,
is a western idea which has only recently been introduced
into China.

After filial piety which ruins communist teaching,
conjugal fidelity is the most important moral element in
the institution of the family in China. Free love, facility
in divorce, the dissolution of conjugal union by the simple wish of one of the parties, the practice of extra-con-
jugal unions, the creation, as we have been often told in
the sovietized districts of groups of "comforters" to
"refresh" the red soldiers in the course of their expeditions, are shocking to the Chinese who otherwise might
be inclined to accept the economic doctrines of the Third

International. The ideal of the moderate-minded Chinese is to work for the prosperity of his family and the continuation of his line.

78. **The Chinese attached to individual property.** Economically speaking, China is still in a backward state: she is still in the stage of agricultural life and family industry. Large scale manufacture and mass production have hardly begun to take root. The working proletariat which constitutes the foundation of communist organizations represents only the smallest percentage of the population. The strong organization of the corporations presents a bulwark almost impossible for the penetration of communism in the family industry. Furthermore the landed property is very well partitioned. The majority of the farmers possess personally or through the family the land they cultivate. There they work with their children and with one or two wage-earners, who form, so to speak, a part of the family. Like all the farmers of the world, they have a simple and clear notion of individual property, a love for the bit of land upon which their ancestors and they themselves have lived, and a strong idea that they should not be deprived of it.

79. **The Kuomintang expresses the political ideas of the population.** The Kuomintang has therefore responded adequately to the political conceptions of the Chinese people when from the beginning it pitted itself against the marxist idea of class war and the dictatorship of the proletariat, and made every effort to realize the programme of the Three Principles of Dr. Sun Yat-sen. It has never deviated from its original stand. It has always professed hostility towards communism, and if in its fight against the latter it has not always achieved the success it desired, the fault was not due to the Kuomintang but to circumstances.

80. **Gravity of the Communist danger.** In spite of the renewed efforts in the course of the last few years for its destruction, communism remains in China a serious danger because it has threatened the country during one of those crisis of social and political evolution which always leaves a nation in a state of temporary weakness, and because the internal crisis is complicated, for the last year, by an external crisis of the greatest importance and magnitude.

It is not easy for any government under similar circumstances to face domestic difficulties in the political, administrative, and financial domain aggravated by the disasters of a flood of unprecedented proportions, and at the same time to stem the tide of a foreign aggression, absolutely unjustified as it was unexpected, while still having to devote its attention to the solution of the communist problem with the firmness it requires.

It is not to be doubted, however, that if a prompt remedy cannot be found, the communist danger may continue to extend to the point of threatening the very foundations of the social organization of China. From what we have said in this memorandum as regards the relationship which exists between the Chinese Communist Party and the Third International and the discipline which the majority of the Chinese Communist leaders receive in the execution of the instructions from Moscow, we can readily see what the political orientation in China would be if the influence of the Comintern really dominates.

81. **Determination of the Chinese Government to extinguish Communism. Necessity of a just solution of the Manchuria dispute.** This political orientation the Government of Nanking is determined to suppress through the campaign which it is launching against the sovietized areas in the central portions of the country. But in order

to assure a successful campaign, it is clear that China should not be handicapped in her important task by any complications arising from the North-eastern horizon. It is necessary that the question of the Three Eastern Provinces should be solved on the condition that the dignity and the supreme interests of China will be safeguarded through the respect of her territorial and administrative integrity, and that any idea of the possibility of new differences arising between our country and the neighbouring Empire will be eliminated.

82. **Economic relief of sovietized regions.** Finally, real success of the campaign against the communists depends perhaps less upon military operations successfully conducted against the Red Armies than upon the rehabilitation of the sovietized regions re-conquered, and upon the economic relief of the regions which communism has devastated. The Government has prepared a programme of public works, particularly as regards the construction of means of communication which would furnish work to the impoverished population, increase the productivity of the country, re-establish peace and order, facilitate the necessary administrative reforms and especially prevent the return of the demoralizing conditions which those regions previously went through and which were the principal reason for the success of communist propaganda.

Peiping, July 29th 1932.

APPENDIX.

A. LAWS RELATING TO THE URGENT SUPPRESSION OF CRIMES AGAINST THE REPUBLIC.

Promulgated by the National Government on January 31st of the 20th Year of the Republic of China (1931) and enforced on March 1st of the same year.

(A translation)

Artcle 1. Whoever, planning to threaten the Republic, by committing one of the following acts, shall be punished by death:

1. Disturbing peace and order,
2. entering into secret relationship with a foreign country in order to disturb peace and order,
3. associating with rebels in order to disturb peace and order,
4. instigating a military person to commit a non-disciplinary act, or to cause him to fail in the performance of his duty or to associate with rebels.

Article 2. Whoever, planning to threaten the Republic by committing one of the following acts, shall be punished with death or life imprisonment.

I. Instigating another person to disturb peace and order or to associate with rebels,
2. conducting a campaign of propaganda against the State by writing, sketching or speech-making.

Article 3. Whoever, committing one of the following acts, shall be punished by life imprisonment or imprisonment of more than ten years:

1. Committing a non-disciplinary act, failing in the performance of his duty or associating with rebels on the instigation of the criminal indicated in No. 4 of Artcle 1,
2. disturbing peace and order or associating with rebels on the instigation of the criminal indicated in No. 1 of Article 2,
3. conducting propaganda on the instigation of the criminal indicated in No. 2 of Article 2.

Whoever having committed one of the crimes specified in the preceding paragraphs on immediately and voluntarily reporting, shall receive an attenuation or exoneration of the penalty.

Article 4. Whoever, having knowledge that a certain individual is a rebel, shelters him without giving notification to the competent authorities, shall be punished by an imprisonment of more than five years.

Whoever, having committed the crime specified in the preceding paragraph, immediately and voluntarily reports, shall receive an attenuation or exoneration of the penalty.

Article 5. Whoever, planning to threaten the Republic by committing one of the following acts, shall be punished with death, or life imprisonment or imprisonment of more than ten years:

1. Obtaining or transporting military supplies for the rebels,
2. revealing or transmitting to the rebels military and political secrets,
3. destroying means of communication.

Article 6. Whoever, planning to threaten the Republic by organizing associations or unions or spreading doctrines incompatible with the " Three Principles of the People " shall be punished by an imprisonment of from at least five years to at most fifteen years.

Article 7. Whoever committing one of the crimes specified by the present law in a region under a state of siege shall be tried by the highest military organ in that region: If he commits the crime within the limits of the suppression of banditry, he shall be tried by a provisional court composed of the magistrate of the district and two judicial officials.

The provisional court shall be established in the district and the magistrate shall be designated as the president of the court.

Article 8. In case a crime is tried by a military organ in conformity with the present law, that organ shall submit a statement of the trial to the competent superior military organ and the sentence shall be executed only after the approval of the latter. If the crime is tried by a provisional court, the court shall submit a statement of the trial to the superior court and the sentence shall be executed only after the approval of the latter; the case shall also be reported to the provincial government for reference.

The competent superior military organ or the superior court if it doubts the judgment passed by the organ which is its subordinate, can give to that organ an order for re-examination, or designate a special delegate to be present at the reconsideration of the judgment.

Article 9. The military organ or police which arrests a person suspected of having committed one of the infractions specified by the present law, shall report the matter immediately to the interested competent authorities.

Article 10. To all that does not fall within the limits of the present law, the provisions of the Penal Code are applicable.

Article 11. The duration of the application of the present law and the date of its enforcement shall be fixed by ordinance.

The provisional law suppressing the anti-revolutionary plots shall be repealed from the date of the enforcement of the present law.

B1. THE STATE OF THE RED ARMIES IN 1930.

Number of Divisions	Number of Rifles	Commander	Place of Activity
1	9,000	Hsu Chi-shen	Border districts of Honan and Anhui
2	4,000	Ho Lung	Border districts of Hunan and Hupeh
3	5,000	Huang Kung-lai	East of Kiangsi
4	3,000	Chou Teh	Center of Kiangsi
5	7,000	Kwang Chi-hsun	West of Kiangsi
6	6,000	Peng Te-huai	Border districts of Hunan and Hupeh
7	9,000	Chang Yun-yi	West of Kiangsi
8	2,000	Ho Cheng-tang	North-west of Kiangsi
9	7,000	Tsai Chen-si	North of Hupeh
10	1,000	Fang Chih-min	North-east of Kiangsi
11	1,000	Kuo Tao-tsou	North-east of Kwangtunge
12	2,000	Lin Pia	Border districts of Honan and Kiangsi
13	2,000	Hu Kou-mien	West of Chekiang
14		Li Chao-shih	Nantung
15		Cheng Tse-ping	Su-Chow
16	3,000	Li Shih-sin	Border districts of Hunan and Kiangsi
17			
18			
19			
20	2,000	Liu Ti-chao	West of Fukien
21	2,000	Tuan Kan-nin	West of Fukien
22	1,000	Chen Yi	West of Kiangsi
Total.........	66,000		

B2. STATE OF RED ARMIES IN MAY, 1931.

Unit	Commander	Political commissariat	Number of men	Number of rifles	Machine guns	Cannons	Trench mortars
1st Army	Hsu Chi-shen	Tsao-Ta-ching	5,000	3,000	32	1	4
2nd Army	Ho Lung	Fen Tai-ying	5,800	4,100	113	2	8
3rd Army	Chou Teh	Mao Tse-tung	14,000	8,800	157	10	16
4th Army	Siao Fang		5,000	3,000	45	2	6
5th Army	Peng Te-huai	Ten Tai-yuan	15,000	8,500	61	3	4
			1,000	800	:	:	:
6th Army	Kuang Chi-hsun	Lih Ke-ming	5,900	4,500	60	4	5
			2,800	1,200	:	:	:
7th Army	Chang Yun-yi	Teng Hsi-hsien	3,000	2,000	52	2	8
Detachment of Li Ming-jui			2,800	1,300	26	:	3
8th Army	Huang Kung-lai	Teng Chien-yuen	5,000	3,200	25	1	2
10th Army	Fang Chih-min	Shao Shih-ping	13,000	4,800	30	1	1
12th Army	Wu Chung-hao	Tan Tseng-ling	5,000	3,000	31	:	4
Army of Tuan Te-chang			2,600	1,500	38	1	2
16th Army	Kung Ho-chung	Wu Tien-yi	6,800	100	30	:	5
20th Army	Mao Tse-tung		19,200	5,850	48	2	4
22nd Army	Chen Yi		5,500	2,100	20	:	2
Total			117,400	57,750	768	29	74

B3. THE STATE OF THE RED ARMIES IN JANUARY, 1932.

Unit	Commander	Centre of Operations or General Headquarters	Number of men	Number of rifles
1st Group of Armies (3rd, 4th and 12th armies)	Chou Teh	Jouikin	50,000	50,000
3rd Group of Armies (5th, 8th and 22nd armies)	Huang Kung-lai	South-west of Fukien	50,000	50,000
7th Army	Li Ming-jui	Lienhwa-Kanchow	10,000	5,000
1st "independent" Division	Liu Wan-tseng	Lienhwa	2,800	1,300
16th Army	Kung Co-chung	Hsiuhui	9,500	4,000
10th Army	Fang Chih-min	North-east of Kiangsi	5,000	3,000
19th Army	Li Seng-ying	Border districts of Kiangsi-Hupeh-Hunan	3,500	2,100
Red Army of the Kiangsi-Hunan border districts.	Cheng Chao	Chaling	4,500	2,300
6th Army	Tuan Te-chang	Region of Hunghu lake	10,000	5,300
2nd Army	Ho Lung	West of Hupeh	12,500	8,600
4th Group of Red Armies	Hsu Chi-shen			
1st Army	Hsu Chi-shen	Border districts of Hupeh-Honan-Anhwei	10,000	7,000
9th Army	Kuang Chi-hsun	North-east of Hupeh	15,000	8,000
14th Army	Tong Fang	South-east of Honan	18,000	6,000
Total...............			200,800	152,600

B4. THE STATE OF THE RED ARMIES IN JUNE, 1932.

Number of Army Corps	Strength	Number of rifles	Commander
1	21,000	12,000	Chou Teh
2	9,000	6,000	Ho Lung
3	12,000	9,000	Peng Te-huai
4	6,000	2,000	Li Nien-hui
5	7,000	5,000	Ki Chen-tou
6	8,000	6,000	Hsu Chi-shen
7	5,000	4,000	Ling Piao
8	7,200	6,000	Tuan Te-chang
9	5,000	5,000	Li Keh
10	4,500	2,000	Chou Kien-pei
11	4,000	3,000	Lo Ping-hui
12	2,000	1,200	Tou Chen-tan
13	2,200	2,100	Tien Tse-huei
Total........	92,900	63,300	

C. THE PROGRAMME OF POLITICAL AND ECONOMIC REHABILITATION IN CONNECTION WITH THE CAMPAIGN AGAINST THE COMMUNISTS.

As has been stated in the text of the present Memorandum, real success of the campaign against the Communists depends more upon the rehabilitation of the sovietized regions, either actually re-occupied or in the course of being re-occupied, and upon the economic relief of the regions which communism has devastated (para. 82). It is now proposd to set forth in the following pages the political and economic programme the National Government has adopted for this purpose.

I. Political Measures During the Period of the Campaign.

The measures adopted consist of the following: 1. Political Rehabilitation. 2. Enforcement of Relief Measures. 3. Strict Supervision.

1. Political Rehabilitation.

Realizing that in the regions devastated by the Communists in Kiangsi the people usually have little corporate organization, the Central Party Headquarters has hastened to devise and adopt schemes for reorganizing popular bodies in the sovietized regions and for the re-adjustment of the methods of popular training in order to curb the efforts of the Communists to delude the common people.

In 1929, the National Government passed the laws for the suppression of banditry by the National Army and the laws for the maintenance of peace for the villages. It also adopted measures for census taking, drew up forms for house-numbers, and regulations governing joint responsibility of neighbours when crimes are committed. Further apprehending that the people may still lack rigorous organization the Government has modified the old practice and passed regulations of *Pao-chia* in the sovietized regions for the purpose of mutual supervision so that there may not be any misprision of felony. There have also been promulgated regulations for the examination of householders in the sovietized regions. Families are investigated according to their order in

the system of *Pao-chia* in every ward,[10] are re-examined once
every month and examined by lot once every three months. This
is to make it difficult for the undesirable elements to mix themselves among the inhabitants and so to lessen the danger of these
inhabitants being led into improper ways of thinking and acting.
The measures enumerated above have been enforced in Kiangsi
Province.

In all the regions devastated by the Communists and since the
establishment of the Party Political Council, the district magistrates, as regards the areas in their respective districts in which
villages had been pillaged by the bandits, houses destroyed or
large numbers of able-bodied men had died or fled away so that
agricultural fields had been laid waste, immediately investigate
into the actual conditions of the land and other taxes and report
to the Party Political Council with a view to reducing their amount
or to postponing their collection in order to relieve the hardship
of the inhabitants.

2. Enforcement of Relief Measures.

As the haunts of the Communists are usually in high and pre-
cipitous mountains, rendering punitive expeditions against them
exceedingly difficult, and as able-bodied men in regions devastated
by the Communists who are suddenly deprived of their means of
livelihood are easily misled by the pretentious and voluble Communists, the Central Government has established as a means of
coping with all demoralizing forces Road Construction Labour
Relief Bureaux in the sovietized regions in Kiangsi province, to
which are sent by the Party Political Council labourers who are
selected from amongst the able-bodied men in the districts under
its jurisdiction, and who are employed in the construction of public highways. On the one hand this plan affords facility to the
campaign against the Communists, and on the other supplies the
afflicted people, especially those who are young and vigorous and
of use to society, with food and clothing so that they may not have
recourse to banditry.

If any great number of refugees who have been harassed by the

---

[10] In this system, each family is given a plate setting forth the name
of its head and other male members therein. Ten families compose a *Pai*,
ten *Pai* form into one *Chia* and ten *Chia* make up one *Pao*.

communists should gather in one locality without food and shelter, the Bureaux of Urgent Relief are established in the districts concerned to keep a record of them and to afford them asylum. The refugees are sent back to their native villages within a fixed period. Those whose villages are still menaced by banditry or who are unwilling to return home though their villages are not within the sovietized regions, are sent to the Road Construction Labour Relief Bureaux for work.

Inhabitants who have been coerced by the communists into joining their rank, on the latter being dispersed or routed by the National Army or surrendering, are escorted by the troops in the front to designated places to be interned in quarters specially established for them.

The labour relief for the sovietized regions is mainly for the construction of public highways. There is established in each locality a relief office attached to the Road Construction Labour Relief Bureau from which as many technical experts or managers as necessary may be detached for service, who draw no additional salary for their concurrent post. Labourers employed in the roads are supplied by the district magistrate concerned from the Internment Quarters for Bandit Prisoners.

The Road Construction Labour Relief Bureau according to the projected roads decided upon is commencing work in sections. The Bureau has also designated certain places to which labourers are sent from the nearest Bureaux of Urgent Relief of designated districts. The Bureau of Urgent Relief in each district supplies labourers in accordance with Article 9 of the "Regulations for Urgent Relief." The Quarters of Internment supplies labourers in accordance with Article 5 of the "Regulations Governing the Disposal of Bandit Prisoners."

Labourers employed in road construction in connection with labour relief are each given a dole of 40 cents a day in lieu of wages which is distributed by the Road Construction Labour Relief Bureau on the spot. The Labour Relief will be suspended with the completion of the projected roads. If by that time the Bureau of Public Highway is required to construct other public roads, all the labourers will be supplied by the Road Construction Labour Relief Bureau from amongst those who have established the best record or who are willing to continue to work. These labourers will be accorded the same treatment as ordinary working men. The remaining labourers not so engaged will be sent back to their respective native places.

3. Strict Supervision.

As a measure of encouragement, the Party Political Council from time to time, strictly supervises and decides upon matters relating to the activities of the local Party headquarters and popular organizations, the administration of local authorities or special organs, the actual state of services rendered by the Party and political workers, the form and contents of the petitions of local popular bodies concerning Party or political affairs, and the measures of reward or discipline of the Party or political workers.

II. Political Measures After the Reconquest of the Sovietized Regions.

The measures adopted in this connection consist of: 1. Pacification of the People. 2. Restoration of Rural Economics.

1. Pacification of the People.

After the reoccupation of a district within the regions where a campaign against the communists has been conducted, the magistrate concerned would, on the one hand, issue proclamations inviting refugees to return to their homes without delay. Those refugees who are devoid of the means of returning to their native places may petition the magistrate of the district where they happen to be with regard to the true state of their affairs so that they may be assisted by him at his discretion in their homeward journey. On the other hand, the magistrate of the reoccupied district selects several persons of good reputation from amongst those inhabitants who have remained in their native city or village who are charged with the duty of ascertaining independently the location and the number of refugees, and to advise the clansmen, neighbours or those who are related to the refugees to arrange for their speedy return. The district magistrate also communicates to the people the measures adopted by the Government for re-assembling the refugees.

With regard to the enforcement of this measure, there has been promulgated the procedure to be followed by the Party Political

Council of the Headquarters of the Commander-in-Chief of the Land, Sea and Air Forces governing the re-assembling of refugees.

Inhabitants who had really been coerced into submission by the communists may file, with the magistrate concerned, and subject to his approval, bonds of sincere penitence to be attested to or guaranteed by their fathers, elder brothers, chiefs of clans or upright and reputable gentry or elders of their respective ward. Those who are really penitent and return home on their own accord, and who have not received any important appointments from the communists or have not committed any serious crimes, may furnish bonds of sincere penitence to be guaranteed by their respective fathers, elder brothers, and five neighbours, such bonds to be submitted to the magistrate of the district concerned for his approval.

With regard to the enforcement of this measure, there have been passed regulations of the Party Political Council of the Headquarters of the Commander-in-Chief of the Land, Sea and Air Forces relating to the reconcilement of people coerced into submission or penitent in the regions where the campaigns against the communists are being conducted.

Inhabitants of districts within the regions for communist suppression, in the event of discovering communists lurking in the locality or any underhand dealings with them, must secretly report the fact to the competent authorities to be dealt with according to law. Those who have brought false accusations out of spite (of malice forethought) are subject to the same penalty for the offences charged. The judge who sits in trial of persons suspected of associating with the rebels, must be particularly careful during the time of examination and must not involve others. If relatives of inhabitants in the various districts have drifted into the sovietized regions and are rendering services to the communists or holding bogus offices under them, the authorities concerned, upon discovering the relatives who remain as residents in the localities to be innocent of any conspiracy, treat them as peaceful citizens and do not involve them into any joint criminal liability.

With regard to the enforcement of this measure, there have been promulgated regulations of the Party Political Council of the Headquarters of the Commander-in-Chief of the Land, Sea and Air Forces with respect to the prohibition of false accusation and joint liability for crimes in the different districts within the regions for the suppression of communists.

2. Restoration of Rural Economics.

Farmers banks have been established, of which the organization, capital and business are as follows:

(1) Organization.—These farmers' banks are divided into provincial and district banks. Provincial banks are established in the provincial capital and the district banks in the different districts. However, prior to the establishment of the district banks, the provincial bank establish branch offices there for the transaction of business.

(2) Capital.—The capital of the bank is temporarily fixed at $5,000,000. Business will be commenced upon $2,500,000 being paid in full out of relief funds. The remaining sum will be subscribed to by the credit co-operative societies in the various localities within five years of their formation, the aim of such banks being their ultimate operation by the people.

(3) Business.—The business is to make loans to credit co-operative societies for short terms (within 8 months) or for medium terms (within three years); to deal in fixed deposits; to transact rural remittance; to collect and to transmit funds for farmers; to issue loan bonds (the total amount of issuance shall, in accordance with the general regulations governing farmers banks, not exceed so many times the total amount of the paid-up capital); and to issue notes in exchange for subsidiary coins in order to meet local requirements.

Delegates are sent to localities recovered from the communists to give guidance to land-owners, farmers cultivating their own land and tenant-farmers in rural communities for the formation, in accordance with regulations governing co-operative societies, of co-operative societies concerning credit, farm product, consumption, transportation and other matters. As a beginning, credit co-operative societies will first be organized, while the other kinds of societies will be taken up only as the actual requirements of the rural communities concerned rise. As to the order of precedence of the various rural communties, those nearest to the city of a district will be given priority for the purpose of showing encouragement.

The organization of a credit co-operative society is briefly as follows:

(1) Its business is to make loans to its members at a low rate of interest with the object of effecting farm rehabilitation.

(2) Its liability is unlimited and shared jointly by all its members.

(3) All land-owners, proprietor-farmers and tenant-farmers are entitled to its membership, but each household is limited to one member only. Each society has at least nine members, and in case there are less than nine men in a village, it can be formed out of two or more villages.

(4) Its capital stock is $10 per share, to be paid in instalments covering a period of five years. Each member subscribes to at least one share. The right of shareholders is in conformity with the units of membership.

(5) The purpose of its loan is temporarily limited to supplying requirements actually indispensable to farm rehabilitation.

(6) Its rate of interest does not exceed a definite low percentage per month.

The organization of a rural co-operative society is briefly as follows:

(1) Its business is to promote mutual benefit and increase production by the setting up of equipments for common use in a rural community, such as public stores, water-wheels, etc.

(2) It assumes the responsibility of a surety.

(3) Its membership consists of all those engaged in agricultural pursuits.

(4) The shares of the society are five dollars each, to be paid up in instalments covering a period of five years.

The organization of a consumers' co-operative society is briefly as follows:

(1) The business of the society has for its object the supply to its members of daily necessaries, and tools required for farm production, particularly farming implements, buffaloes, seeds, etc.

(2) It assumes the responsibility of a surety.

(3) Its membership is open to any one in the village who has a lawful calling.

(4) Its shares are five dollars each payable in instalments for a period of five years.

The organization of a co-operative transportation society is briefly as follows:

(1) The business of the society is for the object of facilitating the movement and sale of farm products of its members.

(2) It assumes the responsibility of a surety.

(3) Its membership is open to all who have farm products for transportation and sale.

(4) Its shares are five dollars each payable in instalments in five years.

III. Establishment of Rural Rehabilitation Committee.

Rural Rehabilitation Committees are established to take charge of districts and villages where lands have been distributed by the communists. The chief duty of such committees is the distribution of farming rights and the adjustment of proprietary rights on agricultural lands. Prior to such adjustments being definitely made, the agricultural lands in a district are placed under the control of the Rural Rehabilitation Committee of that locality for the purpose of distributing them for farming so as to meet the emergency of the case and to avoid non-cultivation. Such a committee is known as Rural Rehabilitation Committee of a certain village or of a certain town. Its organization and function is as follows:—

(1) Organization.—The committees are of three kinds; namely the district committee, the ward committee and the village or mart committee. In a district committee, the magistrate is the chairman, with chiefs of divisions of his office and representatives from the different wards as its members. In a ward committee, the chief of the ward is its chairman with a representative from each of the villages in the ward as members. In a village committee, the chief of the *pao* (1,000 families) is its chairman, with four inhabitants of the village who have lawful business as its members, such members to be elected by householders and chiefs of *chia* (100 families). Regulations governing its organization in

detail will be promulgated separately. In dealing with its affairs, the Rural Rehabilitation Committee is guided by the rulings of the village or mart committee. Things which can not be decided by the village or mart committee are passed upon by the ward committee, and those matters which can not be settled by the ward committee are finally disposed of by the district committee.

(2) Functions.—The functions of such committees are of four kinds. The following is a brief account of the function in connection with the disposal of farming rights of land, leaving the others out of consideration:

The committee in its management of the lands under its control apportions the farming rights according to the number of persons to be supported. An adult can undertake to cultivate so much land as its products are sufficient for his support, the area for which shall be decided by the committee of a locality in accordance with its fertility or otherwise. A minor shall be allowed to cultivate one-half of this amount. The rent payable for each *mou* of land, that is to say, the share of its product to be contributed by the farmer to its owner is decided by the committee in accordance with the local custom. The rent realizable to the land the ownership of which has not been definitely settled is appropriated by the committee for use in the reconstruction of the village or other public utility.

If the family to which farming land has been given to cultivate should consist of only the old and the weak and the women folks without any able-bodied male to undertake the cultivation, the family itself can employ farm-hands to do the farming or the committee can do so on its behalf and attend to all the work for it.

Farmers who have had land distributed to them during the period of communist occupation, excepting those who, having undertaken important work for the red bandits, shall be tried and punished separately, uniformly enjoy the right of undertaking to farm according to the number of mouths to be supported. Products through cultivation of the land harvested prior to the formation of the rehabilitation committee, excluding the portion which the farmer is entitled to keep, is disposed of as land rent according to the procedure stated above.

If owing to the decrease of population in a village or owing to the inhabitants having taken refuge elsewhere and having not all

28

returned, there should be surplus lands left after apportioning for cultivation according to the number of persons, they may be cultivated by farm-hands employed by the committee or by farmers from another village. These lands may be redistributed from time to time upon the successive return of the refugee inhabitants. Lands under the control of the Rural Rehabilitation Committee of a certain village or mart, irrespective of their being cultivated by the proprietors themselves or by tenant-farmers, or distributed for cultivation at the time of communist occupation, are, after the formation of the committee, reported to it, with full particulars of the number of *mao* under cultivation, the location, the number of persons in the cultivators' household, whether aged, young or able-bodied. In the same locality inhabitants, who have not at the time any definite land for cultivation, should also report on the number of aged, young and able-bodied persons in their respective households.

The Rural Rehabilitation Committee, though, in the distribution of lands for cultivation, it is guided by the principle of apportionment according to the number of mouths to be fed, also acts upon the following rules to decide upon the order of precedence in awarding such farming lands.

With the exception of those who are willing to exchange with each other lands for cultivation, the following order of precedence is observed.

(1) The original cultivator before the land was distributed by the red bandits shall have first choice in the apportioning of farming lands.

(2) The original owner whose title has been definitely established and who is willing to cultivate his own land shall have the priority of claim.

(3) Where neither the proprietor-farmer is definitely ascertained, nor is the original cultivator to be found, the one who has cultivated the land after being redistributed by the communists shall be accorded the order of precedence.

(4) Where the proprietor-farmer, the original cultivator and the farmer who has undertaken to cultivate after the land having been distributed by the communists, are all difficult to ascertain, the land shall be assigned anew for cultivation by the committee.

(5) If pieces of land cultivated by the original cultivators, proprietor-farmers, or those who have undertaken to cultivate after the distribution by the communists should exceed the standard of area measured by the number of persons in their respective families, the excessive portion shall be redistributed by the committee to those who have no land to cultivate, or those whose lands are not sufficient.

(6) In assigning lands for cultivation the committee should take into consideration the distance between the habitation of the prospective cultivator and the land to be cultivated.

IV. Replenishment of Buffaloes.

If farmers in the different districts within the regions for anti-communists expedition, who have suffered heavily through the average of the red bandits, are really devoid of the means of purchasing farming buffaloes, such animals are supplied by the Government at a moderate price, which may be paid for from loans obtained from the farmers' banks.

With regard to the enforcement of this measure, there have been promulgated regulations governing the replenishment of farming buffaloes in districts within the regions of communist suppression in Kiangsi.

V. Regulations Dealing With Land Tax, Land Rent, and Farmers' Debts.

The following principles have been adopted for the settlement of disputes arising out of the question of land tax, land rent or farmers' indebtedness:—

(1) Land tax.—Land tax may either be totally remitted, reduced or reprieved under the following circumstances: Taxes in arrear before the 19th year of the Republic (1930) shall be totally remitted. Taxes in arrear after the 20th year of the Republic (1931) leviable in districts where land-distribution had been made by the communists shall be remitted for two years; but in districts where though land-distribution had not been made by the communists, extensive devastation has been committed by them, resulting in the fields being laid waste, the taxes shall be remitted for one year. In districts which have been devastated by the communists

to a less extent, whether the tax should either be given a reduction of half the original amount or a reprieve of half a year is decided upon on reports being made by the magistrate of the district concerned.

(2) Land rent.—Rents in arrear before the 19th year of the Republic (1930) shall be remitted. Rents due during the year shall be remitted if the land is not under cultivation, and shall be proportionally reduced if the land is being cultivated, the rate of reduction to be agreed upon between the land-owner and the tenant-former, or to be decided for them by the co-operative societies of the various villages. The owners of land of more than one hundred *mou* shall contribute three-tenths of the rent accruing to them individually for the purpose of defraying the expenses in the formation of co-operative societies of the various villages, or to serve as foundation funds of such institutions.

(3) Debts of Farmers.—Debts of farmers in districts where land-distribution had been made by the Communists shall all be granted a moratorium of two years, and the unpaid interest of the past shall be reduced or remitted. The highest rate of interest during the moratorium shall not exceed 12%, and the interest above that rate shall be invalid.

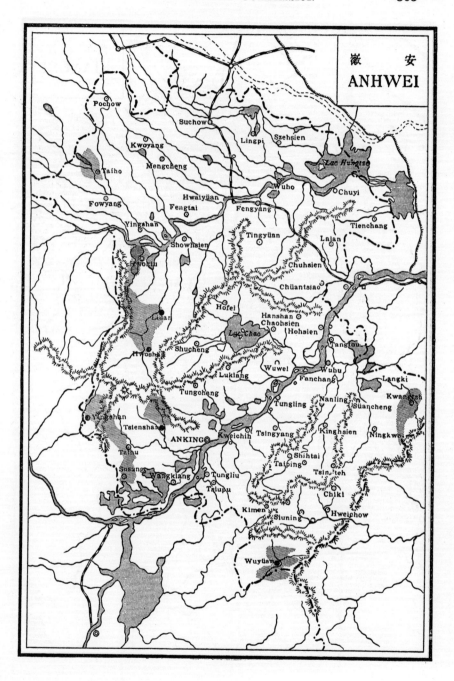

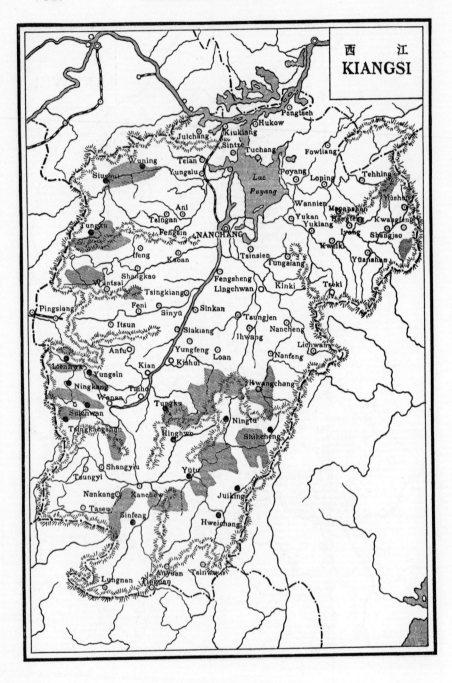

西 江

KIANGSI

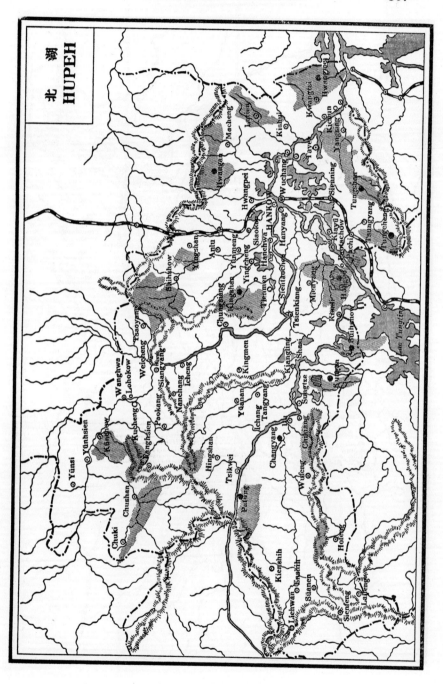

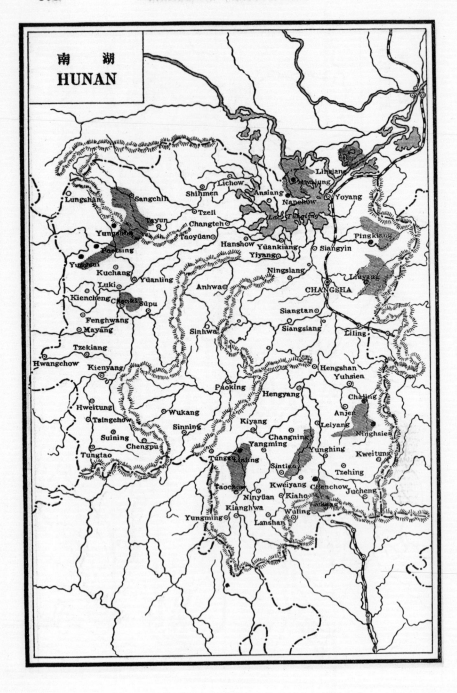

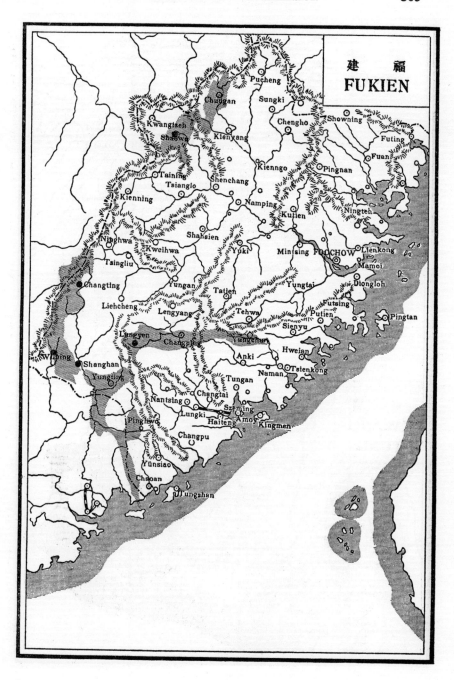

建 福
FUKIEN

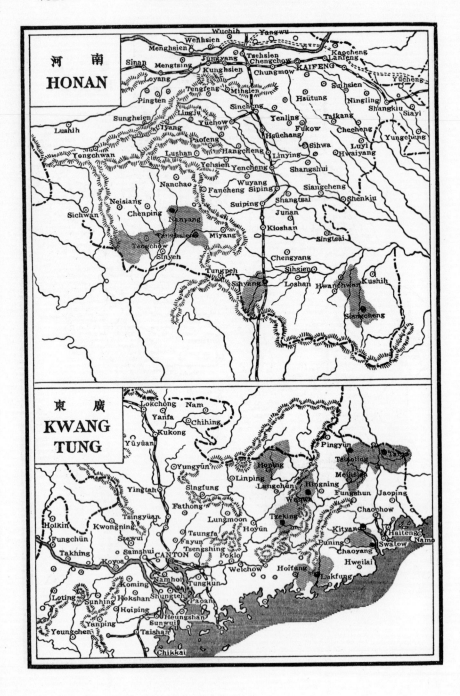

MEMORANDUM

ON

JAPAN'S SEIZURE OF THE SALT GABELLE IN THE THREE EASTERN PROVINCES

Document No. 25   Peiping, August 1932

811

MEMORANDUM ON JAPAN'S SEIZURE OF THE SALT GABELLE IN THE THREE EASTERN PROVINCES.

1. Beginning of Japanese intervention.
2. Seizure of deposits by Japanese.
3. Japanese policy of duplicity.
4. "Orders" from the bogus government.
5. Sub-Inspectorate dissolved by force.
6. Amount of salt revenue seized in five months.
7. Summary.

MEMORANDUM ON JAPAN'S SEIZURE OF THE SALT GABELLE IN THE THREE EASTERN PROVINCES

1. **Beginning of Japanese intervention.** Immediately after the incident of September 18th, 1931, the Japanese military authorities sent 20 soldiers to the Sub-Inspectorate of the Salt Gabelle at Mukden and disarmed its guards. They forced the officials of the Sub-Inspectorate to hand over the safes and accounts of the deposits; the Bank of China was later notified that salt revenue receipts could not be disposed of in any way, not even for administrative expenses, without the knowledge of Japanese military authorities. This was the beginning of Japanese intervention in the Salt Gabelle Administration in the Three Eastern Provinces.

2. **Seizure of deposits by Japanese.** When the so-called "Peace Preservation Committee" was organized in Mukden under the supervision of Japanese authorities, it sent a number of Chinese led by Liang Yu-shu and a number of Japanese led by Yamada Shigeji to the Sub-Inspectorate of the Salt Gabelle demanding that the salt revenue receipts be handed over for paying off the expenses of the local administration. Later, when the Committee was reorganized into the Provincial Government of Liaoning, the same Yamada Shigeji, self-styled as the representative of the Provincial Government, went to the Bank of China at Yingkow on October 30th to force

the Bank to hand over to him a sum of $672,709.56, being the Salt Gabelle deposit in the Bank. The Japanese gave a receipt, the Director and the Deputy-Director of the Sub-Inspectorate not having signed any cheques for the sum drawn.

The Japanese later seized all salt revenue deposits at Yingkow and closed up the Inspectorates of the Salt Gabelle of Kirin and Heilungkiang Provinces. These illegal acts impairing the integrity of the Salt Gabelle Administration were attributed by the Japanese to the independent measures of the "Peace Preservation Committee" and the Provincial Government over which, it was claimed, Japan had no control, but which were in fact directed by the Japanese.

3. **Japanese policy of duplicity.** During the period mentioned above, the Sub-Inspectorate was entirely deprived of its authority. What remained for it to do was to keep account of the salt revenue receipts and to issue permits for the delivery of salt which still held good at places where salt was produced. From appearance, the Sub-Inspectorate of the Gabelle, aside from receiving occasional inspections from Japanese military authorities, still seemed to be functioning without much molestation, and the portion amounting to $217,800 to be paid out every month for foreign loans was duly sent to the Inspectorate-General of the Salt Gabelle at Shanghai with the permission of the Japanese military authorities. In fact, it was all part of Japan's policy of make-believe. On the one hand, she had taken all salt revenue receipts except the sum set aside for paying off foreign loans, while on the other, she tried to mislead the financial circles of the world into believing that Japan was not impairing the rights of foreign investors.

4. " Orders " from the bogus government. According to the report of the Sub-Inspectorate of the Salt Gabelle of Liaoning Province, the Salt Comptroller received, on March 27th, "orders" from the Minister of Finance of the bogus government, to the effect that all deposits, accounts, documents and other properties belonging to the Sub-Inspectorate should be handed over to the bogus government on March 28th, and that, if necessary, force would be used. (The Comptroller was appointed by Marshal Chang Hsueh-liang and forced by the Japanese to carry on his work, but later he fled to Dairen).

On the day mentioned (March 28th), Nagada and Kimura, two Japanese advisers of the "Manchukuo" and four Chinese officials of the Comptroller's Office led a body of 20 policemen and came to the Sub-Inspectorate with a letter from Hsi Hsia authorizing them to take over its control. The translation of Hsi Hsia's letter requesting the Director and the Deputy-Director of the Sub-Inspectorate to make the transfer runs as follows:

"To Mr. Yang Feng-hsiang, Director of the Inspectorate, Mr. Funatzu Fumio, Deputy-Director.

"The new state of Manchukuo instructs you that the Salt Gabelle Administration under the supervision of your office should be handed over to the Salt Comptroller beginning from March 28th, 1932, and that the collection of salt revenue, which was originally undertaken by the Bank of China, should now be handed over to the Official Bank of the Three Eastern Provinces.

"If the officials now working in the Sub-Inspectorate wish to continue their service in the Salt Gabelle Administration of the Manchukuo, they should report their names to the Salt Comptroller's Office and their application will receive serious consideration; but as a preliminary requirement, they should first sever their relationship with the Government of the Republic of China."

(*Signed*) Hsi Hsia,
Minister of Finance of the
Manchukuo.

March 25th of the 1st year
of Tatung.

Meanwhile, in the Comptroller's Office notice was given that all salt merchants should abide by the new regulations and that the forms in vogue issued by the Sub-Inspectorate were no longer valid. Moreover, the new Comptroller sent men to take over control of the organizations established by the Sub-Inspectorate in the various places of salt production.

On March 30th, the Inspector-General of the Salt Gabelle requested the Sub-Inspectorate of Liaoning to protest against the illegal acts on the part of Japan.

5. **Sub-Inspectorate dissolved by force.** On April 15th, the Sub-Inspectorate of Liaoning was dissolved by force. A Japanese adviser to the Salt Comptroller's Office with several Chinese officials and a body of 20 policemen came to the Sub-Inspectorate to take over its control, occupying all premises and seizing all safes, documents, seals, etc. The Japanese adviser then requested the staff to continue their service, but they all refused and left. The Director and the Deputy-Director were forced to leave their duty; a number of the staff followed the Director to Tientsin, waiting for further instructions. The work of the Sub-Inspectorate was completely suspended.

Amount of salt revenue seized in five months. From October 30th, 1931 to April 12th, 1932, Japan seized salt revenue amounting to $7,083,272.53. The integrity of the Salt Gabelle Administration was thus destroyed as well as the system of salt transportation and supply to

Kirin and Heilungkiang Provinces. The payment of foreign loans secured on the salt revenue then became a serious question of uncertainty.

Summary. We may now summarize the above facts in a more concise way as follows:

(1) On September 19th, the Sub-Inspectorate of Liaoning at Mukden was searched by, and its revenue put under the control of the Japanese military authorities.

(2) On October 22nd, the "Peace Preservation Committee" at Mukden sent representatives and several Japanese military officers to the Sub-Inspectorate declaring that the existing system of the Salt Gabelle Administration would be maintained. In the meantime, the Committee proceeded to organize all government organs in Liaoning Province.

(3) On October 30th, the "Peace Preservation Committee" at Mukden, which had been reorganized into the Provincial Government of Liaoning sent some Japanese to seize salt revenue amounting to $672,709.56. This amount plus later seizures up to April 12th totalled more than $7,000,000.

(4) On March 27th, the Salt Comptroller, acting upon instructions of the Minister of Finance of the "Manchukuo", ordered the Sub-Inspectorate to hand over the Salt Gabelle Administration.

(5) On April 15th, a Japanese adviser accompanied by armed forces came to occupy the premises of the Sub-Inspectorate; offices in the various localities were seized and the employees of the whole service in the Three Eastern Provinces were forced to leave.

Peiping, August 3rd 1932.

MEMORANDUM

ON

THE SO-CALLED "INDEPENDENCE" MOVEMENT IN THE THREE EASTERN PROVINCES

Document No. 26   Peiping, August 1932

MEMORANDUM ON THE SO-CALLED " INDEPEND-ENCE " MOVEMENT IN THE THREE EASTERN PROVINCES.

I. Japanese desire for Independence of the Three Eastern Provinces.

1. Japanese appointing Special Ambassador.
2. Japan's desire to annex the Three Eastern Provinces.
3. Minami and annexation.
4. Honjo and annexation.
5. Dohihara and annexation.
6. Royama and annexation.
7. The Mitsui interests and annexation.
8. Other views on annexation.
9. Japan hesitated about direct annexation.
10. Conferences deciding on "independence" before annexation.
11. Yamato Hotel conference.

II. Stages leading to the formation of the Puppet Government.

12. Four stages in the "independence" movement.
13. (1) The Period of Local Association.
14. (2) The Period of Provincial Federation.
15. (3) The Period of Inter-Provincial Conferences.
16. (4) The Formation of the bogus government.
17. Puyi assuming office.
18. Japanese rejoicing.
19. The "Self-Government Guidance Department": its nature and activities.
20. Examples of parades staged by the department.

822 Memoranda Presented to

III. The "Government" under Japanese domination.

IV. Japanese control over the new "state."

V. Concluding remarks.

APPENDIX:

MEMORANDUM ON THE SO-CALLED "INDEPEND- ENCE" MOVEMENT IN THE THREE EASTERN PROVINCES

I. Japanese Desire for Independence of the Three Eastern Provinces.

1. **Japan appointing Special Ambassador.** For the purpose of unifying the Japanese administration in the Three Eastern Provinces, the Japanese Government, we have been told, has recently decided to despatch to the Three Eastern Provinces a Special Ambassador with full powers who shall at the same time be the Commander-in-Chief of the Kwantung Army and Governor of the Kwantung Leased Territory. As Special Ambassador he will be placed under the direction and control of the Foreign Minister and will have power to supervise the Japanese consuls in the Three Eastern Provinces.

2. **Japan's desire to annex the Three Eastern Provinces.** The Japanese plan for the annexation of China's Three Eastern Provinces of 382,000 square miles with a population of 30 millions of whom 95% or more are of the Chinese race may, according to the above information, be considered for the present, to be completed. That plan constitutes a vital part of Japan's continental policy of conquest of very long standing, and the events of September 18th, 1931 gave it an opportunity and impetus that it never had before. It was necessary, however, in the realization of this plan first to sponsor an "independence" movement in the Three Eastern Provinces and to describe the new order of things in

political nomenclature acceptable to the present mentality of the world. In the ten months which have transpired since the fateful evening of September 18th, the Japanese have therefore made very generous use of phrases like "racial consciousness," "self-determination of peoples" and the other shibboleths to which we have all become accustomed as being desirable political ends to achieve. Actually, however, under the cover of these grossly abused terms, the Japanese have been consolidating their plans of conquest. To take only a few recent examples, Japanese of position have publicly given expression to this desire of making the Three Eastern Provinces a part of the Japanese Empire. They represent the general trend of thought among the Japanese as a whole.

3. **Minami and annexation.** General Minami, former Minister of War, who is an advocate of strong policy, is well experienced in Chinese affairs. For many years he served as Commander of the Japanese forces in the Kwantung Leased Territory. He is generally considered as one of the "experts" on Chinese affairs. As early as in July, 1931, when he was still in the War Office, he delivered an address in which he emphasized the gravity of the Manchurian situation and challenged the Government Party on the question of reducing army expenditures. The address aroused considerable criticism in Japanese political circles for its outspokenness. Minami also held secret conferences with the General Staff. Even after he was out of the War Office, he went to the Three Eastern Provinces where he had a tour of inspection and was in conference with General Honjo. The statement which he gave out on December 20th, 1931 during that tour is indicative of his mentality: "The question that remains is one of political control. . . .

Any government set up which does not have the confidence of Japan cannot stand for one day."

4. **Honjo and annexation.** General S. Honjo, who at the outset of the present trouble was Commander of the Japanese "Kwantung Garrison Army," with headquarters at Port Arthur, has had twenty-five years of military experience on Chinese soil. For eight years, he was military adviser to Marshal Chang Tso-lin. He is now Commander-in-Chief of the Japanese forces in the Three Eastern Provinces and has his headquarters in the Japanese section at Mukden. It is from his headquarters that all plans originated and orders given for the setting-up of the various "independence" organizations throughout the Provinces. Even parades and demostrations of the hirelings in support of the so-called "independence" movement are controlled by the headquarters. General Honjo is, indeed, the moving spirit behind the scene.

5. **Dohihara and annexation.** Colonel Dohihara, the third of the triumvirate of important Japanese military men responsible for Japanese activities in support of the separatist movement was stationed in Mukden at the beginning of the present complications. His title was "Chief of the Military Liaison Office in Mukden." Actually he was a sort of Japanese military observer in South Manchuria. For a short while, he was acting Mayor of the occupied Chinese city of Mukden. It was he who kidnapped Puyi from Tientsin and brought him to Dairen where the latter was kept under strict supervision. Like Minami and Honjo, Dohihara has had a long career in China. He has travelled in China extensively and speaking the Chinese language with extraordinary fluency, he had had a full share in fomenting troubles in North China. He was closely connected with

the Anfu Club, with Marshal Chang Tso-lin and his son, and in fact, it was his brain and efforts which contributed so largely to the subjugation of the Three Eastern Provinces to Japanese rule. "The independence of Manchuria and Mongolia," he said on assuming office at Harbin as head of the Special Affairs Department, "is inevitable, for it is the decided policy of the Japanese Imperial Government. Whatever the League of Nations, Chiang Kai-shek or Chang Hseuh-liang might say cannot alter matters."[1]

The spirit which animated this remark was the spirit of the late Mr. Inukai when he said before the House of Peers on March 24th, 1932, "When the new Manchurian Government is organized, naturally it should be recognized by Japan," and of Mr. Araki, the War Minister, when he said, "If in the future anybody should disturb the peace of Manchuria, the Ministry of War will adopt adequate measures of protection." All this shows unequivocally Japan's desire to reduce the Three Eastern Provinces to the position of a protectorate.

6. **Royama and annexation.** Among the so-called intellectuals in Japan, Dr. M. Royama, a professor in the Imperial University of Tokyo, has always sponsored an "independence" movement in the Three Eastern Provinces to be followed by Japanese annexation. As early as January 21st, 1931, he expressed himself in the following terms: "Manchuria is a colony of China, and so it is of Japan. Apart from the propriety of setting up an independent state therein, such enterprise might be feasible in case some Power lends a hand in protecting and guiding it. The question who is the sovereign head is only a matter of detail."

[1] For further details of Dohihara's career *vide Memorandum on the Disturbances in Tientsin: Submitted by the People of Tientsin*, pp. 8-9.

7. **The Mitsui interests and annexation.** Mr. Teijiro Kawamura, Managing Director of the Mitsui Bussan Kaisha, in December 1931, made a special trip through the Three Eastern Provinces and Mongolia, examining their new economic possibilities after Japanese occupation and paying respects to the Japanese troops there. It is a well-known fact that the powerful Mitsui House which dominates the South Manchuria Railway has immense interests in the Provinces. Through its close alliance with the Japanese Kwantung Army and the military clique which dominate the Japanese Throne and Government, the Mitsui House hopes to make the Provinces a receptacle of its extensive economic interests. If the Japanese are free to consolidate their position in the Three Eastern Provinces and Mongolia as they now plan, the Mitsui interests will convert them and the Chinese people in these territories to serve Japanese purposes. Resentful of Chinese development of the Provinces, these Japanese industrialists have had their share in creating the so-called new state of "Manchukuo."

8. **Other views on annexation.** Japanese views on the desirability of an "independence" movement to be engineered by the Japanese and later to be followed by annexation may be found in practically all classes of Japanese. The Chief Secretary of the Japanese People's Diplomatic Association, Nakano Koetsu, in the preface to his book on the Manchurian question said in part as follows: "Japan has destroyed Manchuria and Mongolia through military means, but the Japanese so far have not derived any benefit therefrom. According to the general opinion of the Japanese, therefore, the work of reconstruction under Japanese guidance must be expedited." The High Adviser of the Mukden Self-Government association, Shonosuke, also contributed a

foreword to the work in which he expressed himself in the following terms: "That the whole incident was created by Japan is undeniable. But from the Japanese point of view, it is not simply meant to offer protection to the rights already acquired in Manchuria and Mongolia. Such a view is superficial and unsatisfactory. To be very frank, it is our aim to establish a new Manchuria-Mongolia state. That is our fundamental question."

9. **Japan hesitated about direct annexation.** It was Japan's original intention, immediately after the military occupation of the Three Eastern Provinces, to establish a military Government. That idea received strong support from Honjo and Dohihara and was submitted for consideration to the Japanese Government. The Government, however, actually wavered as to whether the idea was feasible or not. It was actually afraid that it might bring the wrath of an outraged world upon Japan, and thought that it was advisable to be less direct in the conquest of the new territory.

10. **Conferences deciding on "independence" before annexation.** Accordingly, a whole series of conferences were held in different parts of Japan and in the conquered territory participated by all classes of Japanese which decided that annexation should be preceded by an organized "independence" movement. On October 24th, 1931, eminent Japanese both in and out of the Government held at Osaka what was known as "The conference on the Manchurian and Mongolian situation." A similar conference was held on December 5th. Still another was held at Mukden on December 12th, 1931. The resolutions of these different assemblies amounted to the same thing, that it was advisable to compel the four provinces of China's north-east (including Jehol)

to declare their "independence" from the Chinese Central Government under the protection of the Japanese military forces.

11. **Yamato Hotel conference.** Details of this last-named conference are perhaps worthy of being reproduced. The conference was called under the auspices of the *Osaka Mainichi Daily* (Mukden Branch) at the Yamato Hotel. There were present six Chinese officials who have accepted Japanese appointments, twelve Japanese officials, including Komai, five Japanese people's representatives and six *Mainichi Daily* representatives. One Chinese representative (Yu Chung-han) said that the form of the new government should follow the general opinion of the people, whereupon Noguchi representing the Japanese colony of Mukden said it should be a constitutional monarchy. One Japanese representative said that whatever was resolved should receive the consent of the Japanese Government, while another Japanese emphasized the necessity of Japanese emigration to the Three Eastern Provinces and expressed the hope that as soon as the Japanese and Manchurian peoples become friendly enough, the two states should be combined into one. It is evident, then, that even before the puppet government was formed, the idea of annexation had already been forecast in that conference.

II. Stages Leading to the Formation of the Puppet Government.

12. **Four stages in the "independence" movement.** After the general outlines concerning the future of the conquered territory have been decided upon, all that was needed was to organize a new government based on these outlines. It was necessary on the one hand to force as many Chinese as possible into the service of this gov-

ernment so as to give it an appearance of "self-determination," and, on the other hand, to exercise the most rigid control over every department of this government in its centre as well as in its periphery. No attempt therefore was made to concentrate all the energy on the so-called central "government" at Changchun, as the Japanese realized that the provincial governments and especially the local district governments are equally, if not more, important. Before the central "government" was established at Changchun and, with it, the proclamation of the "Manchukuo," there were therefore successive stages through which the "independence" movement had to pass in order that the smallest of social units might be brought within its fold. In the main, there were four stages which Japan went through in the consolidation of her power in the Three Eastern Provinces. They were (1) the period of local association, (2) the period of provincial federation, (3) the period of inter-provincial conferences and finally and (4) the formation of the bogus government.

13. **(1) The Period of Local Association.** (1) The Period of Local Association. When a city was conquered by the Japanese army, the first thing it did was the dissolution of the local government. This having been done, the district magistrate would be forced to swear allegiance to the Japanese. The many signed statements submitted by the magistrates of the different cities in the Three Eastern Provinces to the Commission all bear out the uniformity of this procedure. The next thing would be the organization of the local Peace Preservation Committee or some such organization to maintain the local order. By that time, Japanese control of the locality would be well-nigh complete. Associated with that committee would be what is known as a Special

Affairs Department presided over by a Japanese under the direction of the Japanese High Command. In this way it is clear that even the remotest parts of the Three Eastern Provinces, as long as there are Japanese soldiers, are controlled by the Japanese military. The larger cities were reorganized in the early stages of the military conquest in much the same way. Yuan Ching-kai, for instance, was made the chairman of the local association in Mukden as soon as the city fell into Japanese hands. He was surrounded by Japanese advisers and, of course, had no freedom of action of any sort. In other words, he was a puppet. On November 7th, 1931, the Mukden local association was converted, at the instance of the headquarters of the Kwantung Army, into the provisional provincial government. Japanese control of the organization became from that time still firmer. Although a Chinese in the person of Chao Hsin-po was appointed mayor of Mukden succeeding Dohihara, the number of Japanese ''advisers'' considerably increased, and on the 15th of the month, one of those typical celebrations organized from beginning to end by the Japanese, of which there were going to be so many from now on, was held. The Mayor's office received one day before the occasion over ten thousand paper flags printed with the words ''In celebration of the completion of political control,'' which, upon instructions issued by the Japanese authorities, were to be distributed to the shops and stores along the main thoroughfares of the city.

The celebration came off at 11 a.m. of the 15th and the Japanese managed to persuade about one hundred Chinese to take part. Yuan Chin-kai was compelled to assume the chair. An hour later a big party of Japanese demonstrators arrived on the scene, led by a large number of gendarmes and soldiers. There were in all more than two hundred vehicles of all kinds, carrying well over 5,000 Japanese who distributed hand-bills, shouted slogans, and harangued with megaphones. Among the hand-bills that were picked up, there were many very interesting slogans: "Down with the League of Nations," "Have no fear of the League," "Down with Briand," "We demand the permanent stationing of Japanese troops," "We are against withdrawal," "Be prepared for a war against the world," etc.

14. **(2) The Period of Provincial Federation.** (2) The Period of Provincial Federation. The Provisional Provincial Government of Mukden restored two of the former provincial bureaus, those of industry and finance, and November 15th was formally reorganized into the "Fengtien" Provincial government with Tsang Shih-yi as the Chairman. There was the usual parade conducted by the Japanese to celebrate the formation of the provincial government. The shops and stores were all compelled to hoist a small red flag, bearing the words "In celebration of the Fengtien Provincial Government." Japanese representatives from the Kwantung Army were present and replied to the address of the new chairman. Tsang Shih-yi ever since has been under Japanese surveillance wherever he finds himself and is virtually a prisoner, although things are done in his name by the Japanese.[2]

In Kirin the Japanese appointed General Hsi Hsia as the chairman as early as on September 23rd. General Hsi is noted for his monarchist ideas and the Japanese made a tool of him suspecting him of generally

---

[2] For details, see " Reply to the Questionnaire on Relations between the Central Government of China and the administration of the North-Eastern Provinces, Part III, p. 1 et seq.